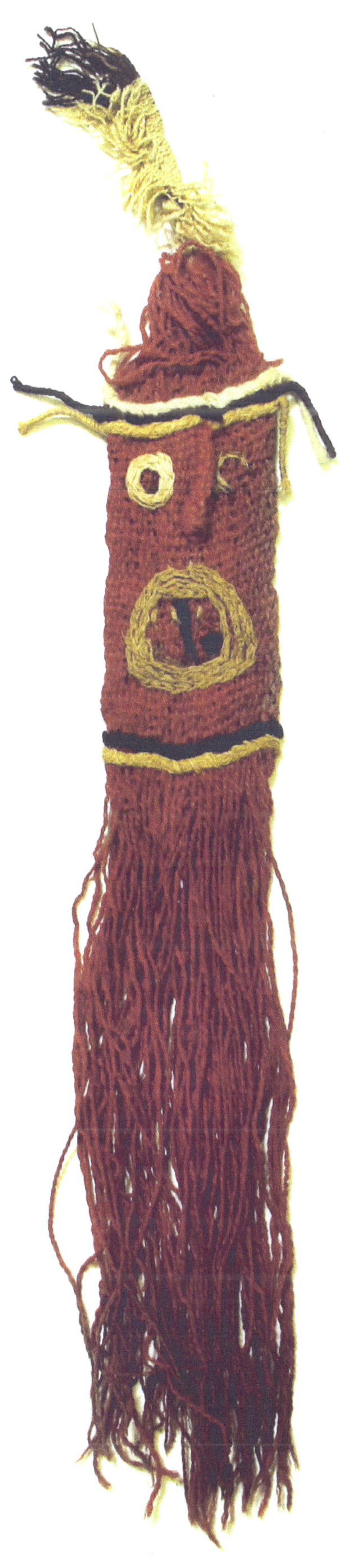

The preColumbian Textiles in the Roemer- and Pelizaeus-Museum Hildesheim, Germany

Lena Bjerregaard

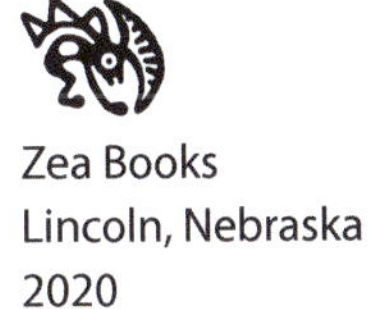

Zea Books
Lincoln, Nebraska
2020

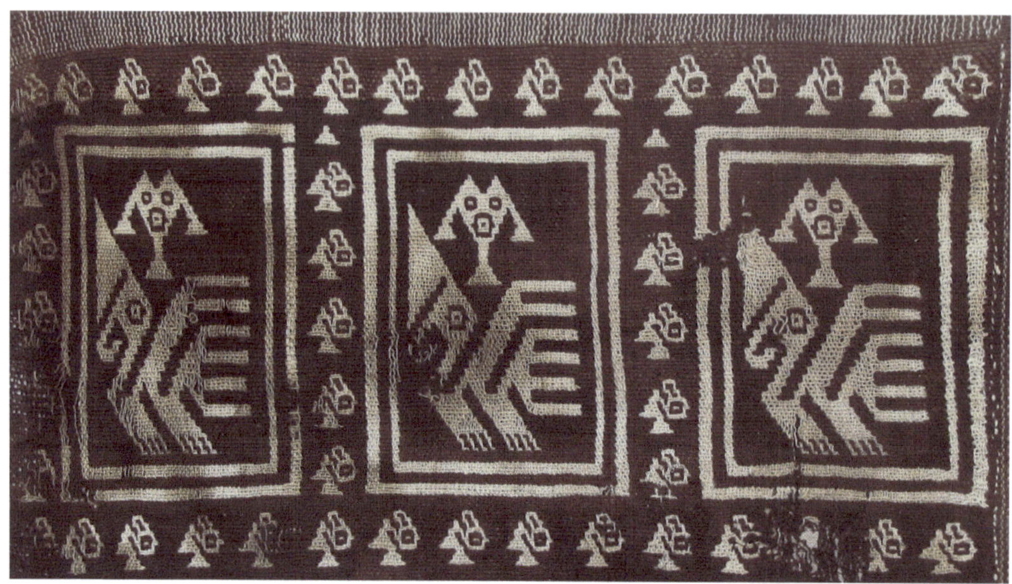

ISBN 978-1-60962-166-7

doi 10.32873/unl.dc.zea.1098

Set in Myriad types.

Zea Books are published by the University of Nebraska–Lincoln Libraries

Electronic (pdf) ebook edition available online at
https://digitalcommons.unl.edu/zeabook/

Print edition available from
http://www.lulu.com/spotlight/unllib

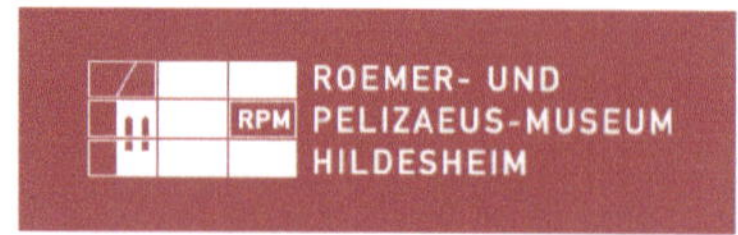

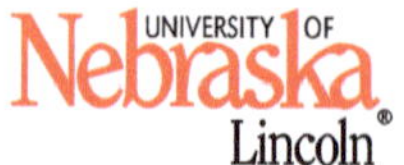

Contents

Foreword by Andrea Nicklisch and Regine Schulz 5

Introduction by Lena Bjerregaard 7

The Roemer- and Pelizaeus-Museum's preColumbian textile collection 8

Determination of styles 9

A brief description of the preColumbian textiles over the last 3000 years 11

Some indications to help identify a preColumbian textile . . 12

Explanation of terms in textile analysis 14

Bibliography 15

Catalogue of preColumbian Textiles in the Roemer- and Pelizaeus-Museum Hildesheim, Germany

Paracas/Nazca – 500 BC – 500 AD 19

Middle Horizon – 400-800 AD 22

Lambayeque – 900-1300 AD 27

Late Intermediate Period – 1200 – 1450 AD 37

Inka – 1400-1550 AD 94

Colonial – 1600 – 1700 AD 103

Recent – 1800-2000 AD 104

Problematic Objects. 106

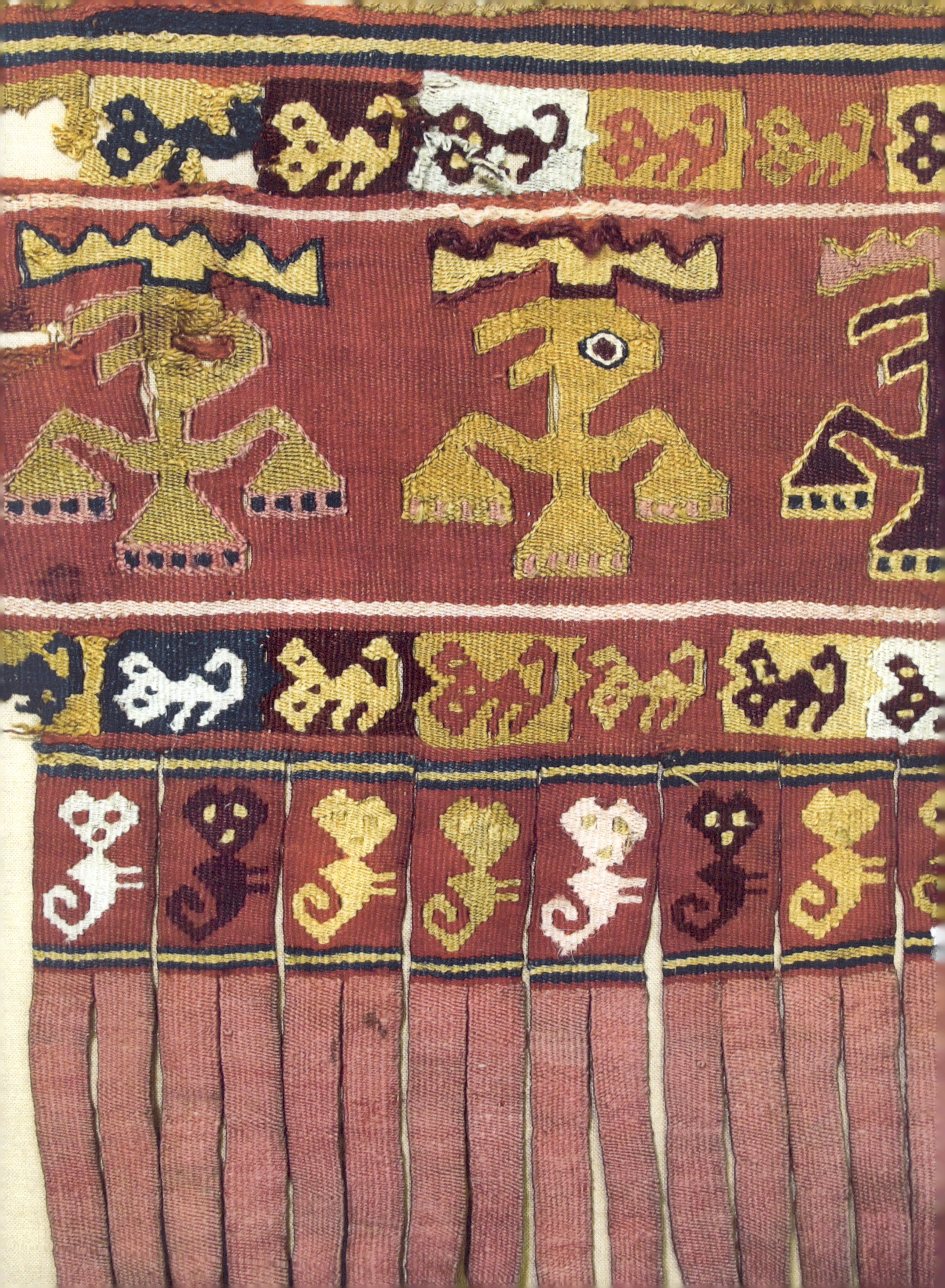

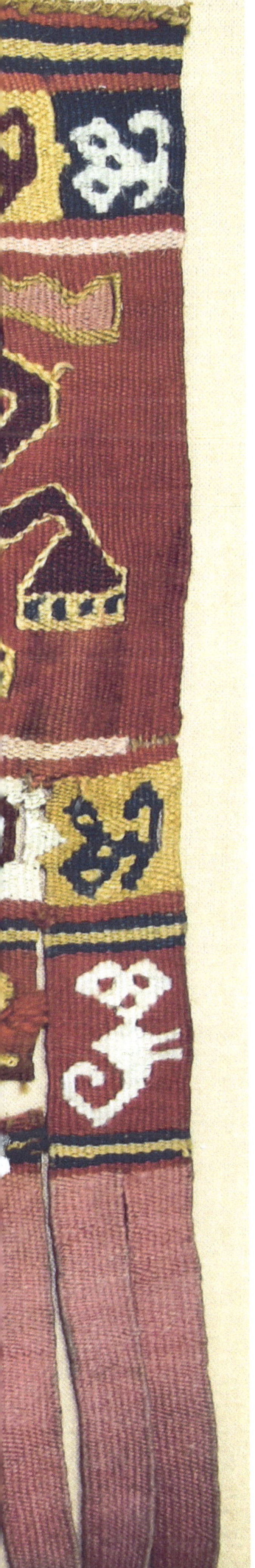

Foreword

Andrea Nicklisch and Regine Schulz

The Roemer- und Pelizaeus-Museum combines two originally separate museums under a single roof: the Roemer-Museum, founded in 1844, and the Pelizaeus Museum which opened its doors in 1911. While the collections of the Pelizaeus-Museum are mainly composed of ancient Egyptian and Graeco-Roman items, the comprehensive holdings of the Roemer-Museum (ca. 310,000 objects) are more multi-faceted. They comprise not only the history of the city and region of Hildesheim but also ethnological and art historical objects as well as natural specimens from all over the world. The founders of the "twin museums", Hermann Roemer and Wilhelm Pelizaeus, intended to create a "World Museum" that covered very diverse aspects of nature and culture. As a result, the collections of the Roemer-Museum reflect – among other things – the world outside Europe. The first annual report of the Hildesheim museum society (1845) listed the "ethnographic collection", which was then part of the art section, as having no more than 28 objects. However, this part of the collection was to grow considerably in the decades that followed and includes today ca. 14,000 objects from all continents.

The pre-Hispanic collection from the South American Andes is one of the highlights of the Roemer-Museum's ethnographic department. It consists mainly of pottery of various pre-Columbian Andean cultures but also includes jewellery, wooden objects, and textiles. In 1905 the new director of the Roemer Museum, Rudolph Hauthal, wrote that he wanted the pre-Hispanic Andean collection of the Roemer-Museum to rank among the best not only in Germany, but ideally also in all of Europe. The first exhibition of that collection was opened in 1906.

The 175th anniversary of the Roemer-Museum in 2019 is a perfect occasion for publishing a selection of important pieces from the Andean pre-Hispanic textiles collection. The museum was thus delighted when Lena Bjerregaard, an internationally renowned expert on pre-Columbian textiles, agreed to examine that group of textiles and to identify the provenance of the individual specimens. This will enable an international public to gain knowledge about this collection, which was as yet largely unpublished. In addition, Lena Bjerregaard's study shows the connections between collectors and collections in German museums in the late 19th and early 20th century.

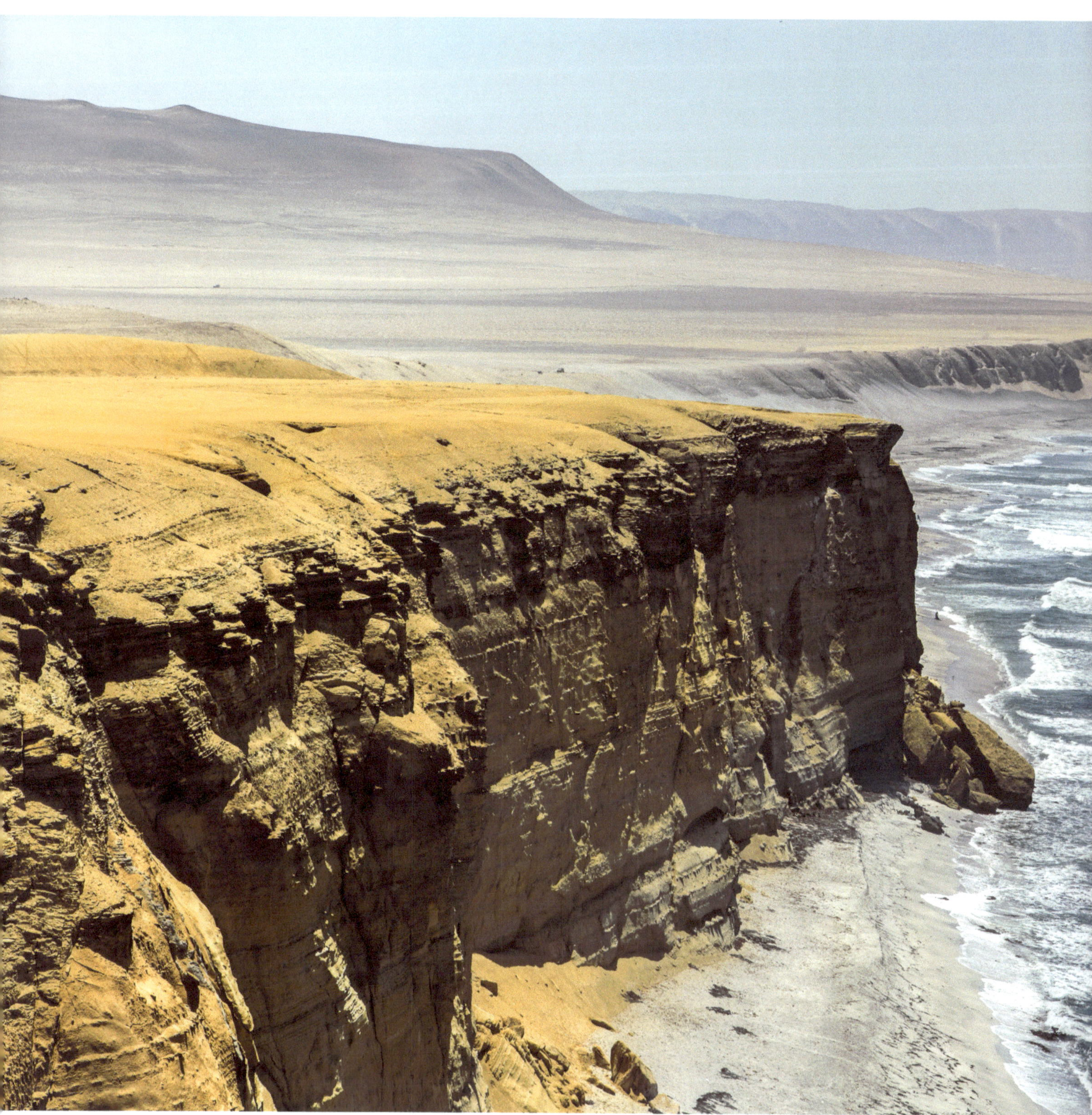

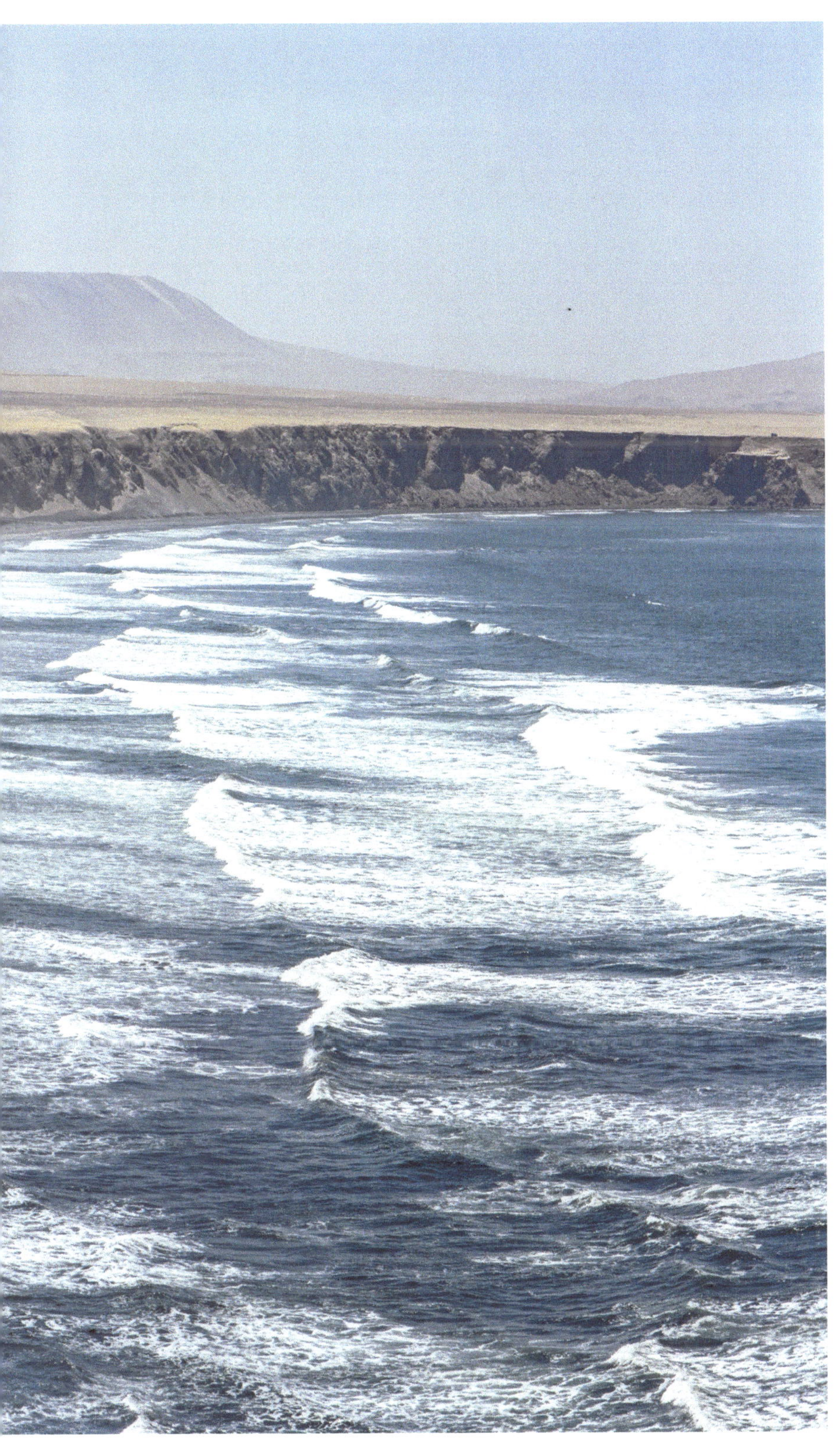

Introduction

Along the coast of Peru is one of the driest deserts in the world. Here, under the sand, the ancient Peruvians buried their dead wrapped in gorgeous textiles. As organic material keeps almost forever when stored without humidity, light and oxygen, many of the mummies excavated in the last hundred years are in excellent conditions. And so are the textiles wrapped around them. Their clear colors are still dazzling and the textile fibers in good condition.

Textiles were highly valued objects in ancient Peru – used for expressing status and diverse messages in these non-literate but highly organized and very developed cultures. Much energy, innovation and aesthetic sensibility were invested in the textiles.

The preColumbian peoples had access to exquisite materials: the local fibers were camelid fibers (alpaca and vicuña), cotton and plant fibers (agave, for instance). The camelid fibers have very little scales compared to sheep fibers, and are long, soft and lustrous. The Peruvian cotton grew in 5 different colors.

The ancient Peruvians were also master dyers and have for thousands of years dyed their yarn with indigo blue, madder red, cochineal red, sea snail purple and yellow from many kinds of plants. And so they produced some of the finest, most beautiful and most interesting textiles in the world.

Instead of writing, they kept the order in their world encoded in textile fibers.

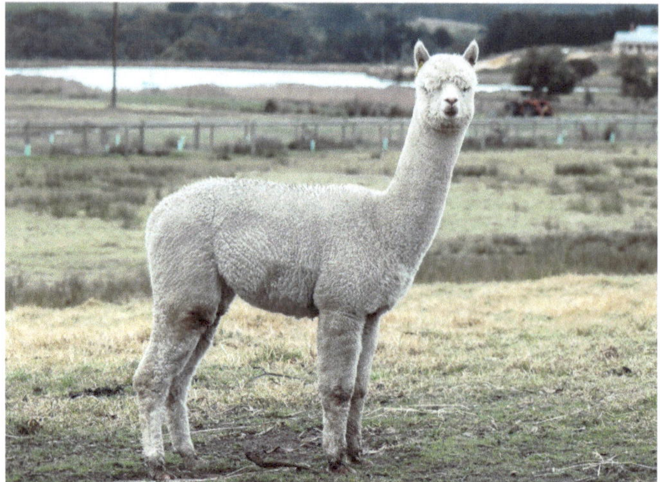

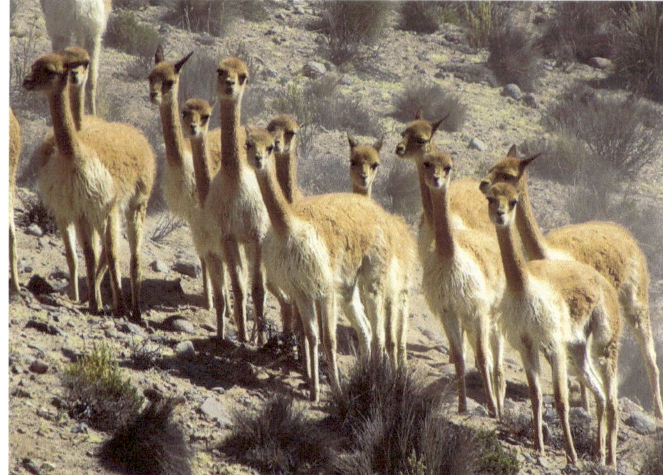

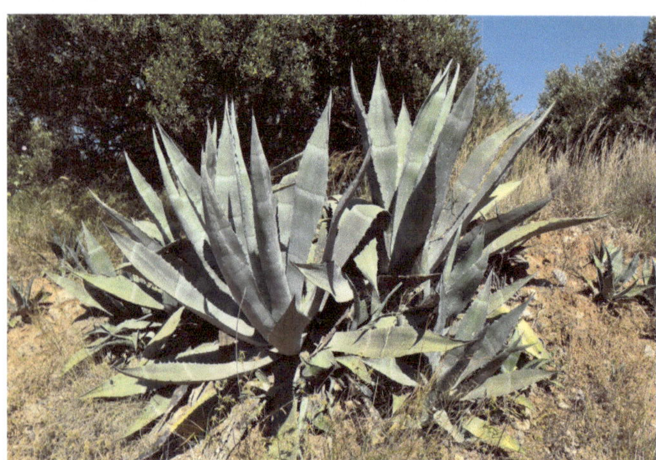

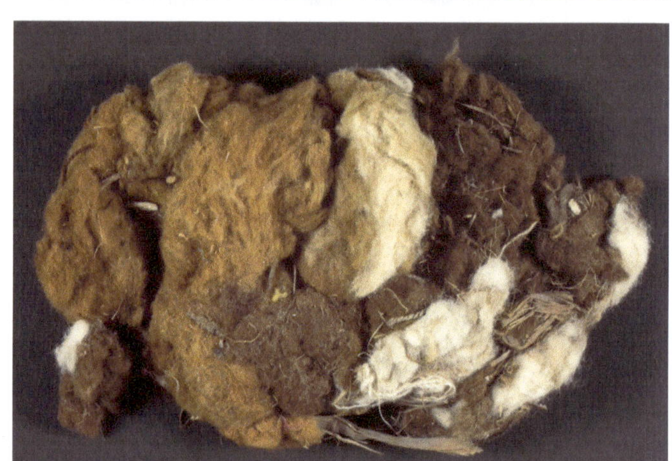

The Roemer- and Pelizaeus-Museum's preColumbian textile collection

The Roemer- and Pelizaeus-Museum in Hildesheim houses a collection of 405 preColumbian textiles. Most of them are fragments, but a few complete pieces are present.

I have chosen 133 pieces for this publication, to represent the collection at its best.

Almost all the textiles have no information on either the collector or the donor and also have no geographic provenience. Some of them are very, very similar to other fragments (very likely from the same textile) in the collection that Wilhelm Gretzer sold to the now Ethnological Museum in Berlin in 1899 and 1907 and could have been from his collection. Gretzer was a close friend of the then director of the Roemer Museum, Prof. Rudolf Hauthal, and at the time it was a common practice both for collectors and museums to cut up the ancient archaeological textiles and sell or give them away as

Photos

Previous pages: Paracas National Reserve, Peru (masT3rOD, Wikimedia, CC-BY)

Above, clockwise from top left: Alpaca (Notnoisy at Wikimedia, CC-BY); Group of vicuñas in Peru (Marshallhenrie, Wikimedia, CC-BY-SA); Peruvian brown cotton (Cornell University Anthropology Collections, 899.1.8.); *Agave deserti* in Palm Canyon, California (Stan Shebs, CC-BY-SA).

"design samples" or as it was called in Germany "Doubletten". This custom has scattered fragments of archaeological textiles in many museums and collections worldwide, and recently researchers have begun to register and at least digitally reunite these fragments in order to reconstruct the form of a complete piece.

The museum's collection has samples from many different places and cultures – from 2000 years ago and up into recent times. There are one Paracas/Nazca (500 BC-500 AD), 4 Middle Horizon (400-800 AD) pieces, 15 Lambayeque (900-1100 AD), 11 Inka (1450-1550 AD), 1 colonial (1550-1800 AD) and 2 fine objects from 1800-1900 AD. There is even a falsified object – a feathered shield put together partly from preColumbian feathered strings, but in an improper way.

All the rest (about 370 pieces) are from the Late Intermediate Period (1100-1450 AD). These textiles can largely be defined geographically as north-, central- or south coast textiles. However, there was much trade, inspiration and subcultures involved – and it is often very difficult to say exactly where a textile was found, or made. I have tried my best – with a little help from my friends.

Wilhelm Gretzer mostly delivered his textiles to the museums with stated provenience – and most of them came from Pachacamac on the central coast. Pachacamac was, however, a ritual place in use over thousands of years and by many different cultures. For this reason, often textiles in north and south coast styles have Pachacamac as provenience in the museum collections he furnished. In the late intermediate period (12-1450 AD) various cultures coexisted – on the central coast the Ychsma and Chancay cultures have only quite recently been defined by researchers, and also on the north coast different cultures were competing side by side during that period.

Determination of styles

In order to determine the style of a preColumbian textile without provenience many different parameters are used.

The *iconography* of the textile is considered. And then the materials and the techniques that differed from culture to culture.

Materials:

The fibers used to create textiles in ancient Peru were camelid hair, cotton and other plant fibers. The highland cultures (Wari/Tiwanaku, Inka) had easier access to camelid fibers, as most camelids lived in the highlands. Each of these cultures at their time dominated large areas of Peru/ Bolivia/ Chile/

Ecuador and spread their artistic influence from north to south and from the Andes to the coast. The coastal cultures like Moche, Lambayeque and Chimu in the north and Ychsma and Chancay on the central coast were not so geographically widespread. They were cotton growers, and used camelid fibers more sparingly as added decoration on cotton fabrics.

Plant fibers were much used on the coast during the late intermediate period. For instance, the many central coast hairnets were made in *Fourcraea andina* – a South American agave.

Techniques:

The spinning/plying techniques differed in ancient Peru and can provide information on the culture/style.

Cotton was mostly spun locally – a sign of this is that within the different cultures mostly the spinning and plying direction were the same, but differed from culture to culture. Cotton fibers were/are spun holding the spindle vertically resting it in a bowl. Often the seeds are extracted while spinning. Cotton yarns were either S or Z spun, S or Z plied and could be used un-plied, either single or paired.

Spinning and plying camelid fibers was/is done vertically on a drop spindle. Cotton fibers are spun horizontally with the tip of the spindle normally resting in a bowl/gourd.

Almost everywhere throughout the Andean world, camelid fiber yarns were two Z-spun yarns plied together in the S direction. They were often probably imported to the coast from the Andes already spun and plied.

Cotton yarns diverged from culture to culture much more in the direction of spinning/plying.

The weaving and other non-woven techniques were many – as a matter of fact preColumbian artisans used practically all the techniques known in Europe before the industrialisation – and a few more very complicated techniques unknown in Europe (such as discontinuous warp and weft).

Most textiles were woven on the backstrap loom – the first loom everywhere in the world. It consists basically of 2 sticks between which the warp is mounted. The top stick is tied with a rope to some stable pole/poles and the bottom stick is attached around the weaver's hips. She/he then controls the tension of the warp by her body movements. Two or more sheds are then inserted in the warp – most textiles in ancient Peru were plain weave (warp-faced or balanced, gauze weave, double weave) but also complicated warp patterns and twill were woven on the backstrap loom. On a backstrap loom every technique can be made. The length of the warp is unlimited, but the width of the fabrics cannot be more than ca 80 cm – the span that one weaver can manage. Larger textiles were created by sewing together several woven panels.

At least two cultures – Wari/Tiwanaku and Inka – also used a large two-beam loom. On that they wove their large tunics in tapestry and the women's very large wrap-around dresses. This loom can produce very wide textiles and several weavers can work side by side on the same textile. A tunic was woven sideways – so the tunic had the warp horizontal when worn.

The non-woven techniques are more time-consuming than weaving and usually used for smaller objects, such as headdress elements. They were created with few tools, such as a needle or awl. With endless variations of braiding, plaiting, looping and knotting the preColumbian people created bands, slings, lace-like trimmings and hairnets.

The looping techniques used in Europe were mainly used for coarse mittens and hats, but in Peru (Paracas/Nazca especially) this technique was immensely refined and used for creating tiny colorful 3-dimentional borders and even whole textiles. The technique 'orcis' that was used in Europe in recent times to create white plate dividers was used in ancient Peru to create plant fiber hairnets painted with shellfish purple. Fist-braiding for bands and ornamental slings was done in round, square and rectangular forms by manipulating up to 80-90 yarns over one hand. This technique is to my knowledge only used elsewhere in Japan for the round bands tying the belt of the kimono, and by the herders of Tibet, who also make rectangular fist-braids for slings.

A few techniques from the old world have not been found in preColumbian Peru: tablet weaving, crochet and knitting. Tablet weaving was used in ancient Mesopotamia and reached north to the Vikings, who used it for decorative bands. Crochet probably developed from "tambouring" and reached Europe in the 1700 century from the Middle East. Knitting also comes from Mesopotamia and only reached Europe in the 16th century.

A brief description of the preColumbian textiles over the last 3000 years

The earliest clothing

For thousands of years before our era women wore string skirts – the oldest ones are found in the Tarapaca desert in northern Chile and are from 7000 BC. and sometimes dyed red with madder on cotton or camelid fiber.

Around the year 0 the coastal people in southern Peru/northern Chile changed their costume. The men had been wearing only loincloths and the women string skirts, but both genders around that time seemed to have left this custom for the tunic, probably inspired by the highland people.

The tunic

The tunic was – in many variations – worn by both men and women in the preColumbian world.

Through the following millenia, the men wore a tunic mostly with a vertical warp, vertical neck slit and vertical arm slits. The women wore a tunic mostly with a horizontal warp, horizontal neck- and arm slit. Horizontal stripes were generally reserved for women and vertical for men, though exceptions occurred.

The men's tunics were worn loose and the women's either loose or held together by a belt. The tunics could be short or long, narrow or wide, changing with time and culture. Mostly the women wore longer tunics reaching below the knees and the men shorter ones. The men wore a loincloth under the tunic, so their tunics could be very short. In some cultures women also wore wrap-around dresses.

Techniques

Most preColumbian cultures used many different textile producing techniques. In the following only a few, very characteristic techniques will be mentioned.

Some indications to help identify a preColumbian textile.

Paracas/ Nazca 500 BC-500 AD

Camelid fiber or cotton plain weave fabrics with camelid fiber embroidery in stem stitch in vivid colors. Short wrap-around skirts for men and short tunics, turbans and large mantles with embroidery along the edges, and sometimes all over. The early imagery was geometric and later more naturalistic anthropomorphs mixed with animals – a flying shark-man, for instance.

Intricate 3-dimensional looping was used to create garment edgings and occasionally whole textiles. Preferred colors were red and blue, but all colors were used, and many more techniques.

Moche 100-650 AD

Not many Moche textiles are found today. The climate on the north coast with its recurrent floods is not good for preserving organic material.

But the textiles that remain prove that their textile craft was elaborate. Tapestry weavings depicted many natural scenes – among them many images of human sacrifice. Geometric patterns were also prevalent, and techniques like double weave, discontinuous weave, gauze and brocade. The plain weave was set up with single spun, paired warps.

Middle Horizon 500-900 AD

The Wari/ Tiwanaku originated in the highlands and influenced all coastal Peru.

The large tapestry woven tunics were woven on the vertical two beam loom.

The iconography was not as naturalistic as Moche/ Lambayeque. The tapestry tunics were in their images abstracted following specific and precise rules and could only be "read" by specialists. Some of the tapestries had a fineness of 70-80 camelid wefts per cm.

Lambayeque 900-1100 AD

The Lambayeque tapestries have very natural figurative images, representing both ritual but also everyday scenes. Flowers and animals were a common image – often with roots and tentacles stretching out from the fabric. The yarns were not as tightly packed as the Wari/ Tiwanaku tapestries. The large tunics were woven in plain weave cotton, and had sewed-on patches of tapestry, often with 3-dimentional decorations. The green color (indigo and some yellow plant dye) was very predominant. Unlike the other preColumbian weavings the Lambayeque used a very variable spin and ply.

Late intermediate: 1200-1500 AD

The coastal textiles were mainly cotton with smaller decorations in camelid fiber. The techniques were many – brocade, gauze weave and double weave in brown and tan were predominant. The large brocaded animals wearing a crescent feather imitation headpiece were abundant on the north coast. On the south coast tiny geometric intertwined patterns in tapestry and brocade were in vogue. The central coast sported intricate gauze woven shawls, complicated knotted hairnets painted with sea shell purpur, or cotton tapestries with edgy representations of seabirds and fish.

The male tunics from the coast in this period were rather short and could be with or without sleeves. They often had an added fringe at the bottom (looped fringe is an Ychsma indication).

North coast (Chimu) textiles had mainly single spun, paired warps – whereas Central coast (Ychsma/ Chancay) and south coast mostly used 2-ply yarns.

Late Horizon: 1450-1550 AD

The Inka wove their tunics and wrap-around-dresses on vertical two beam looms. Inka designs are "minimalistic" compared to the designs of earlier cultures and have mostly geometric motifs. A large step fret decoration was often woven around the neck and a band with geometric "tukapu" squares often decorated the center of male tunics. These tukapus are said to indicate messages – such as the hierarchical and geographic status of the wearer.

But they are so far not fully understood. The Inkas kept track of everything happening in their world in Quipus – a system of plied and knotted yarns – mostly in cotton. They also have not been fully deciphered.

Camelid fibers are predominant in the Inka textiles and many are woven in discontinuous weave. The Inka also braided exquisite slings. They wore them around the head and with time these slings became so large and elaborate that they were unfit for herding/hunting and only served as decorative headbands.

Colonial: 1536 – 1800 AD

Male tunics and female wrap-around dresses continued to be worn for centuries after the conquest. The tapestry designs became influenced from Europe and lost their edgy shapes. Rounded forms, silk yarns and Christian symbols indicate that a textile is definitely made after the conquest.

Explanation of terms in textile analysis

S: is a single spun yarn, spun in S direction.
Z: is a single spun yarn, spun in Z direction.
2S: is two single spun yarns – spun in Z and plied in S.
2Z: is two single spun yarns – spun in S and plied in Z.

In the indications of thread count, the warp measure is before the weft measure.
In the indications of size of a textile, the warp measure is before the weft measure.

The thread count is average (3 counts per textile)

All measurements are in centimeters.

Warp/weft rep is also called warp or weft faced.

Supplementary weft patterns are:

- Lancée: a supplementary weft pattern on top of a woven fabric, where the supplementary weft yarns reach from selvedge to selvedge.
- Brocade: the supplementary wefts only cover part of the warp.

The definitions of the techniques are from Irene Emery (see bibliography).

Bibliography

Bergh, Susan (2012) *Wari, Lords of the Ancient Andes*, The Cleveland Museum of Art, Thames & Hudson, New York.

Bjerregaard, Lena (2001) Doubletten — puzzles that could maybe some day be reconstructed, *Baessler-Archiv*, band 49, Berlin.

Bjerregaard, Lena (2002) *Pre-Columbian Treasures in the National Museum of Copenhagen*, Corpus Antiquitatum Americanensium/The National Museum of Denmark, Copenhagen.

Bjerregaard, Lena (2006) Haar als Symbol und Werkstoff; Haar-Objekte in den Staatlichen Museen zu Berlin, *Journal-Ethnologie* 6.

Bjerregaard, Lena (2010) Fist-braided bands used as headgear in pre-Hispanic Peru, *Archaeological Textile Newsletter* 51:2-13, University of Copenhagen.

Bjerregaard, Lena (2011) Pre Columbian Hairnets in the Ethnological Museum, Berlin, *Baessler Archive*, no. 57, Berlin.

Bjerregaard, Lena (2011) Redecillas Purpuras de la Costa Central, *Jornadas V de Textiles Precolombinos*, Universidad Autonoma Barcelona.

Bjerregaard, Lena (2016) Lambayeque-style textiles in the Ethnologisches Museum, Berlin, *Nuevo Mundo Mundos Nuevos*, online http://nuevomundo.revues.org/69290

Bjerregaard, Lena (2016) Non-woven Textile Techniques in Pre-Columbian Peru, *Archaeological Textile Review* 58:86–97.

Bjerregaard, Lena (Ed.) (2017) *PreColumbian Textiles in the Ethnological Museum in Berlin*, Zea Books, Lincoln, NE, online https://digitalcommons.unl.edu/zeabook/52/

Boetzkes, Manfred, Wolfgang Gockel and Manfred Höhl (Eds.) (1986) *Alt-Peru. Auf den Spuren der Zivilisation*, Katalog-Verlag EA Quensen GmbH, Lamspringe.

Boetzkes, Manfred (Ed.) (1994), *Welten in Vitrinen. 150 Jahre Roemer-Museum*, Catalogue from Roemer-Museum Hildesheim.

Boone, Elisabeth Hill, ed. (1996) *Andean Art at Dumbarton Oaks*, Vol 2., Washington, D.C.

Boytner, Ran (1998): *The Pacatnamú Textiles: A Study of Identity and Function*. Ph.D. dissertation, University of California, Los Angeles.

D'Harcourt, Raoul (1962) *Textiles of Ancient Peru and Their Techniques*, University of Washington Press, Seattle.

Donnan, Chris B. (1986) An Elaborate Textile Fragment from the Major Quadrangle, *The Pacatnamu Papers*, vol. 1, pp. 109-114. Museum of Cultural History, University of California, Los Angeles.

Dransart, Penelope and Helen Wolfe (2011) *Textiles from the Andes*, British Museum Press, London.

Emery, Irene (1966), *The primary structures of fabrics*, Thames and Hudson, London.

Frame, Mary (1986) Nasca Sprang Tassels: Structure, Technique and Order. *Textile Museum Journal* 25, 67-82, Washington, D.C.

Frame, Mary (1997) *Textiles Chuquibamba*, Museo de Arte, Lima.

Frame, Mary (2003) What the women were wearing: A deposit of early Nasca dresses and shawls, *Textile Museum Journal*, 42/43:13-53, Washington, D.C.

Frame, M., F. Vallejo, M. Ruales, and W. Tosso (2012) Ychsma textiles from a Late Horizon burial at Armatambo, *Ñawpa Pacha* (Institute of Andean Studies, Berkeley, CA) 32(1): 43–84.

Frei, Karin, and Lena Bjerregaard (2017) Provenance investigations of raw materials in preColumbian textiles from Pachacamac; strontium isotope analyses, in *Actas VII Pre-Columbian Textiles Conference in Copenhagen 2016*, pp. 387-398, Zea Books, University of Nebraska–Lincoln, https://digitalcommons.unl.edu/pct7/22/

Gayton, A. H. (1955) A new type of ancient Peruvian shirt, *American Antiquity*, vol. 20, Utah.

Haeberli, Joerg (2002) Siguas 1: A newly identified Early Horizon Culture, Department of Arequipa, Peru, *TSA Symposium Proceedings*, http://digitalcommons.unl.edu/tsaconf/392

Hecker, Gisela (1995) *Die Grabungen von H. Ubbelohde-Doering in Pacatnamu, Nordperu*, Berlin.

Jiménez Díaz, María Jesús (2009) *Tradición de tradiciones, La coleccíon del Museo de América*, Madrid.

Keck, Rudolf W. (Ed.) (1994) *Gesammelte Welten. Das Erbe der Brüder Roemer und die Museumskultur in Hildesheim (1844-1994)*, Verlag Gebrüder Gerstenberg Hildesheim.

King, Heidi (2012) *Peruvian Featherworks*, Metropolitan Museum of Art, New York.

Kurella, Doris, and Inés de Castro (2013) *Inka Könige der Anden*, Linden-Museum, Stuttgart.

Lavalle, J. A., and G. J.A. González (1993) *The textile art of Peru: Collection*. Lima, Peru.

Lavalle, José Antonio de, and Rosario de Cárdenas Lavalle, eds. (1999), *Textiles Milenarios del Peru*, Lima.

Makowski, Krzysztof, Alfredo Rosenzweig, María Jesús Jiménez Diaz, and Jan Szemiński (2006) *Weaving for the Afterlife, Peruvian Textiles from the Maiman Collection*, Vol. I, Israel.

Makowski, Krzysztof et al. (2010) *Señores de los Imperios del Sol*, Banco de Crédito del Perú, Lima.

Montell, Gösta (1929) *Dress and Ornament in Ancient Peru*, Göteborg.

Oakland, Amy (2008) The string or grass skirt: an ancient garment in the southern Andes, *Textile Society of America Symposium Proceedings*, paper 120.

Oakland Rodman, Amy and Gioconda Arabel Fernandez Lopez (2005) North coast style after Moche: Clothing and identity at El Brujo, Chicama Valley, Peru, in Ricard Martin Reycraft, ed., *Us and Them: Archaeology and Ethnicity in the Andes* (64th annual SAA, Chicago, April 1999), Cotsen Institute of Archaeology, University of California, Los Angeles.

Paul, Anne (1990) *Paracas Ritual Attire, Symbol of Authority in Ancient Peru*, University of Oklahoma Press.

Pease G. Y., Franklin (1999) *Los Incas: Arte y Símbolos*, Banco de Credito del Perú, Lima, 1999.

Phipps, Elena, et al. (2004) *The Colonial Andes*, The Metropolitan Museum of Art, New York.

Phipps, Elena (2013) *The Peruvian Four-Selvaged Cloth*, Fowler museum Textile Series, No. 12, Los Angeles.

Pillsbury, Joanne (2002) *Inka Unku: Strategy and Design in Colonial Peru*, Studies in the History of Art, Cleveland.

Prümers, Heiko (2007) *Zeitschrift für Archaeologie Aussereuropäischer Kulturen 2*, Textiles de la Tumba del „Señor de Sipán", Peru, pp. 255-324.

Reid, James (1986) La Textileria Nasca, *Culturas Precolumbinas*, eds. José Antonio de Lavalle, Banco de Crédito del Perú, Lima.

Reiss, Wilhelm, and Alphons Stübel (1880) *Das Todenfeld von Ancon*, Berlin.
Rickenbach, Judith, and Nikkibarla Calonder (2007) *Textilien aus dem alten Peru: die Sammlungen der Abegg-Stiftung und des Museum Rietberg,* Schweitz.
Rowe, Ann P. (1977) *Warp-patterned Weaves of the Andes,* Textile Museum, Washington, D.C.
Rowe, Ann P. (1984) *Costumes and Featherwork of the Lords of Chimor,* Textile Museum, Washington, D.C.
Rowe, Ann P. (1995-96) Inca Weaving and Costume, *Textile Museum Journal,* Textile Museum, Washington, D.C.
Rowe, Ann P. (2014) Technical reflections of highland–coastal relationships in late prehispanic tunics from Chillon and Chancay, *Textiles, Technical Practice, and Power in the Andes,* London.
Rowe, John Howland (1979) Standardization in Inca Tapestry Tunics, *Junius B. Bird Pre-Columbian Textile Conference 1973*, figs.1-3, pp. 246-47.
Shimada, Izumi (1985), Excavations on Huaca Grande: An Initial View of the Elite of Pampa Grande, Peru, *Journal of Field Archaeology* 12.
Shimada, Izumi (1995) *Cultura Sicán. Dios, riqueza y poder en la costa norte del Perú, Lima*: EDUBANCO, Fundación del Banco Continental para el fomento de la Educación y la Cultura, 1995
Stone-Miller, Rebecca (1992) *To Weave for the Sun, Andean Textiles in the Museum of Fine Arts,* Boston.
Strelow, Renate (1996) *Gewebe mit Unterbrochenen Ketten aus dem Vorspanischen Peru* (*Pre-Hispanic Peruvian Textiles with Discontinuous Warp*), Neue Folge 61, Museum für Völkerkunde, Berlin.
Young-Sánchez, Margaret (1969) *The Chancay Textile Tradition: Textiles from Lauri in the Collection of the Amano Museum,* Lima.
Young-Sánchez, Margaret (2004), *Tiwanaku, Ancestors of the Inca,* Denver Art Museum/ University of Nebraska Press.
Young-Sánchez, Margaret and Fronia W. Simpson (2006) *Andean Textile Traditions, Papers from the 2001 Mayer Center Symposium at the Denver Art Museum,* Denver Art Museum, Denver, Colorado.

Exhibition catalogues: No author

Paracas, tresors inedits du Perou ancient (2008) Musee quai Branly, Paris.
Inka. Textiles and ornaments of the Andes. (2019) Royal Museums of Art and History, Bruxelles

Conference papers:

Ed. Solanilla Demestre, Victoria (2000), *Actas I, Jornadas Internacionales de Textiles Precolombinas,* Universitat Autonoma de Barcelona.
Ed. Solanilla Demestre, Victoria (2002), *Actas II, Jornadas Internacionales de Textiles Precolomblnas,* Universitat Autonoma de Barcelona.
Ed. Solanilla Demestre, Victoria (2006), *Actas III, Jornadas Internacionales de Textiles Precolombinas,* Universitat Autonoma de Barcelona.

Ed. Solanilla Demestre, Victoria (2009), *Actas IV, Jornadas Internacionales de Textiles Precolombinas,* Universitat Autonoma de Barcelona.

Ed. Solanilla Demestre, Victoria (2011), *Actas V, Jornadas Internacionales de Textiles Precolombinas,* Universitat Autonoma de Barcelona.

Ed. Desrosiers, Sophie (2017), *Actas VI, Pre-Columbian Textile Conference 2014,* Quai Branly, Paris, Mundo Nuevo – Nuevos Mundos, Colloques. https://nuevomundo.revues.org/69877

Ed. Bjerregaard, Lena and Ann Peters (2017), *Actas VII, Pre-Columbian Textile Conference 2016,* Copenhagen, Zea Books, University of Nebraska–Lincoln. https://digitalcommons.unl.edu/zeabook/59/

Ed. Bjerregaard, Lena and Ann Peters (forthcoming 2020) *Actas VIII, Pre-Columbian Textile Conference 2019,* Royal Museums of Art and History, Bruxelles, http://digitalcommons. unl.edu/zeabook/

Unedited:

Prümers, Heiko, (1983) *Präkolumbische Textilien von der Mittleren Küste Perus aus der Sammlung des Roemer Museum Hildesheim.* M.A. Dissertation.

PARACAS/NAZCA – 500 BC – 500 AD

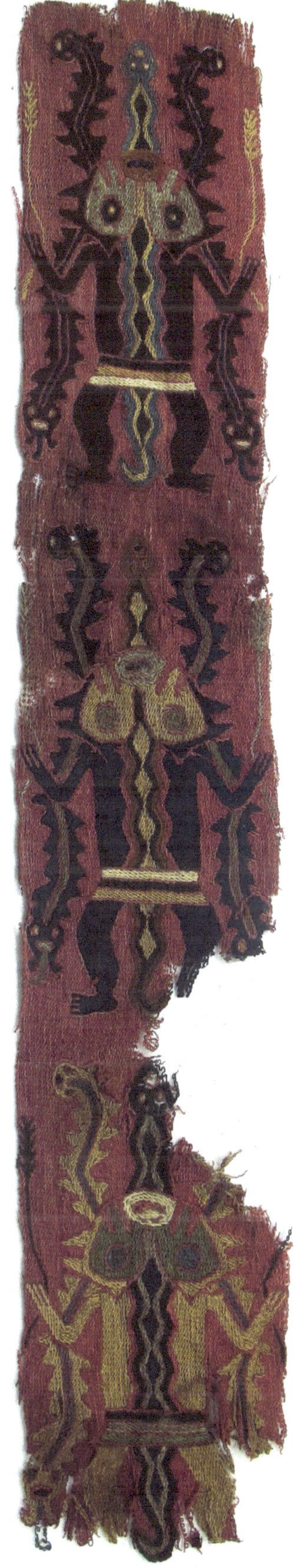

Museum number: Dauerleihgabe STIFTUNG NIEDERSACHSEN, coll. Zarnitz, L/SN 12

Item: Edge band from turban or skirt.
Style: Paracas /Nazca, 500 BC-500AD
Size: 35 x 6 cm
Material/technique: Plain weave with soumack embroidery over 2 yarns, under one.
Cotton plain weave: 2S. Threadcount is 14 x 14 per cm. Embroidery: Camelid fiber 2S.
Further description: the cotton backing material is almost gone. It can not be stated what is warp and what is weft.

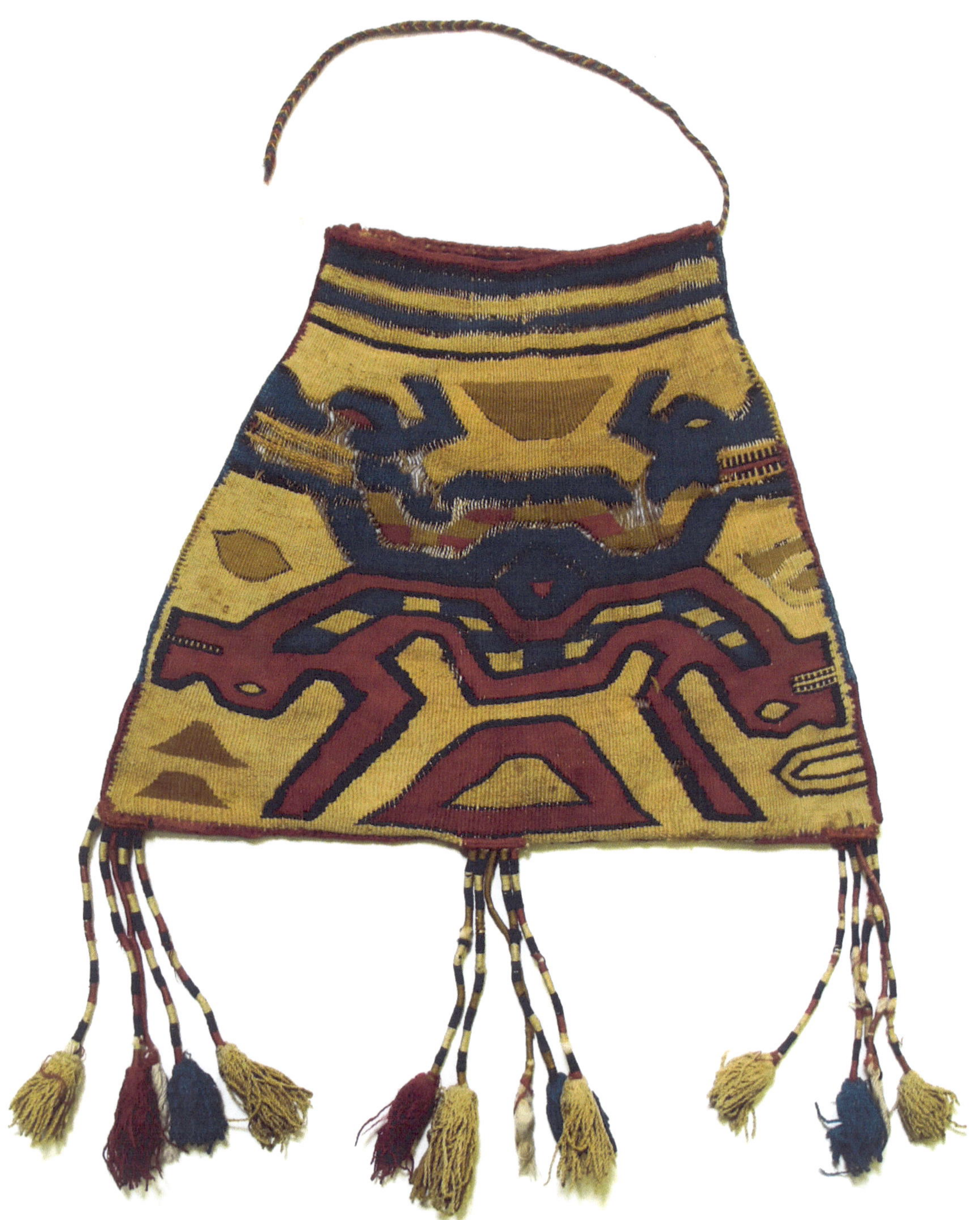

Museum number: V 8.961

Item: Bag
Style: Nazca
Size: 23 x 30 cm
Material/technique: Tapestry weave. Warp: cotton 2S (a brown and a white twined together). Weft: camelid fiber 2S. The threadcount is 8 x 30 per cm.
Further description: The edges of the bag are sewn together/ adorned on edge (top) and fold (bottom) with loop stitch embroidery. At top is a flat 4 braid – for strap – attached at one edge, fragmented at other. At bottom 3 groups of wrapped yarns ending in a tassel. 4 yarns in each group. These are cotton yarns 2S wrapped with camelid fiber 2S. These wraps with tassels are 13 cm long.

Museum number: V 9.300

Item: Woven tassel
Style: Nazca
Size: 35 x 8 cm
Material/technique: A plain weave (camelid fiber 2S) cloth 8 cm wide is folded along the warp center, so it is double and the two weft edges are partly sewn together along the right side. The threadcount is 12 x 5 per cm.
17 cm loose warp-fringe below – at top 4 cm warp loops.
The woven part is adorned with chain-stitch and cross knit loop stitch.

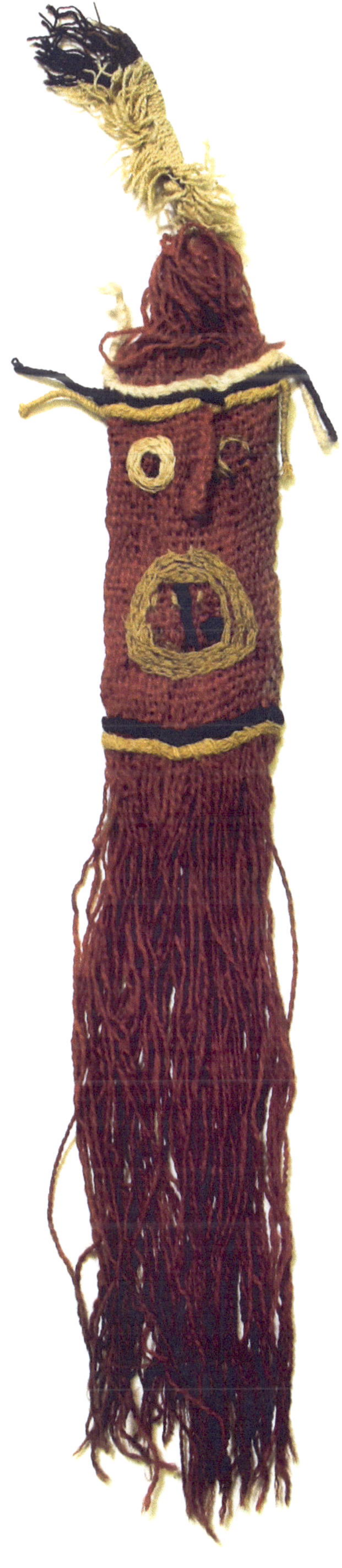

MIDDLE HORIZON – 400-800 AD

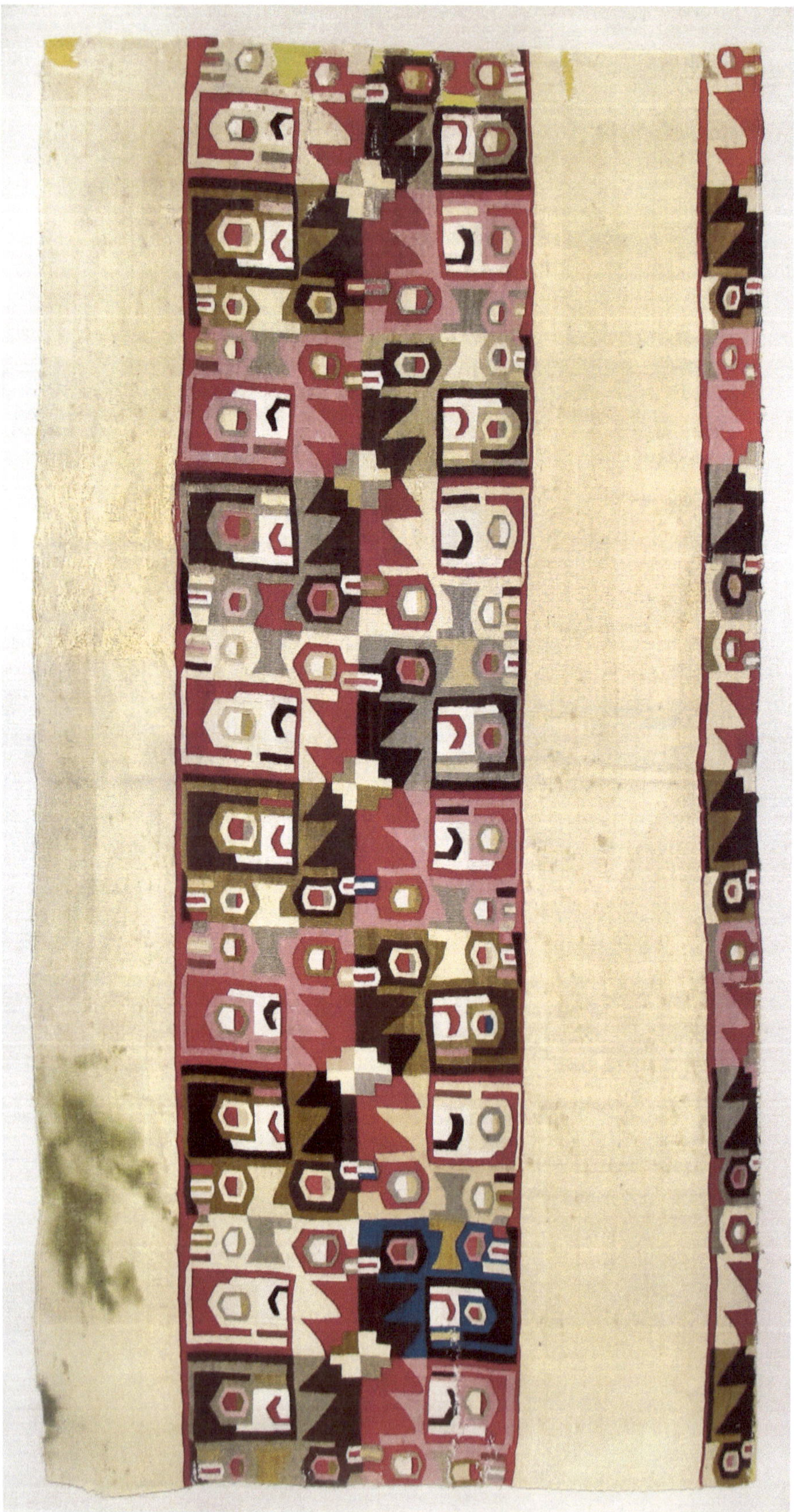

Museum number:
Leihgabe STIFTUNG NIEDERSACHSEN, Schenkung Zarnitz/Pelling

Item: 1/4th of a tunic
Style: Wari
Size: 56 x 108 cm
Material/technique: Interlocked tapestry. In various places in the white parts there are "lazy lines" (maybe – an indication that several weavers were engaged side by side).
Cotton 2S warps, camelid fiber 2S wefts. The threadcount is 12 x 48 per cm.
Further description: At intervals two or more warps are tan instead of white – but somehow not following/indicating the pattern. The side designs are not completely aligned with the center patterns. But close (0,5 – 1 cm apart)
Notice the sparse blue....
The fragment has NO warp-selvedges but fragments of weft-selvedges at both sides. Also some side edge embroidery is left: at one end 38 cm of embroidery (an 8-shape stitching to another cloth), then 30 cm loop stitch embroidery (indicating the arm hole), and the last 38 cm without any embroidery.
Thus indicating that the textile here has the shoulderline in the horizontal center – and is then cut off horizontally 54 cm down the front and back of a tunic panel.
The textile is a long term loan of the Savings Bank Foundation of Lower Saxony.

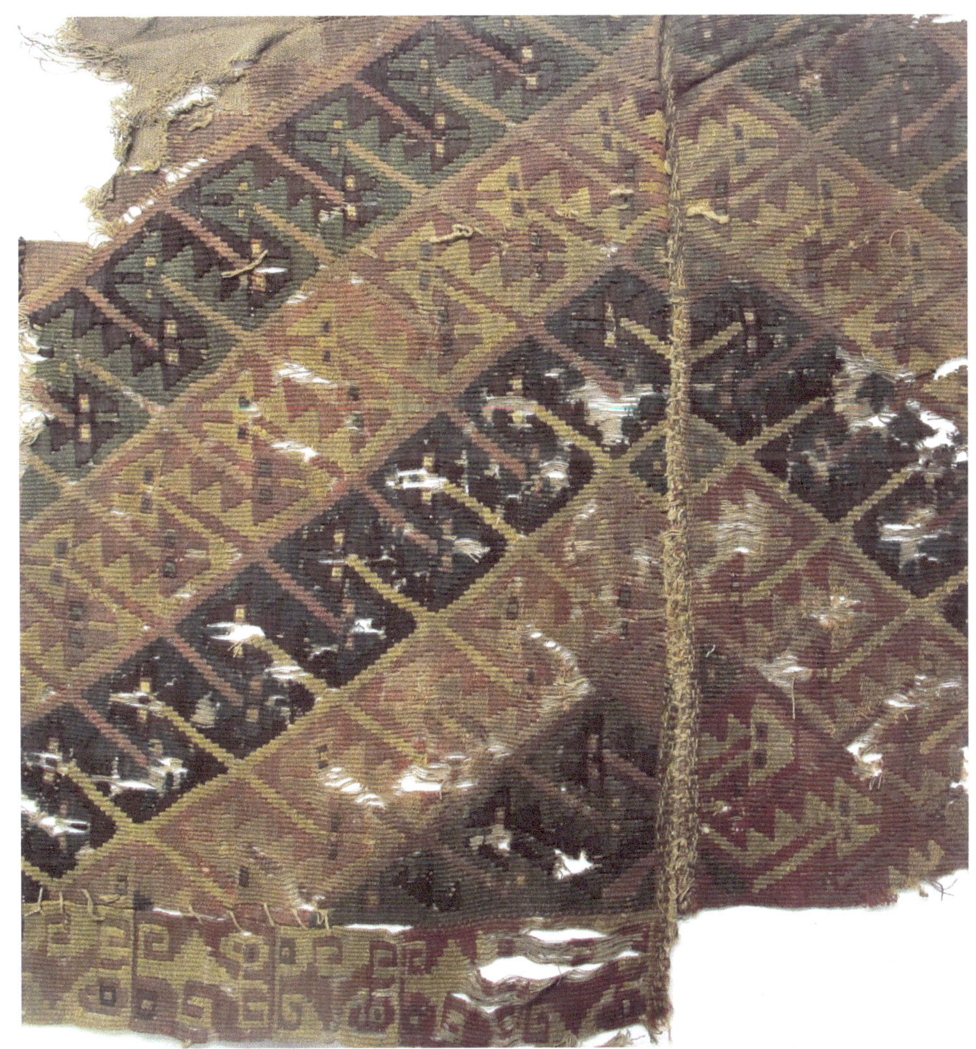

Museum number: V 8.957

Item: Fragment
Style: Late Middle Horizon, Central coast
Size: 45 x 35 cm
Material/technique: Two panels sewn together. Slit tapestry, warp cotton 3Z, weft camelid fiber 2S. At lower left edge is a piece of plain weave cotton (Z yarns). The threadcount is 18 x 11 per cm.

Museum number: V 9.061

Item: Fragment
Style: Late Middle Horizon, South Coast
Size: 22 x 11 cm
Material/technique: Interlocked (every 2 mm) tapestry, warp 2S cotton; weft 2S camelid fiber. The threadcount is 9 x 42 per cm.
Further description: V9050 is a fragment of the same textile.

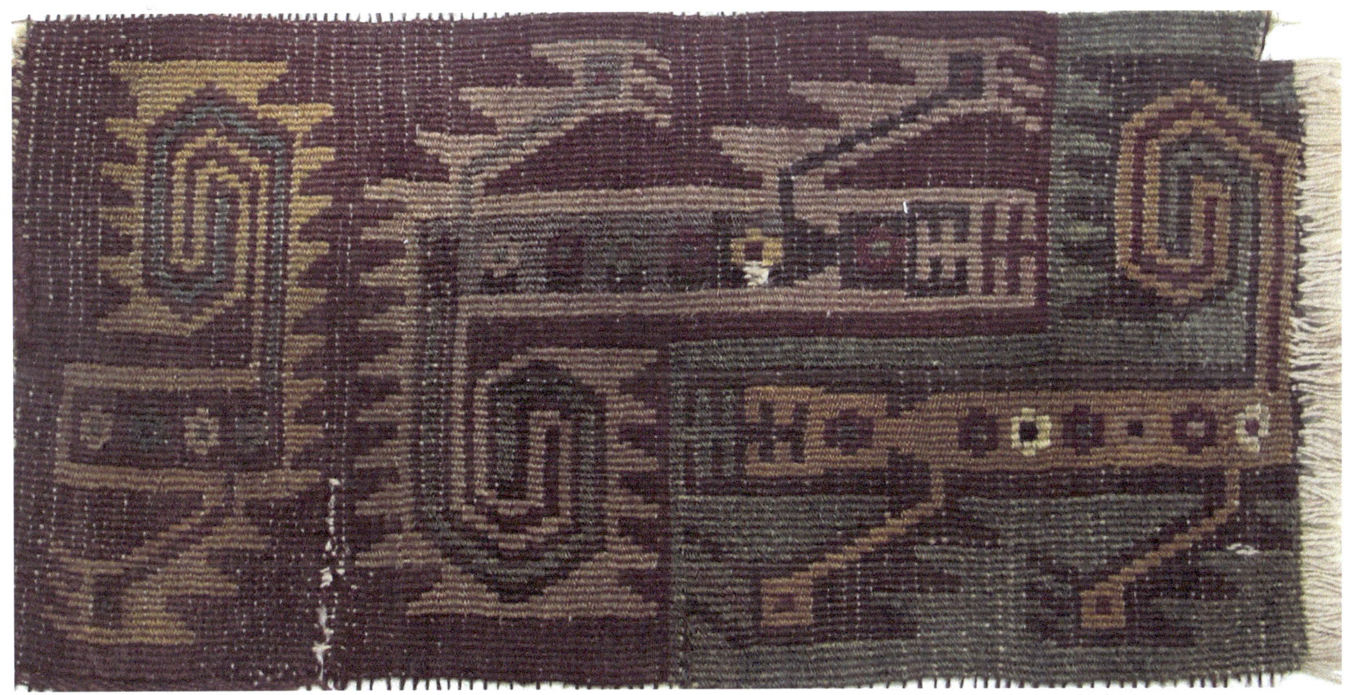

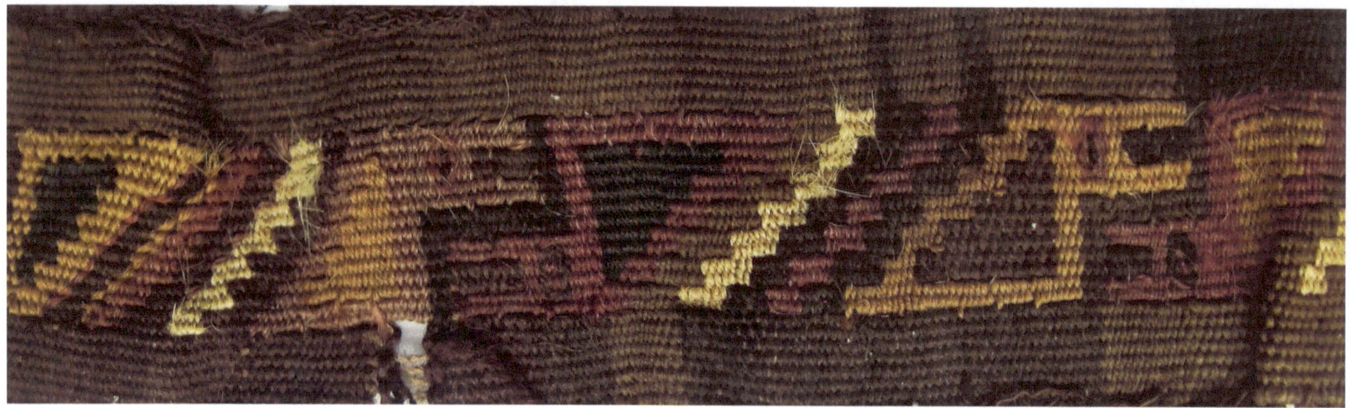

Museum number: V 9.054

Item: Band
Style: Middle Horizon
Size: 47 x 2,5-3 cm
Material/technique: Interlocked tapestry (every 5 wefts), warp cotton 2Z, weft camelid fiber 2S. The threadcount is 12 x 42.
Further description: At one end is warp selvedge, at two sides are side selvedges. Fragments of a plain weave cotton material (S, threadcount: 20 x 20 per cm) at the sides – to which the band has been stitched.

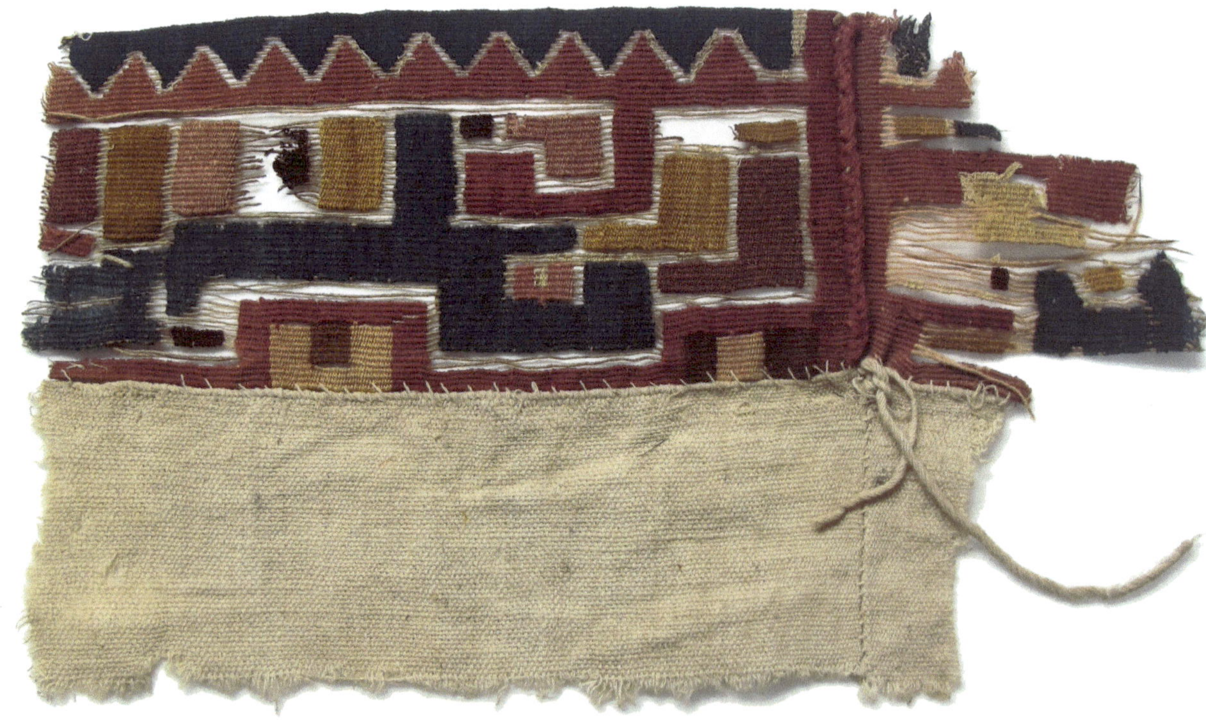

Museum number: V 9.082

Item: Fragment
Style: Middle Horizon, North or South Coast.
Size: 25 x 13 cm
Material/technique: The fragment consists of two panels sewn together. Each panel has:
1. an interlocked (every 6-7 mm) tapestry band. Warp in the larger panel is camelid fiber 2S, in the smaller panel camelid fiber 2Z. Weft 2S camelid fiber in both panels. The two panels are sewn together with loop stitch embroidery. The threadcount is 9 x 46 per cm.
2. a plain weave cotton textile (two panels), warp is paired, both warp and weft are single S. The threadcount is 9 (paired) x 10 per cm. The warp selvedge is stitched on to the tapestry band (that has warp lengthwise).

Museum number: V 9.145

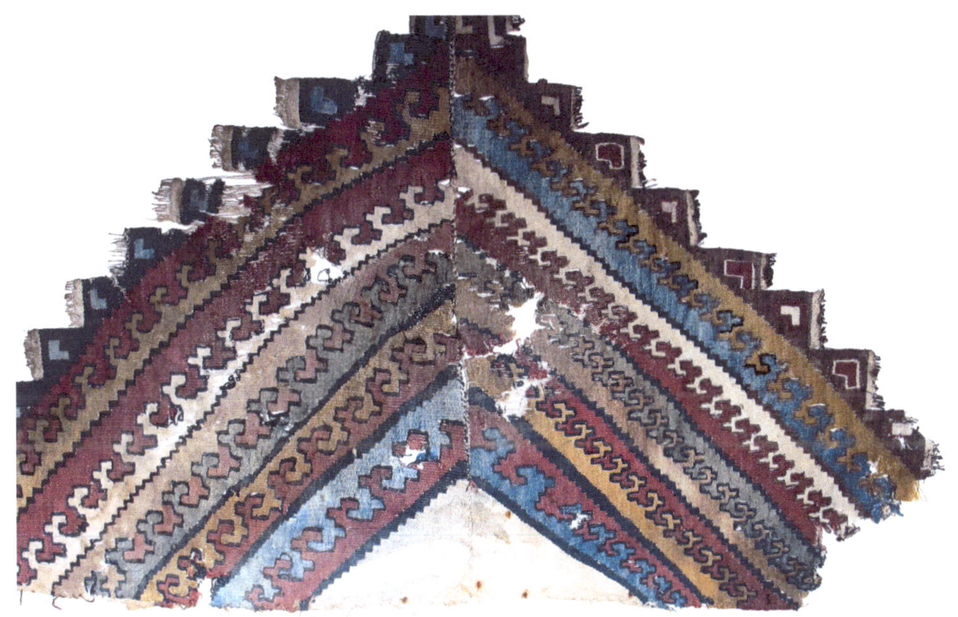

Item: Fragment
Style: Late Middle Horizon, Central/ North Coast,
Size: 68 x 37 cm
Material/technique: The textile is in plain weave cotton 2Z (both warp and weft). The threadcount is 7 x 12 per cm in the plain weave. The textile has tapestry patterning with a threadcount of 7 x 26 per cm. The tapestry warp is the plain weave warp and the weft is 2Z cotton.
Further description:
The textile consists of two fragments sewn together along their warp selvedges. This sewing is probably not original – the tapestry patterning seem not to belong together. Both fragments have a side selvedge aligned vertically to the right in photo.
In Textile Museum, Washington is a similar complete tunic (TM1969.38.1). It is a short tunic with sleeves. The tapestry part consist of 4 pieces that have been appliqued to a basic cotton textile with seams at shoulder and center front and back.

Museum number: V 9.228

Item: Fragment
Style: Middle Horizon
Size: 28 x 29 cm
Material/technique: 4 dovetailed tapestry bands (7 cm wide) stitched together. Cotton 2S warp, camelid fiber 2S weft. The threadcount is 7 x 40 per cm.
Further description: No warp selvedges.
Litterature: Raoul D'Harcourt, 1966, pl. 8, Tiwanacu.

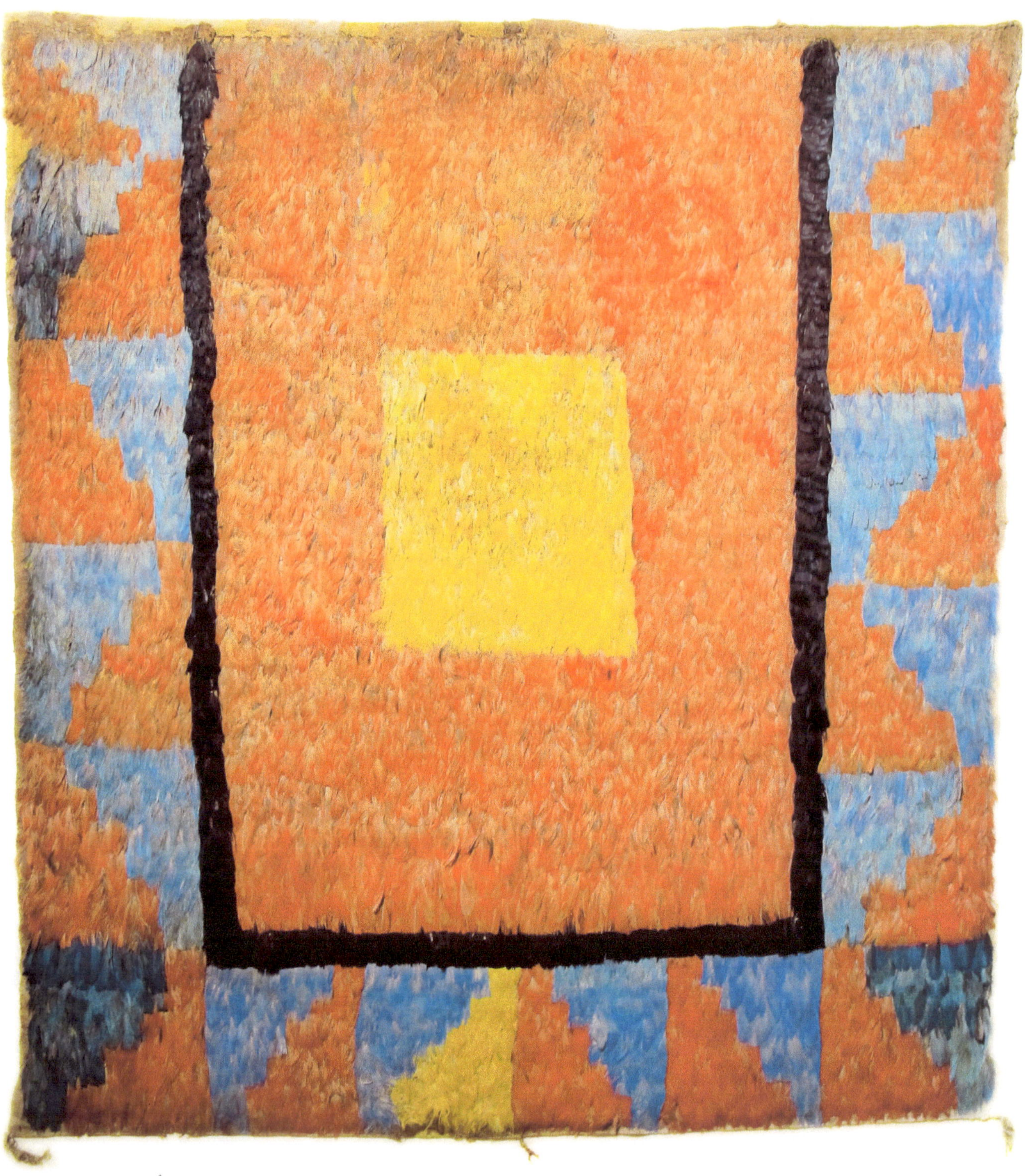

Museum number: V 10.399 a

Item: Half of a tunic
Style: Central or South coast, 400 – 600 AD
Size: 106 x 100 cm
Material/technique: The base cloth of the textile is cotton 2S woven in plain weave. The thread count is 10 x 7 per cm.
Feathers in different colors are stitched on as feather fringes made with two tying cords.
Gift by the Museum Society on the occasion of the 150th anniversary of the Roemer-Museum, 1996.

LAMBAYEQUE – 900-1300 AD

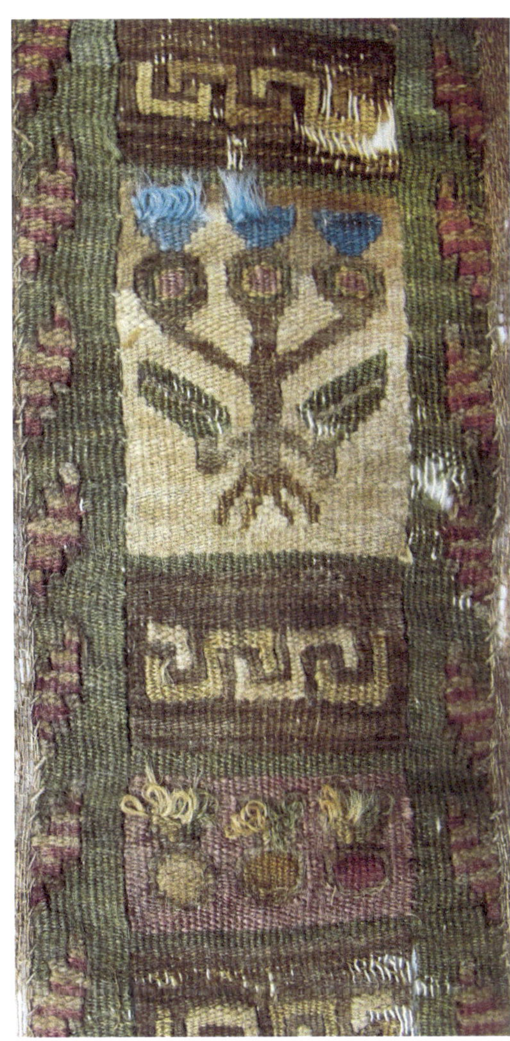

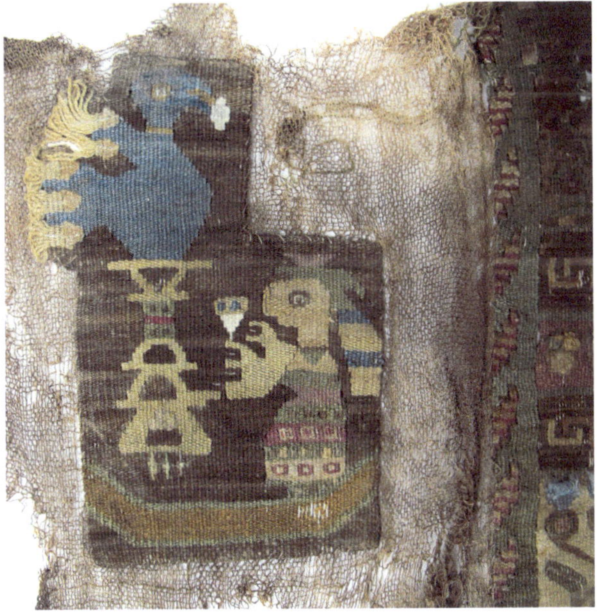

Museum number: V 9.353

Item: Fragment of tunic
Style: Lambayeque
Size: 51 x 36 cm
Material/technique:

1. The foundation fabric of the tunic is cotton, plain weave, S (warp and weft). The threadcount is ca 12 x 8 per cm
2. The center band – 7 cm wide – has warp cotton S, weft camelid 2S. The threadcount is 9 x 40 per cm.
3. The patches are tapestry, warp cotton S, weft cotton S and camelid fiber 2S. The treadcount is 9 x 24 per cm.

Further description: The textile is a fragment from the front side of a tunic with appliqued center band and patches. The iconography on the patches seems to be a person (maybe a woman because of the foot long garment – or a man in ritual clothes?) offering something to a turkey on a piedestal.

The pattern on the center band is trees or plants with flowers (maybe cotton), vegetables, and geometric patterns.

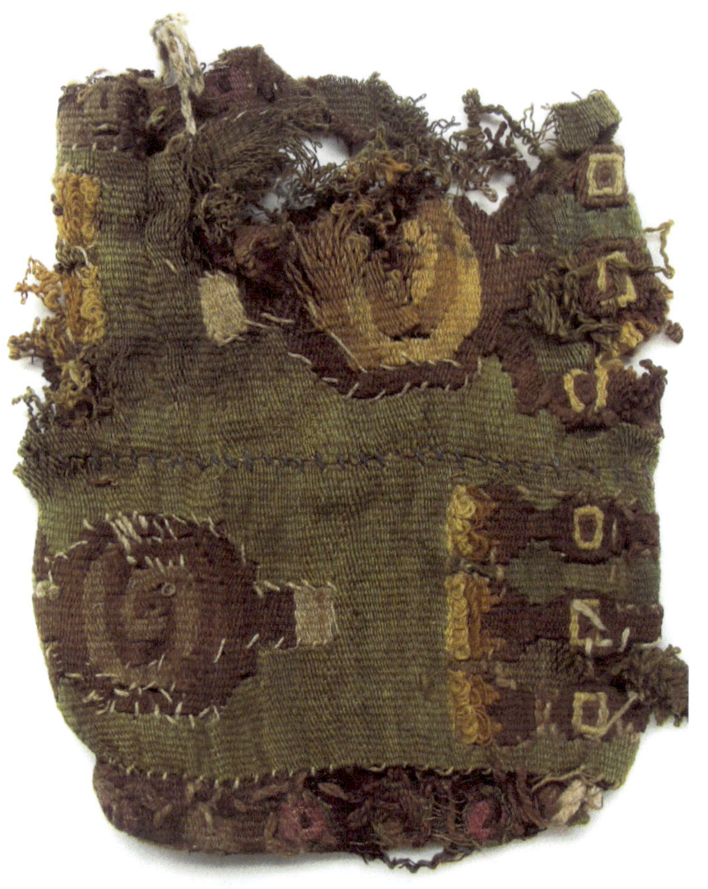

Museum number: V 9.309

Item: Bag
Style: Lambayeque
Size: 18 x 15 per cm
Material/ technique: Slit tapestry with occational 3-dimensional looping (for flowers). Warps: cotton S, wefts: camelid fiber S.
Further description:
The bag is a reuse of bands: In the center two 7 cm wide bands from a tunic center band, and at top and bottom two cm wide bands.

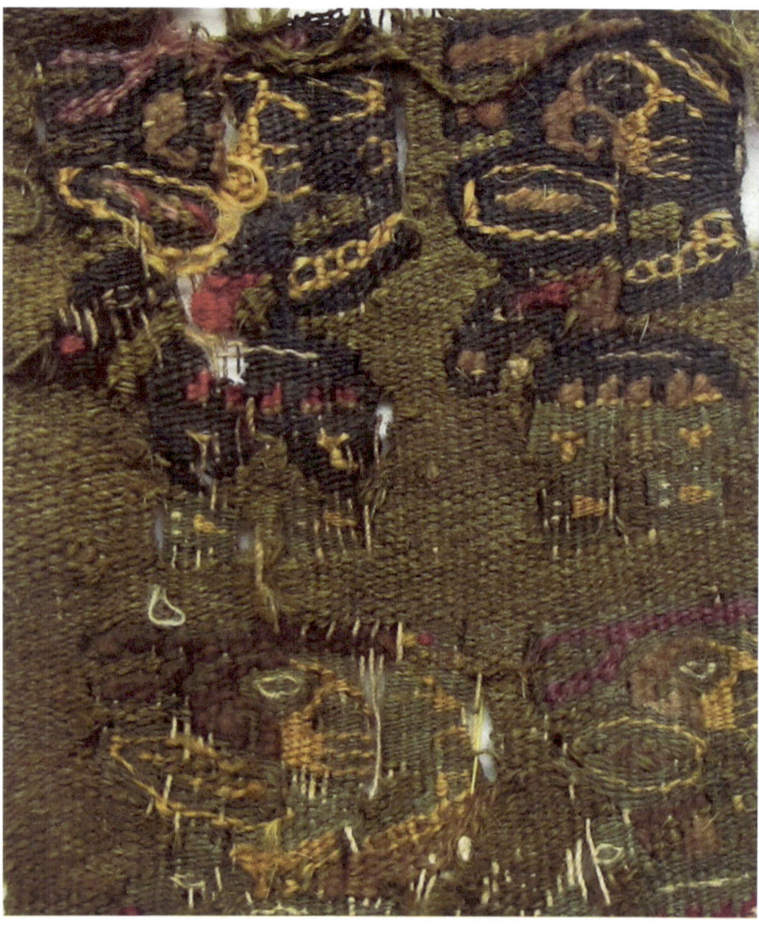

Museum number: V 9.294

Item: Fragment from center band of tunic
Style: Lambayeque
Size: 16 x 6 cm
Material/technique: Tapestry: warp cotton, 2Z, weft camelid fiber 2S. The threadcount is 11 x 26 per cm.
There are fragments of sewing threads on the two side selvedges.
Further description: The iconography is of anthromorphic figures with bird's heads and carrying bundles.
V 9.294 and V 9.193 are from the same textile.

Museum number: V 9.279

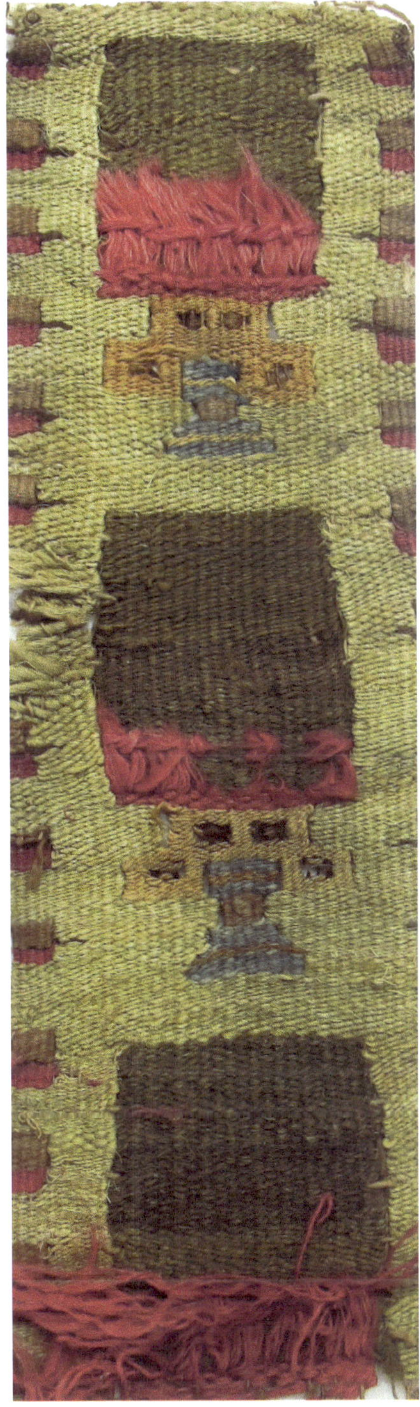

Item: Fragment from center band of tunic
Style: Lambayeque
Size: 21 x 7 cm
Material/technique: Slit tapestry, warp cotton S, weft camelid fiber 2S. The threadcount is 6-7 x 30 per cm. Along the side selvedges are fragments of sewing threads used to attach the band to a foundation textile. A few threads of this fabric (cotton S) are left in place.
The iconography is of a stylized high status person (large ear spools, pyramid base) wearing a huge hat.

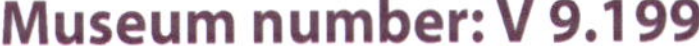

Museum number: V 9.199

Item: Fragment of tunic
Style: Lambayeque
Size: 44 x 10 cm
Material/technique: The fragment consists of 3 parts: all only have side selvedges.

1. in the center is a cotton S plain weave band 5 cm wide. The threadcount is 22 x 9 per cm.
2. to both sides (lengthwise) of this band is sewn a tapestry band (no fringe) 3 cm wide with step fret patterns. 2Z cotton warps. Wefts: 2S camelid fiber and paired Z cotton. The threadcount is 6-7 x 20-28 per cm.

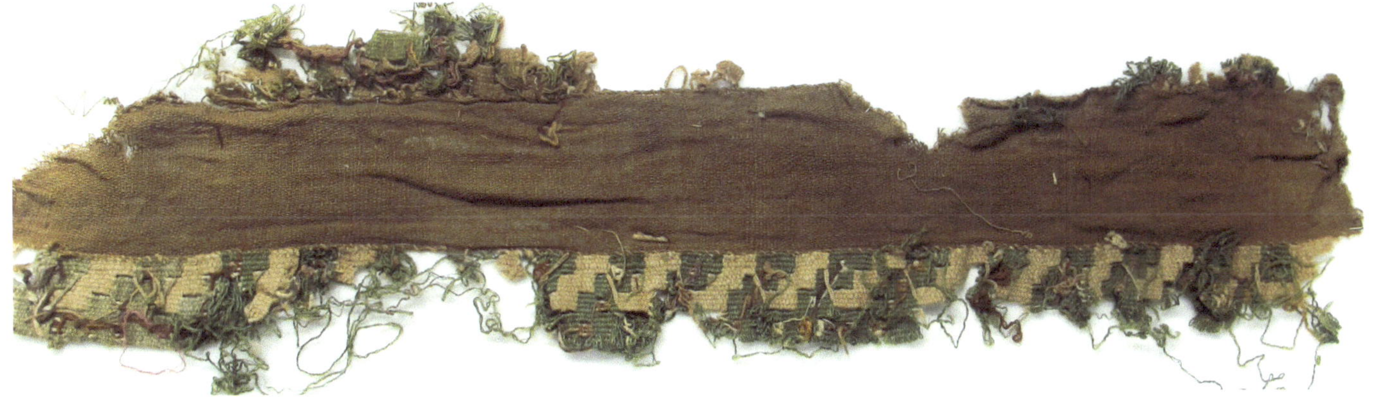

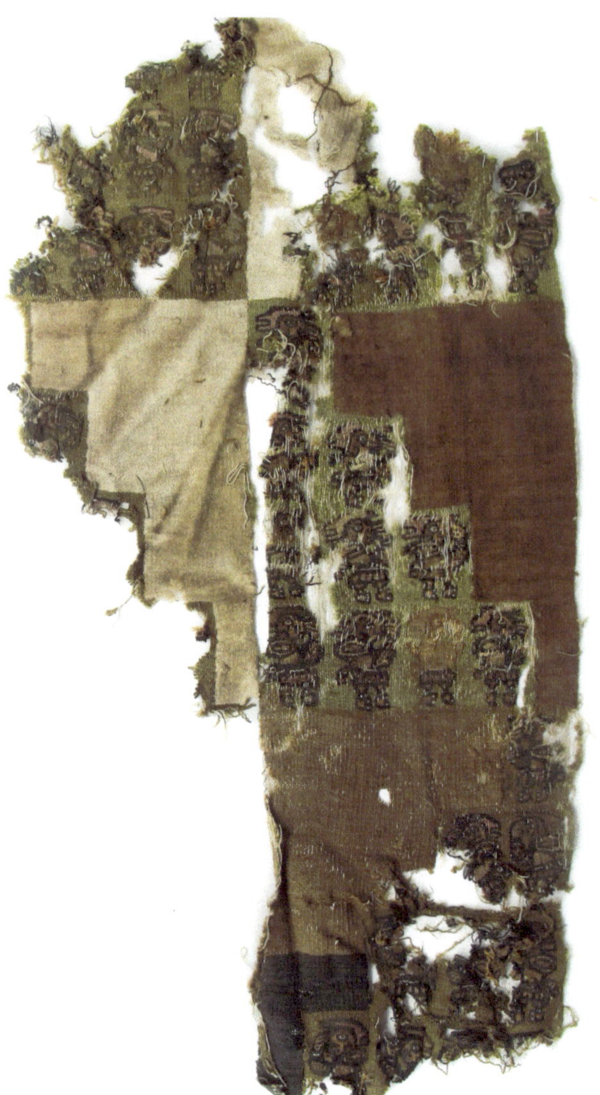

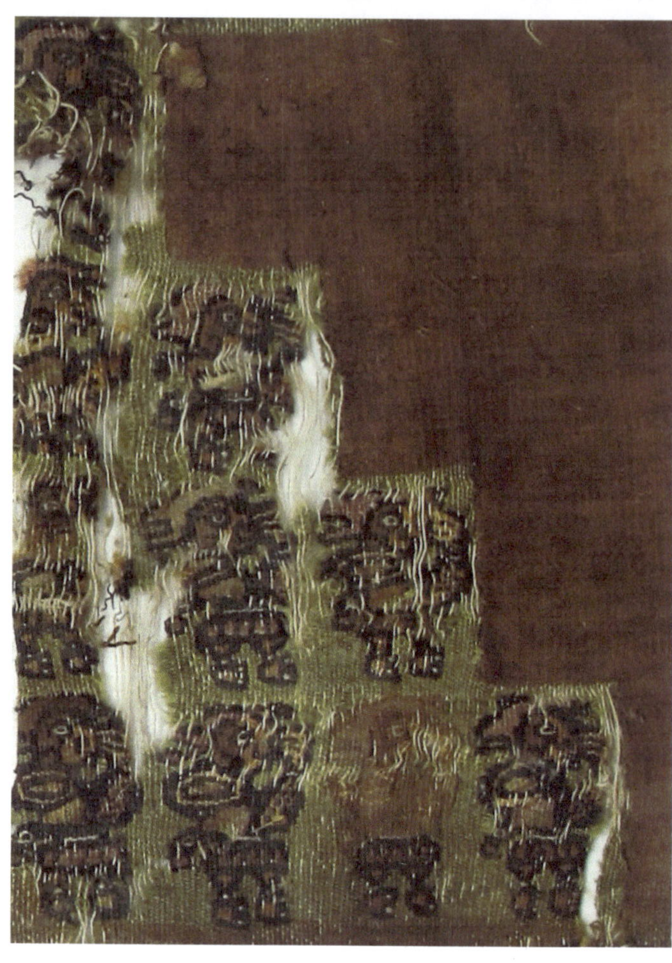

Museum number: V 9.193

Item: Fragment of tunic
Style: Lambayeque
Size: 43 x 22 cm
Material/technique: Slit tapestry, warp cotton 2S, weft camelid fiber 2S. The threadcount is 11 x 26 per cm.
Further description: anthropomorphic figures with human/bird's head figures and monocrome step fret patterns.
V 9.193 and V 9.294 are from the same textile.

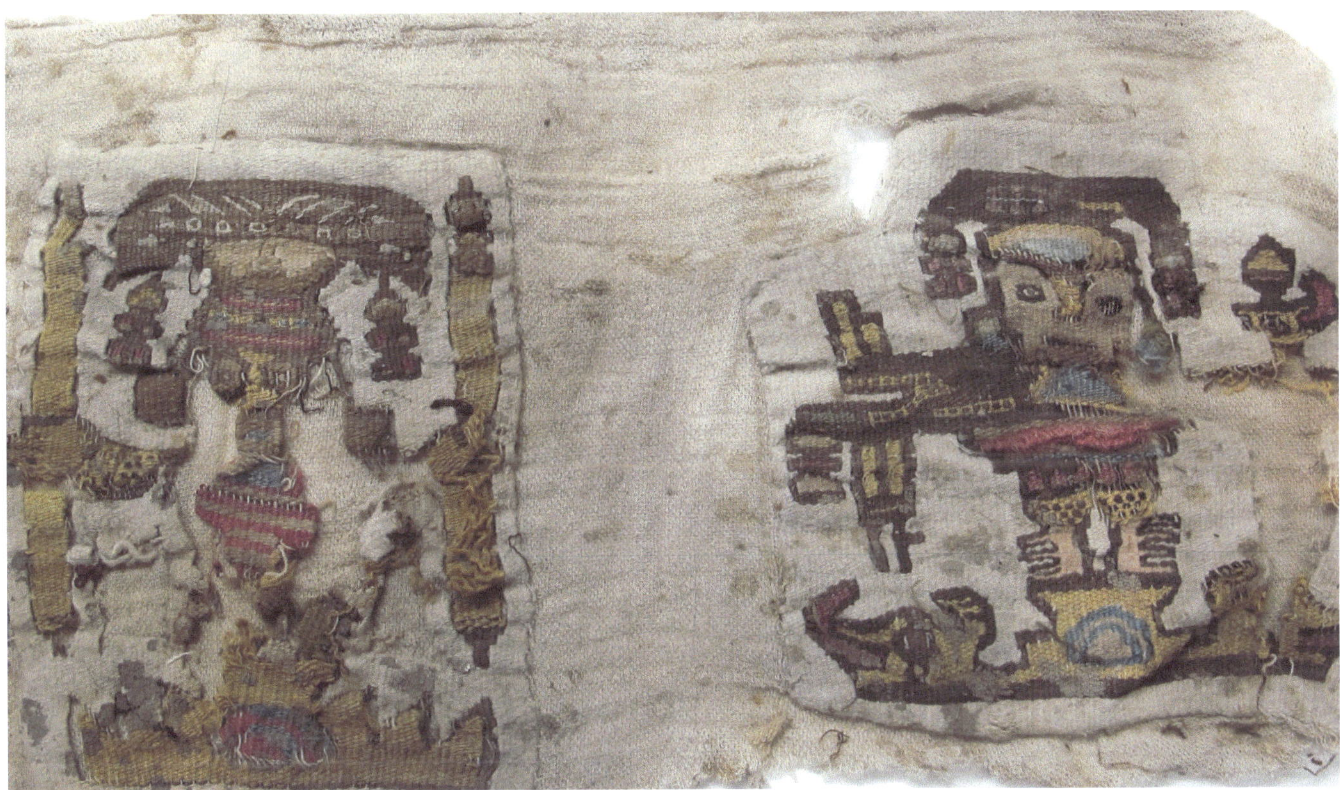

Museum number: V 9.171

Item: Fragment of a tunic

Style: Lambayeque

Size: 24 x 58 cm

Material/technique: The fragment is from a tunic.

The foundation material is loosely woven plain weave cotton S – the warp is paired. The threadcount is 18 (paired) x 12 per cm.

Further description: Patches of slit tapestry (16 -14 x 13) are appliqued on a foundation textile. The motifs are "the great lord" (or God) standing on a step fret construction, wearing a feathered headdress and ear spools and carrying staffs in both hands. On the right patch is a stripe of looped wefts on the person's stomack.

The two other patches are similar – and the right (although representing the same) is a very different design.

The patches have cotton warp – the two right are S and the left is Z spun. The wefts are camelid fiber 2S and 2Z cotton.

The 3,5 cm wide sideband is also slit tapestry. Warp S and weft camelid fiber 2S and paired cotton Z.

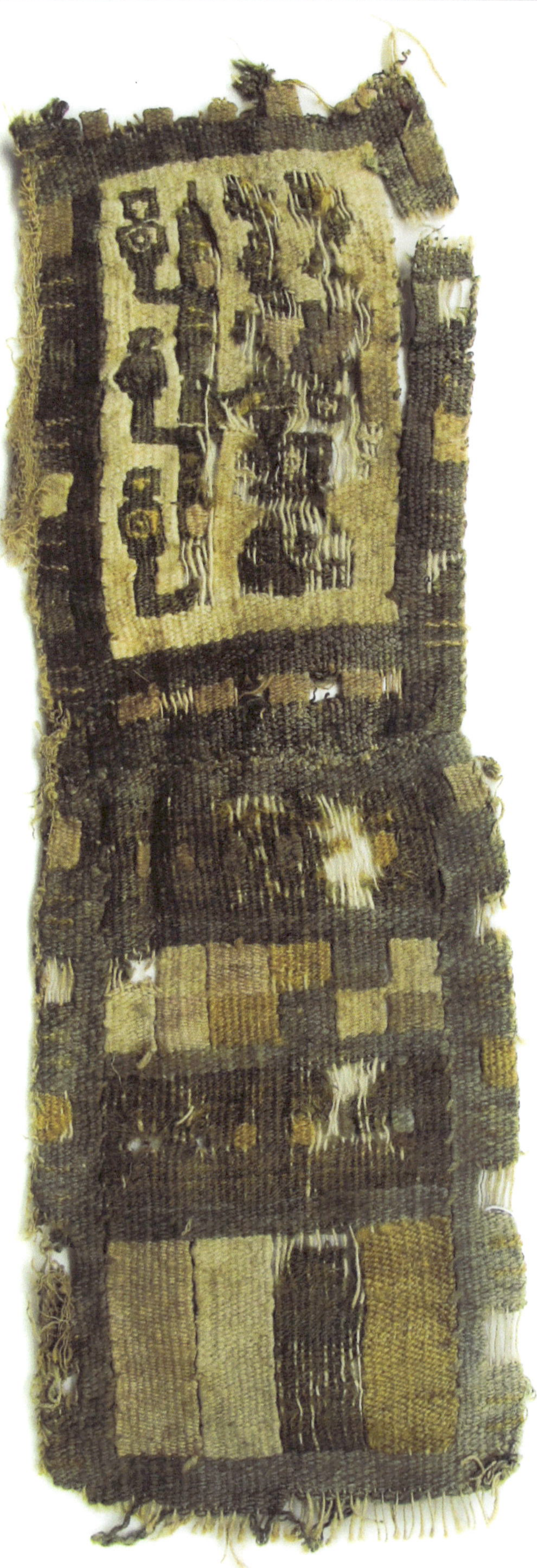

Museum number: V 9.114

Item: Fragment
Style: Lambayeque
Size: 30 x 10 cm
Material/technique: slit tapestry, warp cotton 2S, weft cotton 2S and camelid fiber 2S. The threadcount is 7 x 20 per cm. Two fragments of 14,4 cm are sewn together along the warp selvedge. Along the right weft selvedge is a smal fragment of a loosely woven, plain weave cotton textile, stitched on.
Probably the item is a center stripe from a tunic.

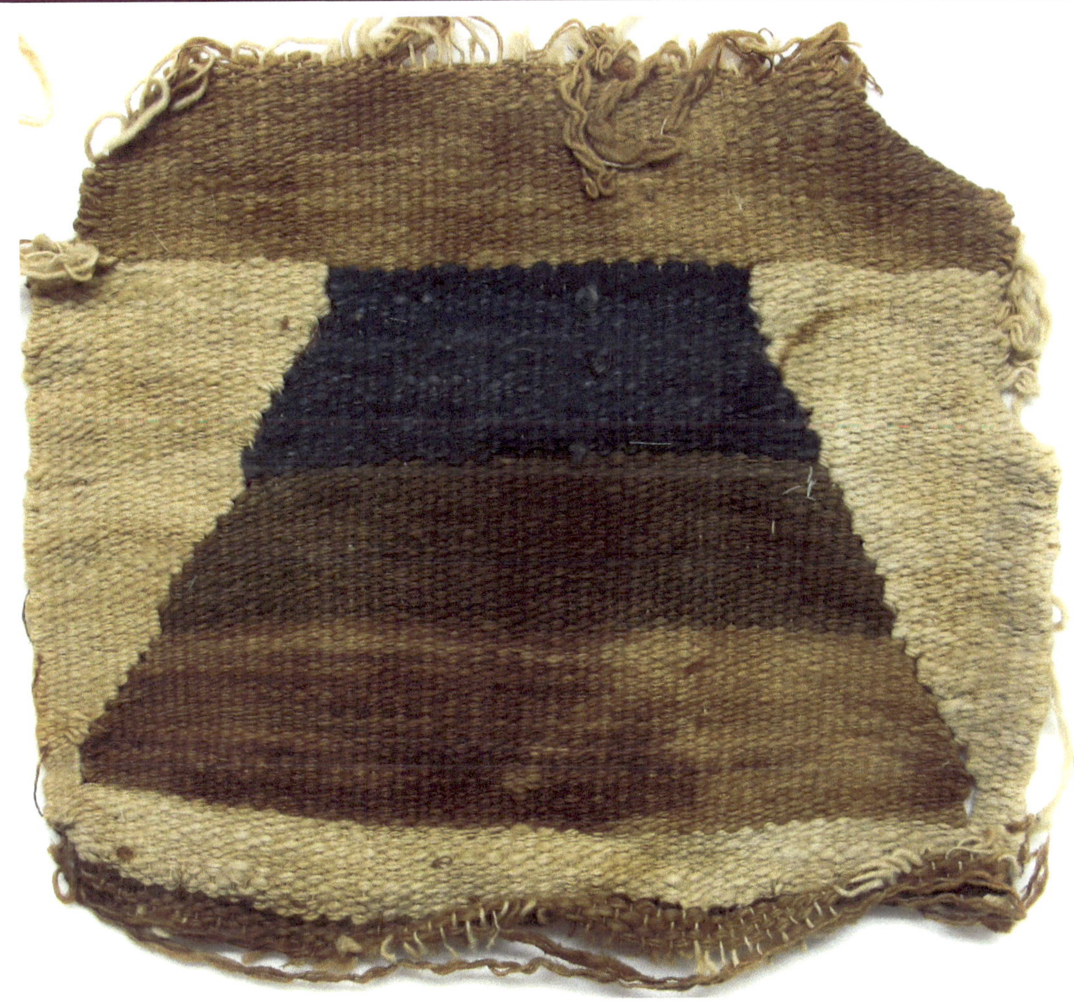

**Museum number:
V 9.098**

Item: Fragment of patch
Style: Lambayeque
Size: 13 x 14 cm
Material/technique: Tapestry with warp cotton S and weft cotton paired S.
2 side selvedges, with fragments of sewing threads used for attatching it to the foundation textile.
The image is of a pyramid – an abstract power symbol.

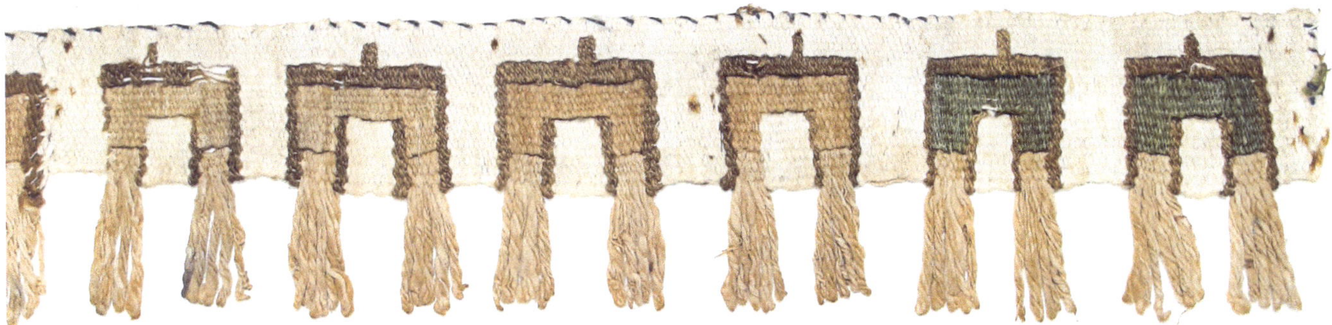

Museum number: V 9.100

Item: Fragment of a band
Style: Lambayeque
Size: 62 x 7 cm
Material/technique: Tapestry with weft fringes. Warp: cotton S, weft: cotton Z and camelid fiber 2S.
The threadcount is 5 x 30 per cm.

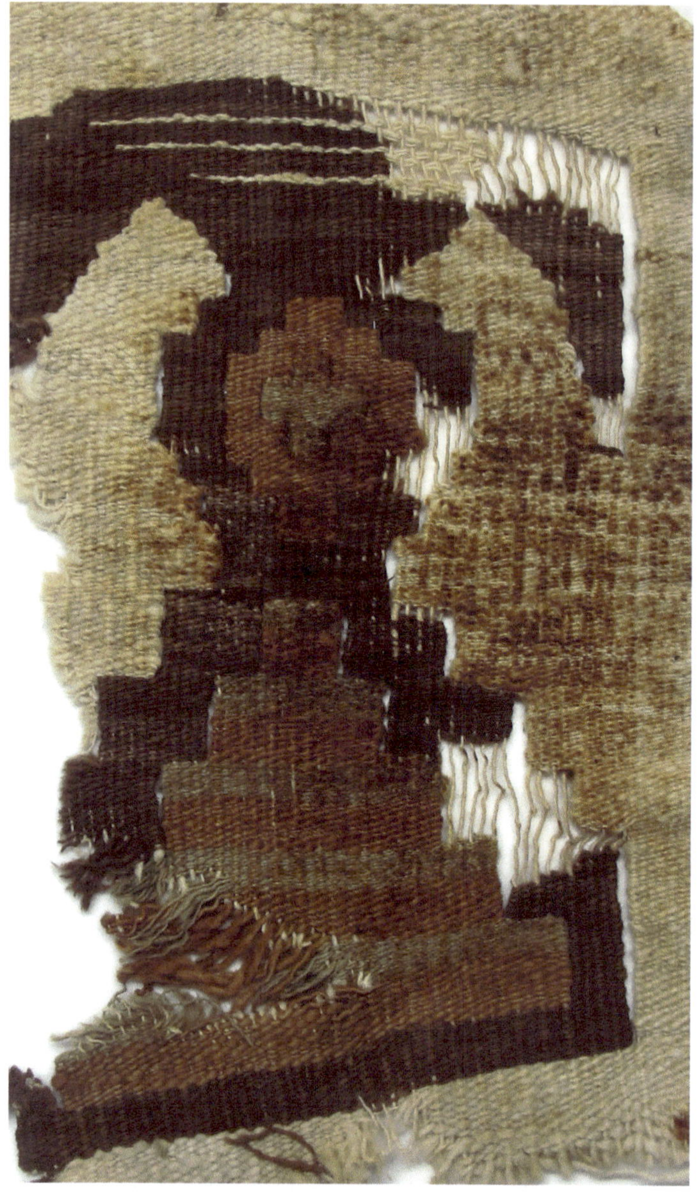

Museum number: V 9.093

Item: Patch
Style: Lambayeque
Size: 18 x 12 cm
Material/technique: Tapestry, warp cotton S, weft cotton S, single and paired.
The fragment is probably from a tunic. The image is a status person/god (step fret pyramid with face with crescent headgear as an abstract power symbol). The patch has side selvedges – along one are sewing threads for attatching to the foundation textile.

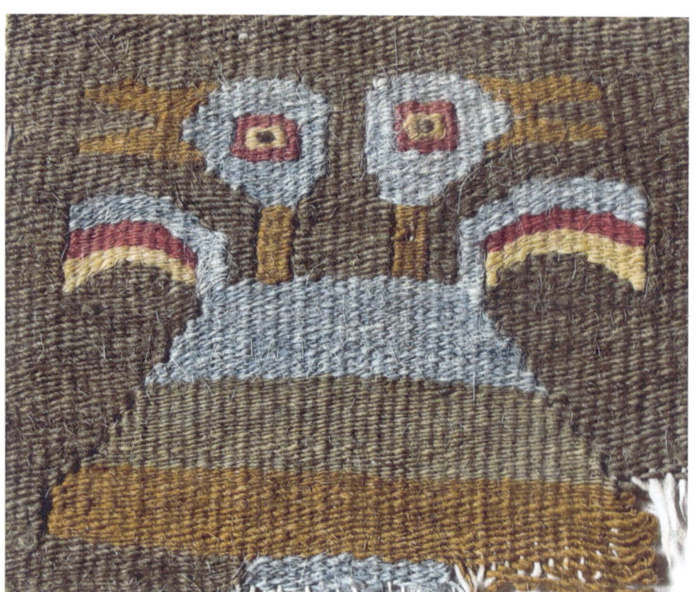

Museum number: V 9.091

Item: Fragment of patch for tunic
Style: Lambayeque
Size: 12 x 12 cm
Material/technique: Tapestry, cotton S warp, camelid fiber 2S weft. The threadcount is 5 x 34 per cm.
Two side selvedges – no warp selvedges.

Museum number: V 9.092

Item: Patch for tunic
Style: Lambayeque
Size: 20 x 12,5 cm
Material/technique: The patch is in cotton tapestry weaving and has the warp S, and the weft S and Z. The red spot is camelid fiber 2S.The threadcount is 6 x 22-32 per cm.
At both warp ends the patch is cut and bent down with a 0,5 cm seam. Two side selvedges.
Further description: The patch is probably from a tunic. Pattern is a status person/god (step fret pyramid and face with crescent headgear – an abstract power symbol). The patch has side selvedges – along one are sewing threads for attaching it to the base textile.

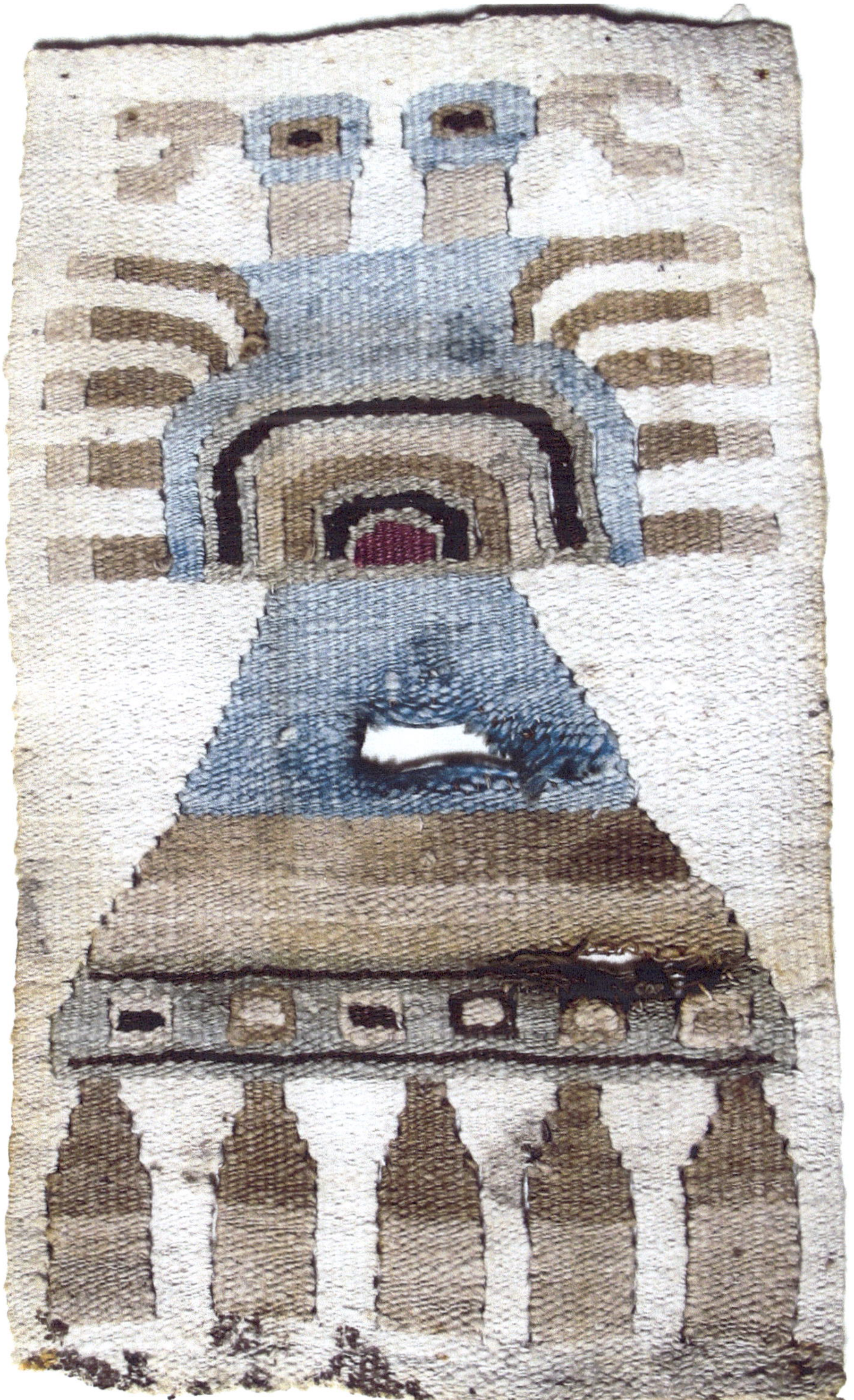

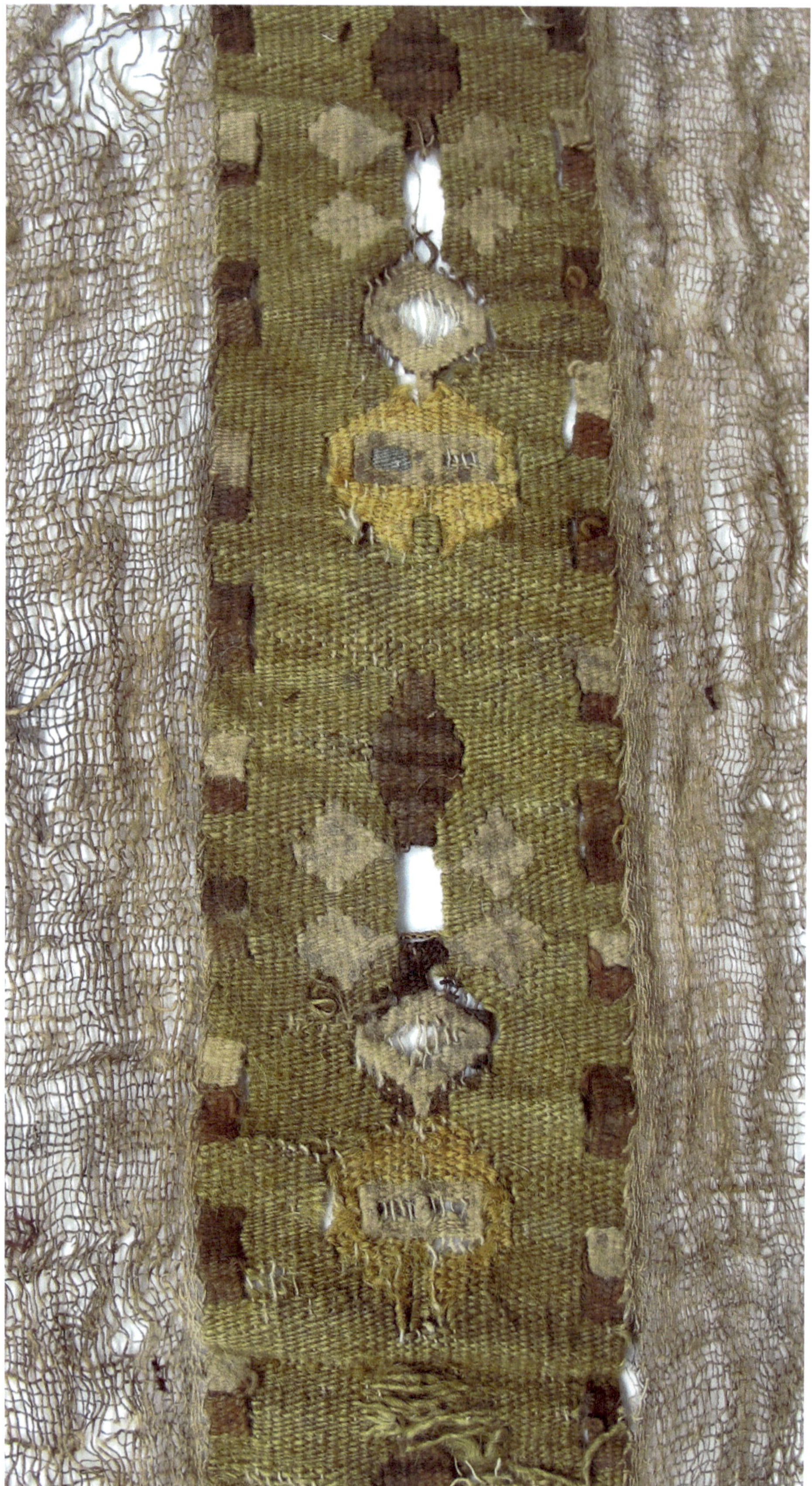

Museum number: V 9.175

Item: Fragment of tunic
Style: Lambayeque
Size: 54 x 38 cm
Material/ technique: The fragment is from a tunic made in cotton S loose plain weave. The threadcount is 6 x 6-8 per cm. This foundation material of the tunic has 3 different colored warp stripes, and at top a fragment of a horizontal tapestry band with fringe (indicating that it is the back upper part of the tunic). This band is 5 cm wide, has warp S cotton, and weft 2Z camelid fiber. The threadcount is 6-7 x 20 per cm.
The vertical center band - 6 cm wide – is in slit tapestry with cotton warp S, and camelid fiber weft 2S. The threadcount is 6-7 x 20 per cm.

Late Intermediate Period (1200 – 1450 AD)

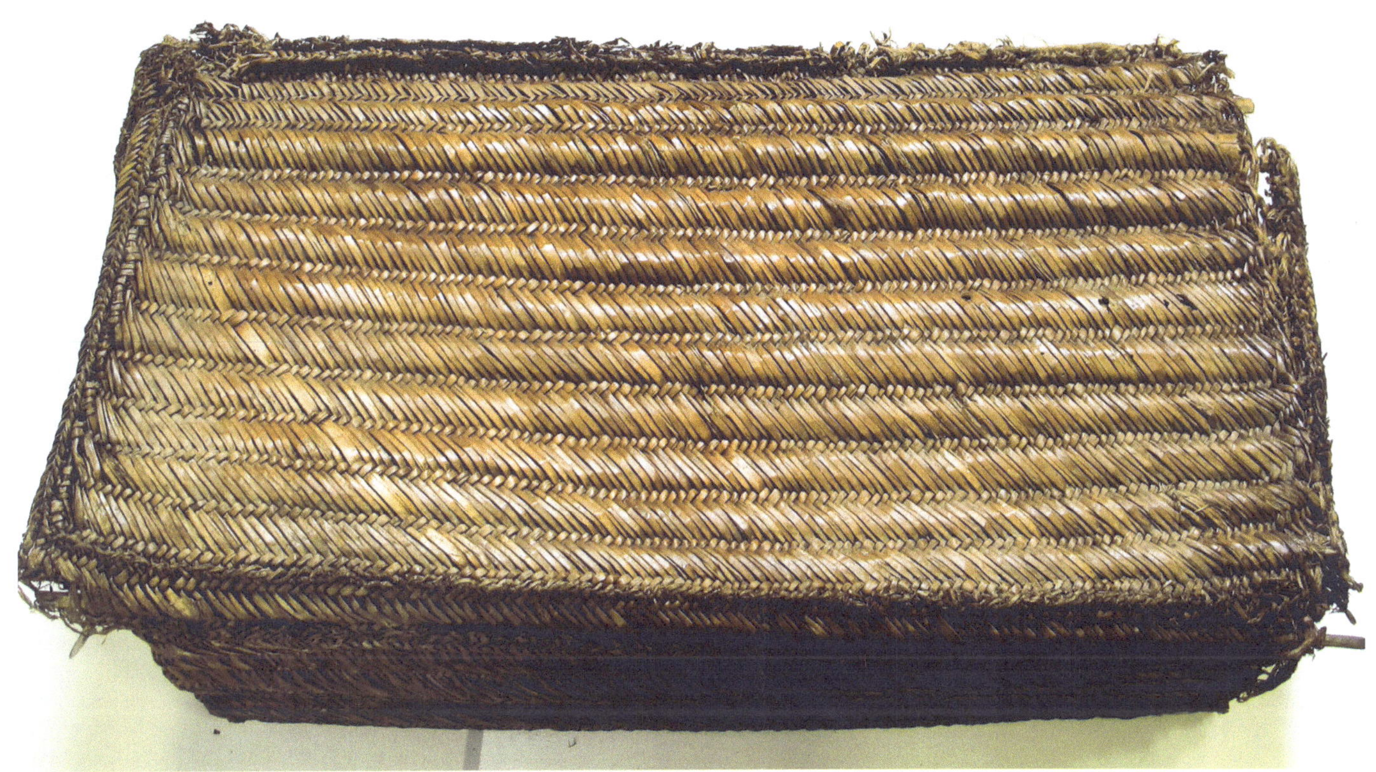

WORK BASKET

Museum number: V 5.466

Item: Work basket
Style: Late Intermediate Period, Central Coast/ North Coast
Size: 53 cm (long) x 29 cm (wide) x 23 cm (height)
Material/technique: The very large workbasket is made of plaited reed.

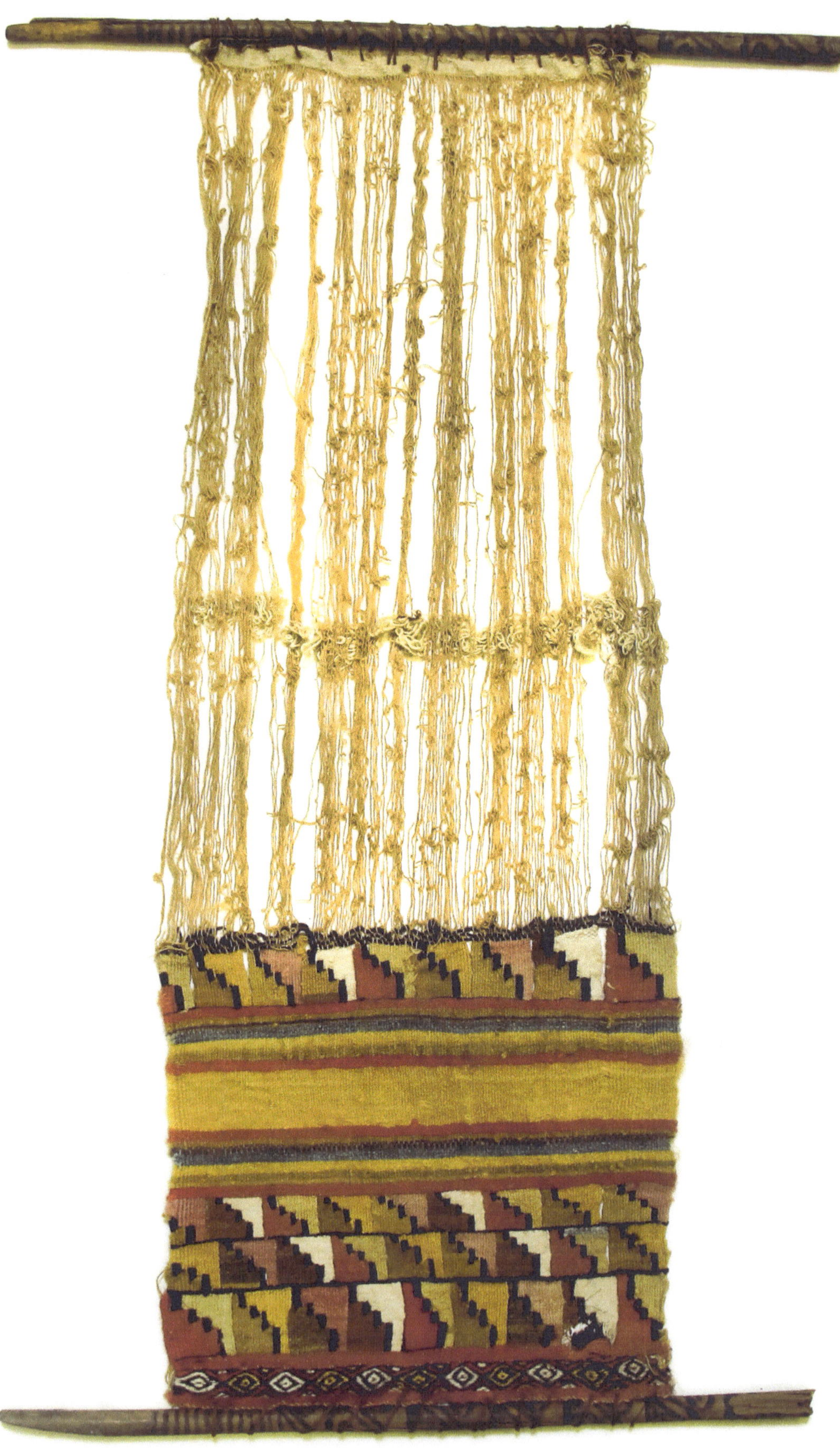

The workbasket contains:

Museum number: V 10.191 in workbasket

Item: Loom
Style: Late Intermediate Period, Central coast
Size: Loom sticks 27 cm, weaving 17 cm
Material/technique: Weaving set up on top and bottom beam.
The weaving is slit tapestry. Warp: cotton S, weft camelid fiber 2S. The threadcount is 10 x 36 – 40 per cm.
At bottom is 1 cm of weft brocade lancée (supplementary weft). At top 1 cm plain weave. The heddle (cotton 2S) is still in place.

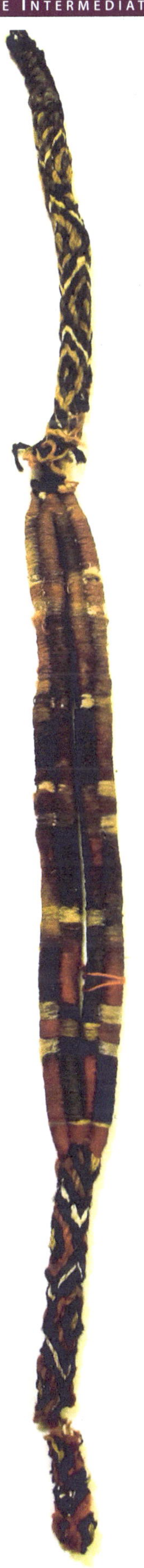

Museum number: V 9.345 in work basket

Item: Fragment of sling
Style: Late Intermediate Period, Central coast
Size: 46 x 2,5 cm
Material/technique: The sling consists of the following:

1. a 4 cm fragment of a square braid, camelid fiber 2S. In this the multicolored yarns for the fistbraid are hidden.
2. 12 cm round fistbraid
3. 20 cm sling cradle – consisting of the fistbraided yarns divided in four, wrapped and sewn flat next to each other to create the 2,5 cm flat sling cradle. In the middle is a 15 cm split.
4. 12 cm round fistbraid – like on the opposite side of the cradle.

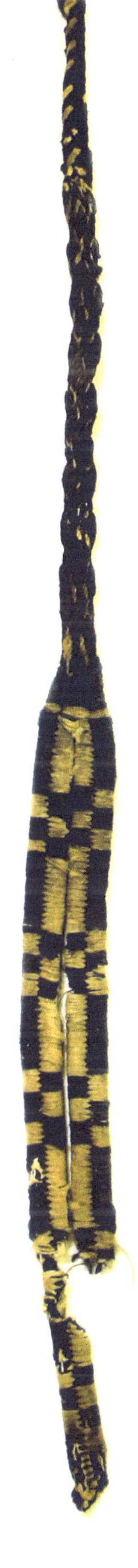

Museum number: V 4.566, a in work basket

Item: Fragment of sling
Style: Late Intermediate Period, Central coast
Size: 44 x 2,5 cm
Material/technique:

1. 5 cm square braid, camelid fiber 2S (fragment)
2. 15 cm round fistbraid
3. cradle: the fistbraiding yarns are divided in 4, wrapped and sewn flat together. The cradle is 23 cm long – and broken. The slit starts in the undestroyed end one cm above the fistbraid.

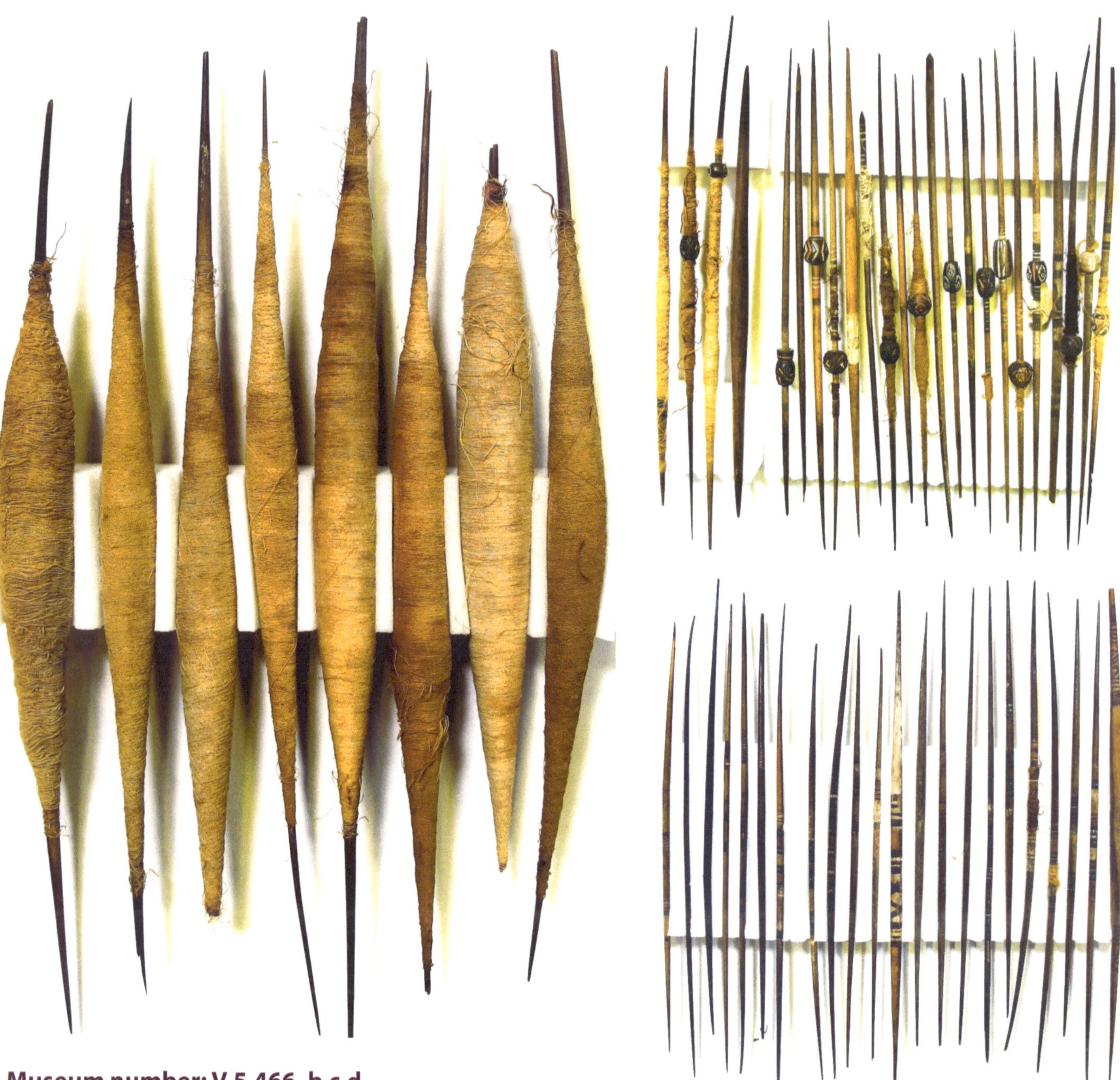

Museum number: V 5.466, b,c,d in work basket

Item: 54 Spindles – 19 with cotton yarn S, and 35 without yarns.
Style: Late Intermediate Period, Central/North Coast
Size: 32 – 22 cm long

Museum number: V 5.466, e in work basket

Item: Reed bag filled with camelid fiber yarns.
Style: Late Intermediate Period, Central coast
Size: 27 x 13 cm
Material/technique: The bag is made in plaited reed and is filled with 2S camelid fiber yarns.

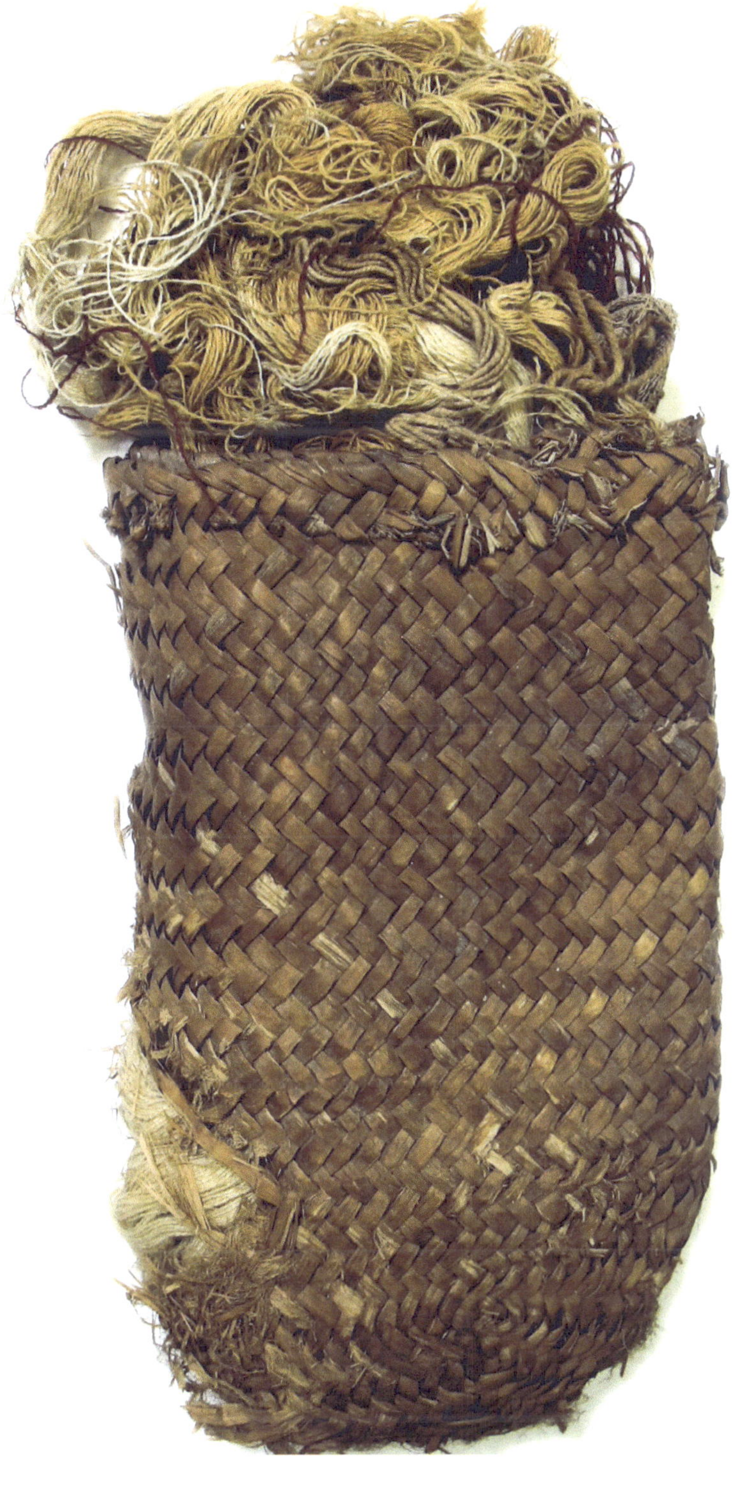

Museum number: V 5.466, f in work basket

Item: Fragment of a band
Style: North Coast/Central coast
Size: 22 x 2,5 cm
Material/ technique: Tapestry – cotton Z warp, camelid fiber S weft . The threadcount is 8 x 45-50 per cm.

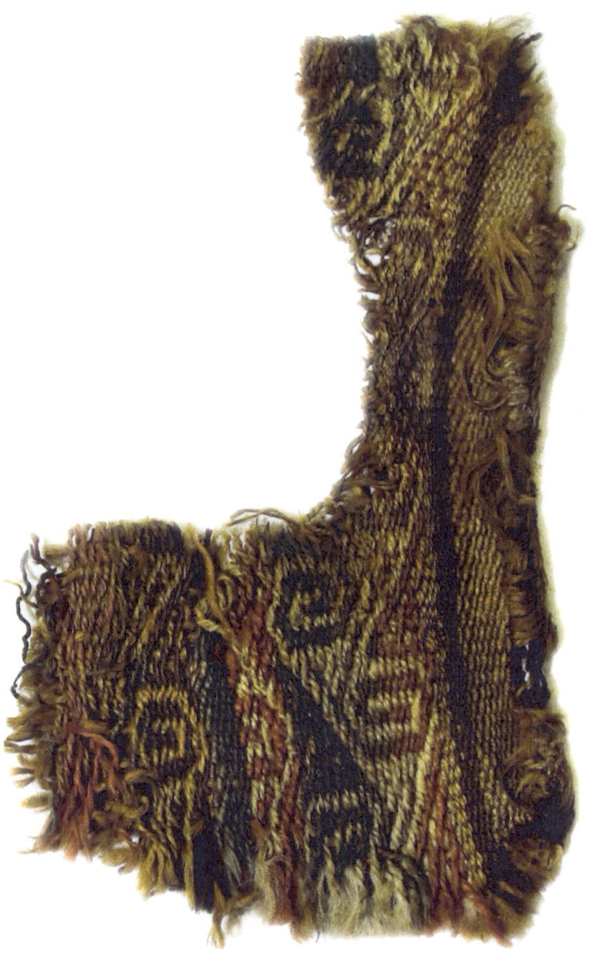

Museum number: V 5.466, g in work basket

Item: Fragment of weaving
Style: Central Coast
Size: 12 x 7 cm
Material/technique: complimentary warp patterned, camelid fiber 2S weaving fragment. Along one side selvedge it has loopstitch edge embroidery (like neck and arm openings of tunics) so it is probably a fragment of tunic. The threadcount is 10 – 5 per cm.

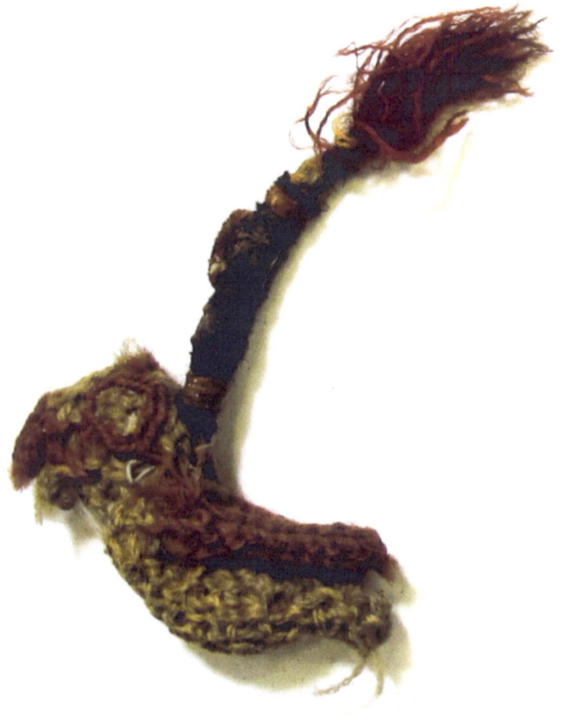

Museum number: V 4.566, h in work basket

Item: Bird ornament
Style: Central coast
Size: bird: 3 cm x 5 x 1,5 cm; tassel: 6 cm
Material/technique: The bird is made in looping (Wings: cross-knit-looping and body: simple looping). Eyes are embroidered with running stitches. The tassel has a wrapped stem (4 cm long). All is in 2S camelid fiber.

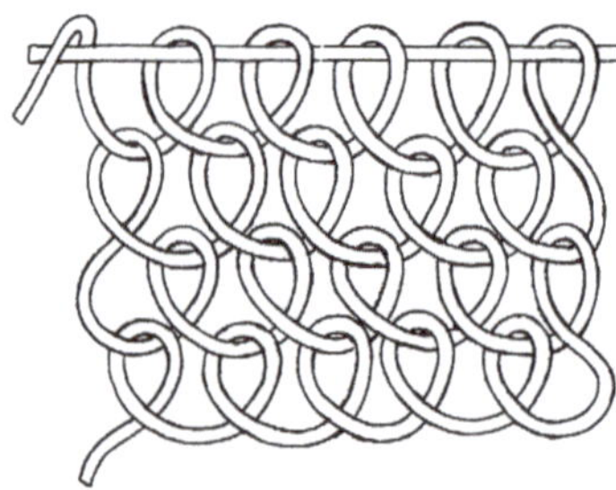

Simple looping

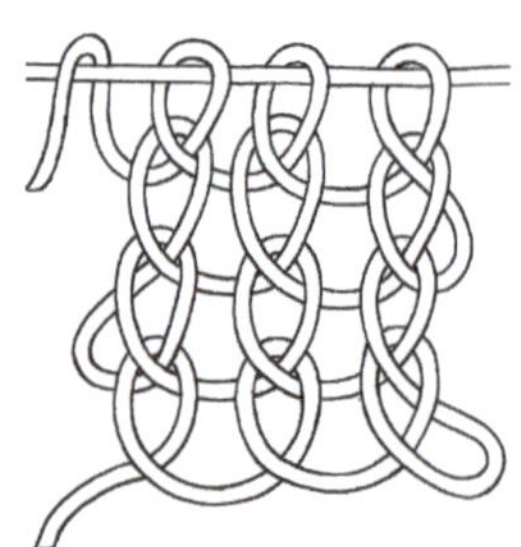

Cross-knit-looping

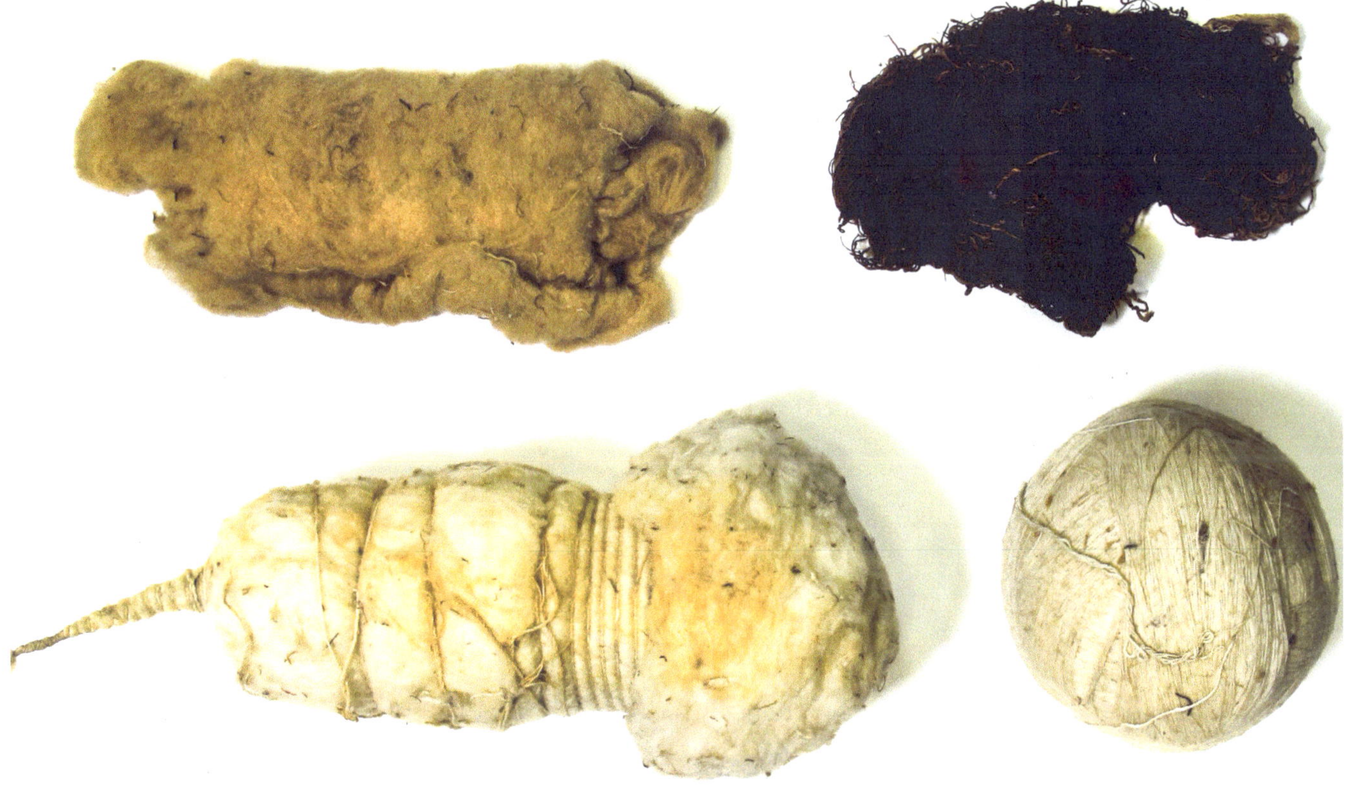

Museum number: V 5.466, i
in work basket

Item: unspun cotton (brown (21 cm x 9 cm) and white (Ø 28 cm x long 29 cm) – ready for spinning.
A bowl of white cotton yarn Z spun (Ø 10 cm)
Bundle of camelid fiber yarns (red 2S) and brown cotton (S)

Museum number: V 5.466, j
in work basket

Item: Sling
Style: Central coast
Size: 190 x 1,5 cm
Material/technique:

1. 86 cm (complete with loop) square 8 strand braid in S plant fiber (probably Fourcraea andina).
2. 6,5 cm round fistbraid, plantfiber and added 2S camelid fiber yarns.
3. Cradle 15 cm long (with 14 cm slit) in wrapped plantfiber yarns divided in four and sewn flat together. The wrapping is plantfiber and cotton Z.
4. 15 cm square 8 strand braid, plantfiber, changing into 60 cm round 4 braid. This is broken at end.

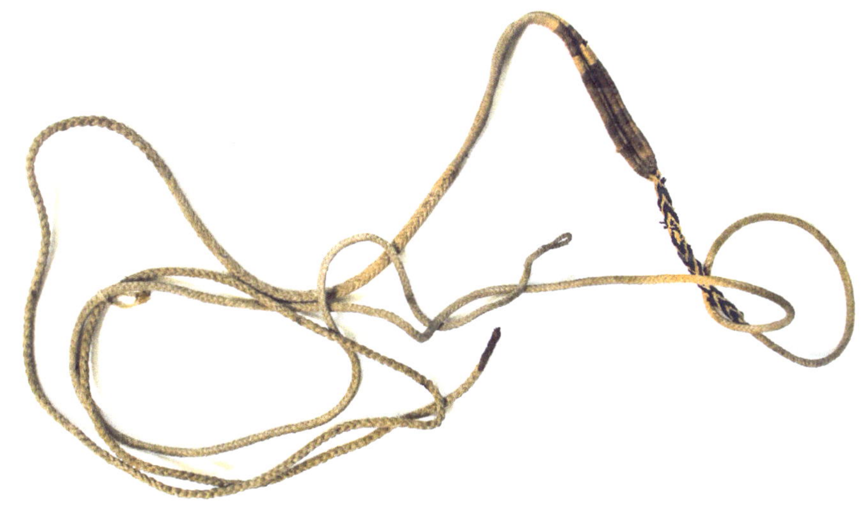

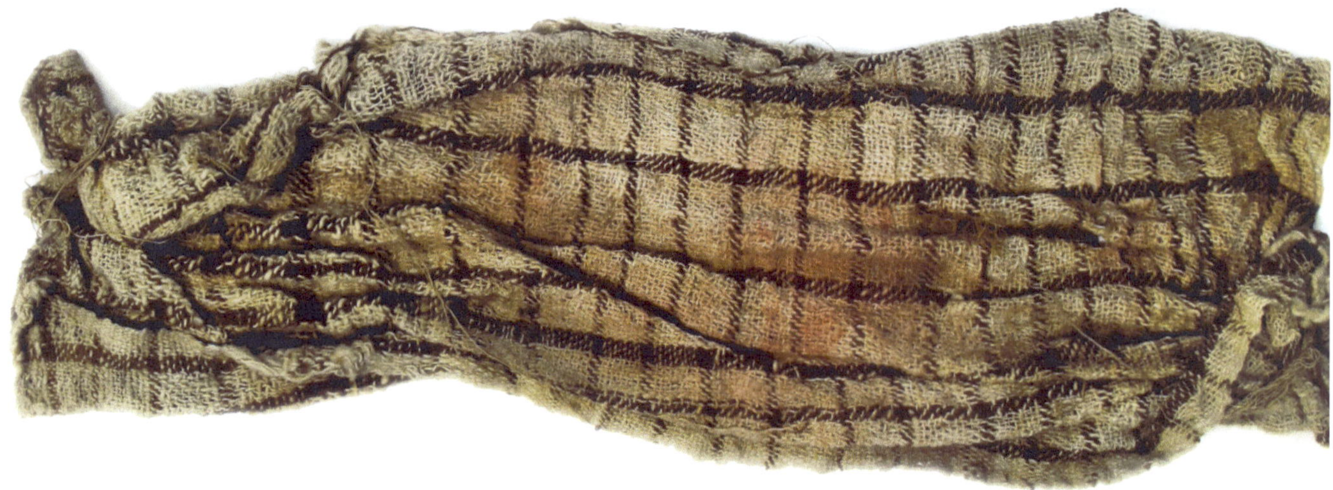

Museum number: V 5.466, k in work basket

Item: Textile with 4 selvedges
Style: North Coast/Central coast
Size: 35 x 19 cm
Material/technique: Plain weave Z cotton. The threadcount is 10 x 9 cm. The cloth has four selvedges. It is stained with Cinnobar.

Museum number: V 8.963

Item: Fragment of a band
Style: Central Coast
Size: 38 x 8
Material/technique: Slit tapestry, warp cotton 2S, weft camelid fiber 2S. The threadcount is 10 x 60 cm. Two side selvedges and no warpselvedge

Museum number: V 8.964

Item: Fragment probably from a funerary shroud.
Style: Central coast
Size: 63 x 34 cm
Material/technique: Plain weave in cotton S for both warp and weft. The threadcount is 22 x 16 cm. On to this textile is appliqued 9,5 - 10 cm squares in tapestry with warp cotton S and weft camelid fiber 2S. The squares are placed diagonally on the foundation cloth.
The fragment is part of VA 55944, Wilhelm Gretzer collection, Berlin.

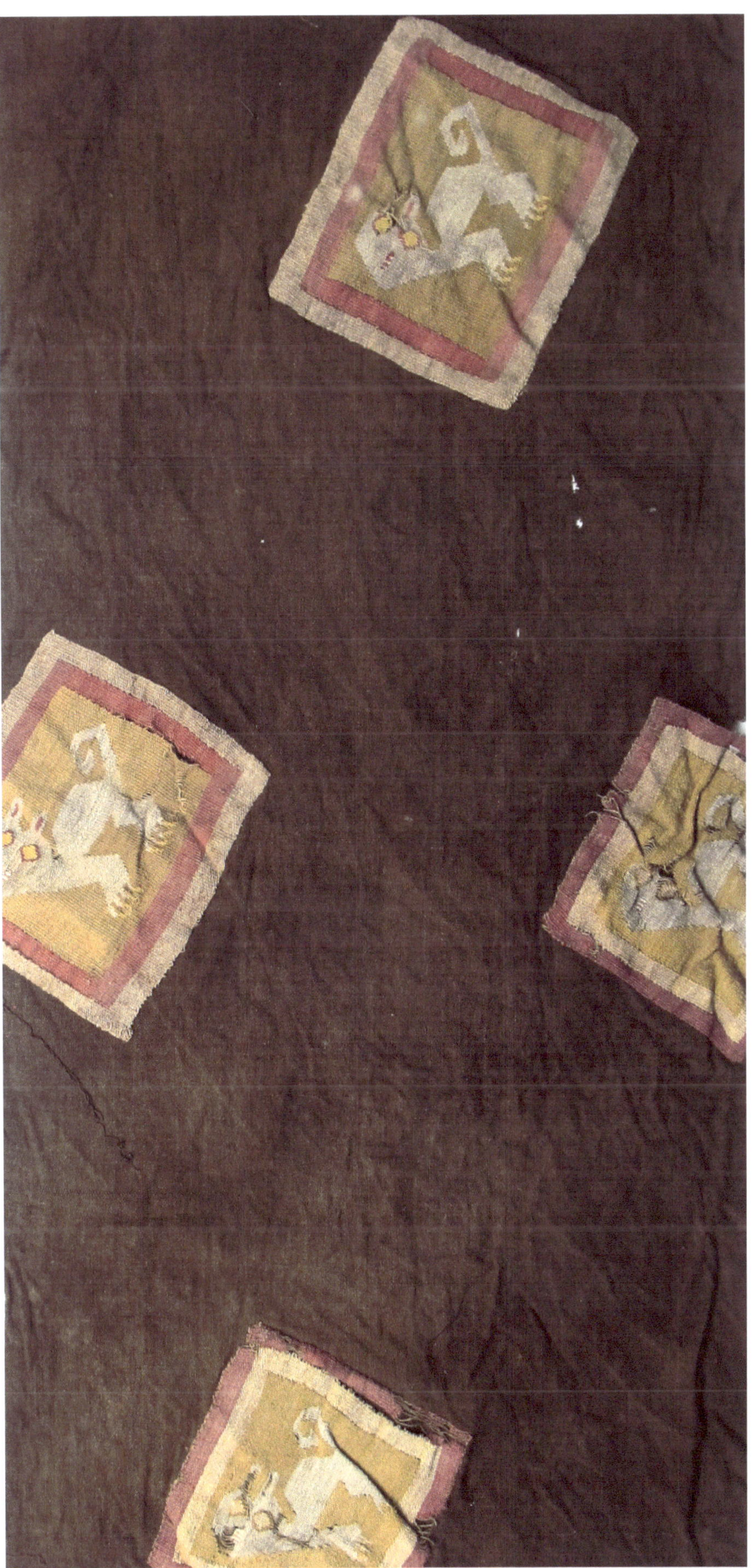

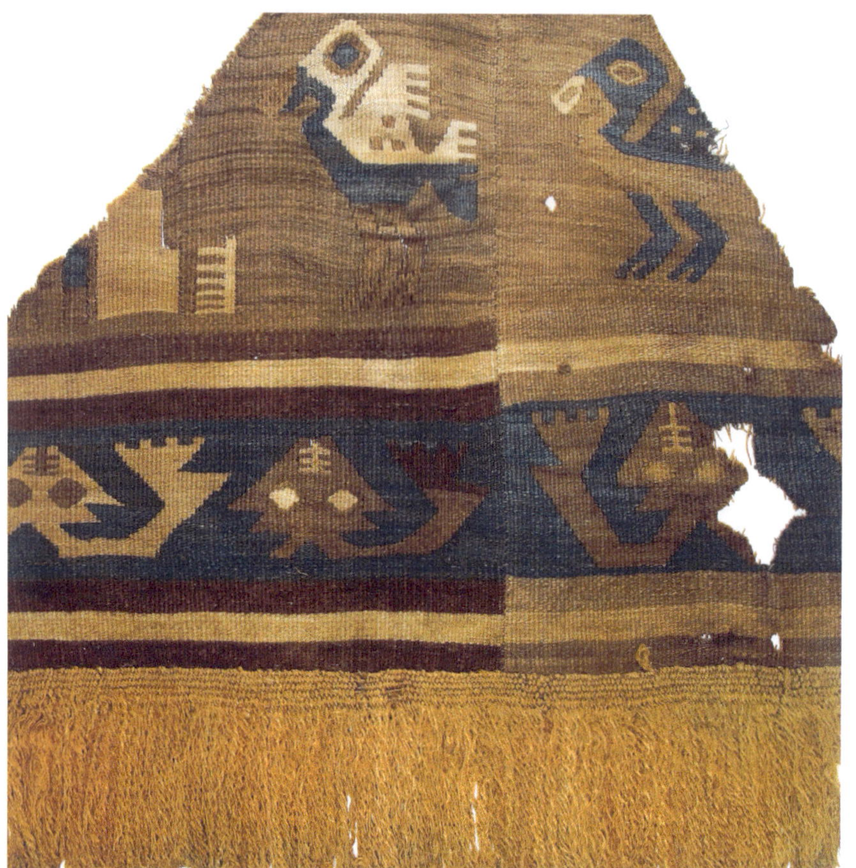

Museum number: V 8.965

Item: Fragment
Style: Central coast, Ychsma
Size: 23 x 24 cm
Material/technique: Two panels sewn together and with a 5 cm wide looped weft fringe at bottom. Warp selvedge at bottom (by fringe). The technique is slit tapestry, warp 2S cotton, weft 2S camelid fiber. The threadcount is 10 x 60 per cm. Probably the textile is the bottom of a tunic.

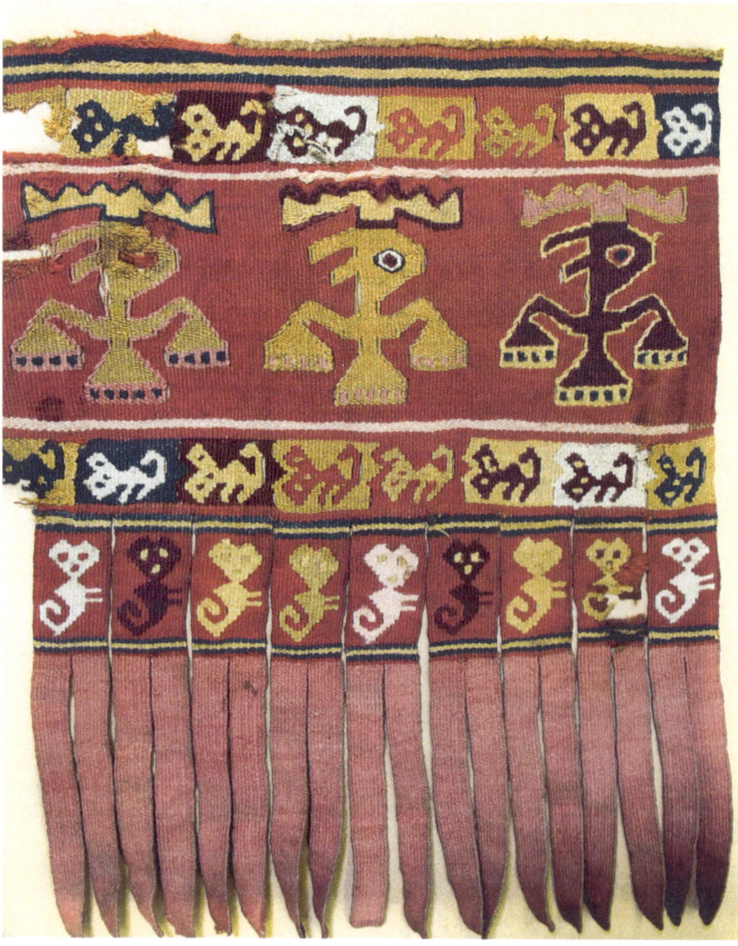

Museum number: V 8.971

Item: Fragment
Style: Central coast
Size: 29 x 29 cm
Material/technique: Slit tapestry with warp cotton 2S and weft camelid fiber 2S. The threadcount is 8 x 28 cm. The fragment has at bottom woven fringes (9,5 x 1 cm). And above that 4,5 cm slits (2 cm wide) – each being the width of two woven fringes.
Warp-selvedge at top and bottom, weft selvedge right side (when fringes down).

Museum number: V 8.976

Item: Fragment
Style: Central coast/ north coast
Size: 63 x 24 cm
Material/technique: Discontinuous warp and weft in cotton Z, S, paired Z (in weft) and 2S – seemingly at random. The fragment has one warp selvedge and two side selvedges. Both warps and wefts are interlocked in each other.

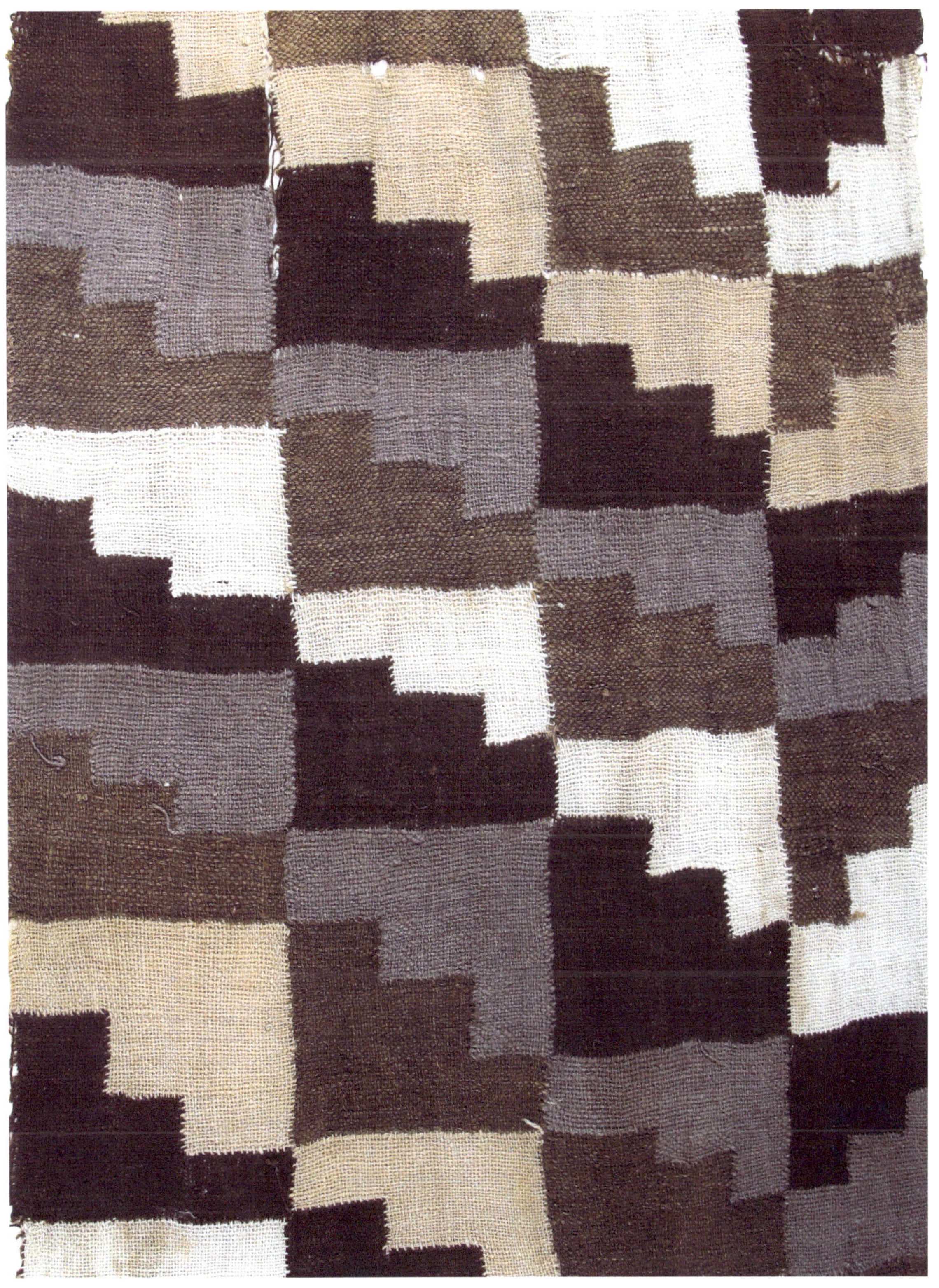

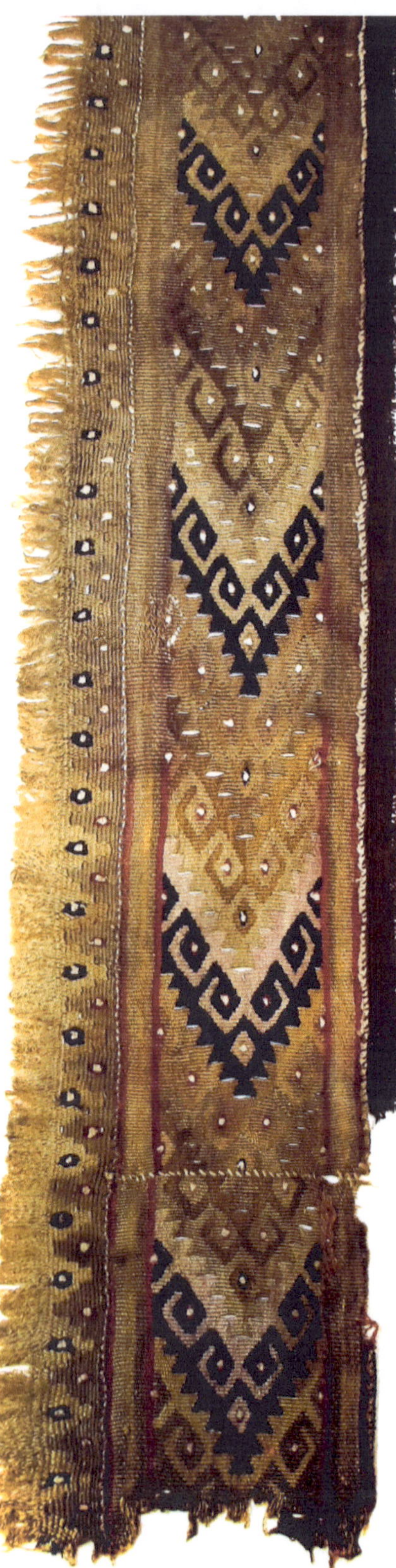

Museum number: V 8.977

Item: Fragment
Style: Central coast, Ychsma
Size: 12,5 x 52 cm
Material/technique: The textile is probably the lower part of a tunic.
At bottom: 3,5 cm looped weft-fringe with tapestry. This band has warp along the center band.
Above: 7,5 cm wide slit tapestry band. Consisting of two panels. The warp is on the short side
At top are fragments of plain weave cotton.

Museum number: V 8.984

Item: Fragment from tunic.
Style: Central coast, Chancay
Size: 26 x 13 cm
Material/technique: The textile is probably from the bottom edge of a tunic. The fragment consists of :

1. A weft faced plain weave band with cut weft fringe. Camelid fiber 2S, woven 1,5 cm, the rest loose wefts. The threadcount is 7 x 20 per cm.
2. A brocaded band 6 cm wide with warp and weft in 2S camelid fiber. The threadcount is 9 x 40 per cm.
3. Stitched to the band are fragments of a plain weave cotton textile with warp S, weft Z and a threadcount of 8 x 14 per cm.

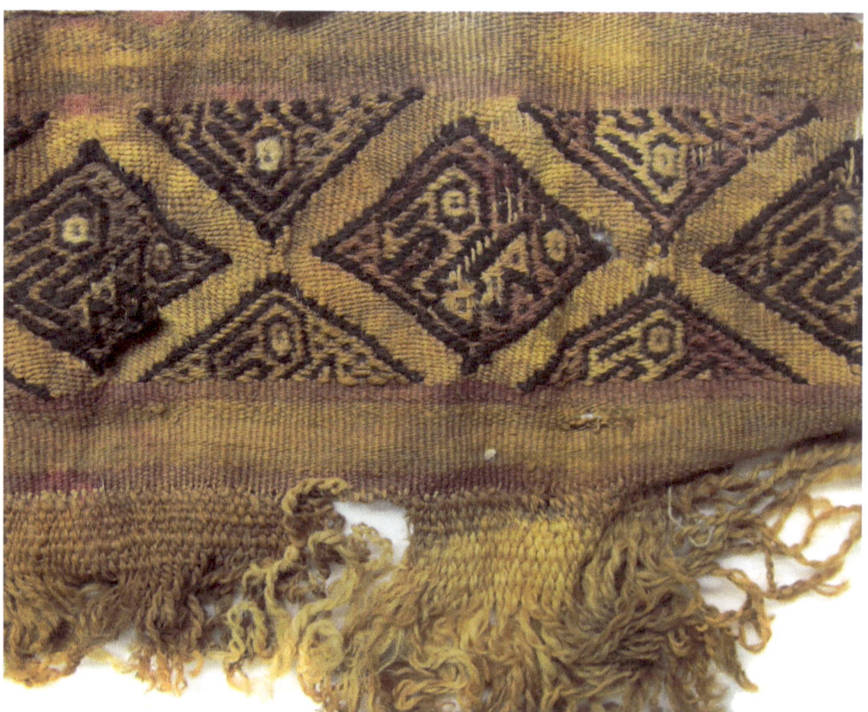

Museum number: V 8.985

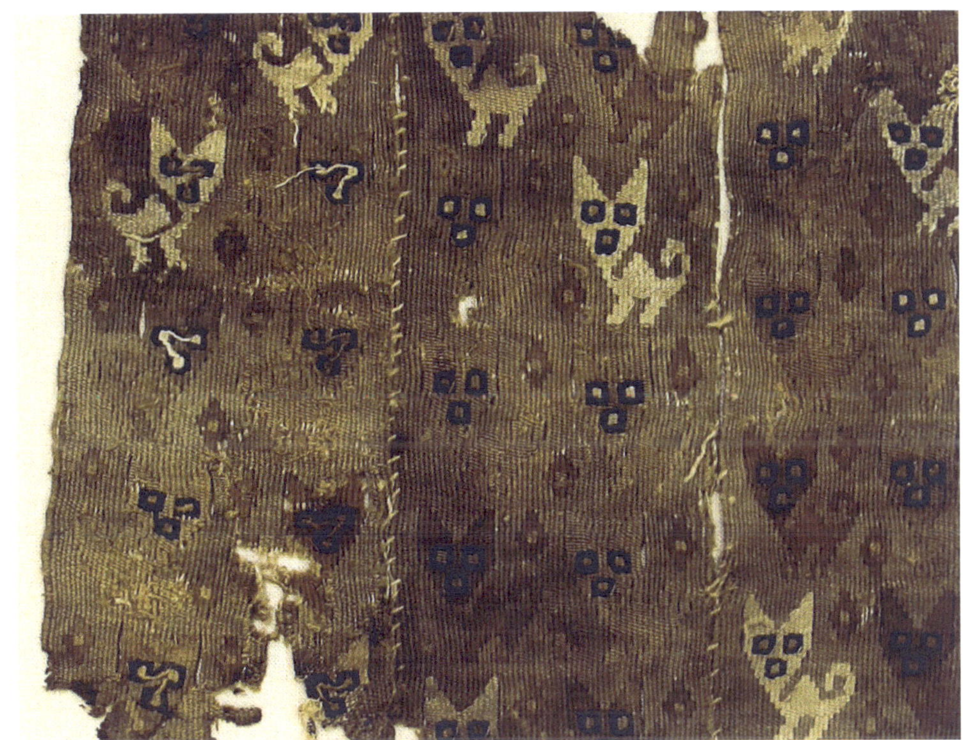

Item: Fragment
Style: Central coast
Size: 30,5 x 19,5 cm
Material/technique: Textile in slit tapestry. The warp is 2S cotton (twined from two colors: tan and white). The weft is camelid fiber 2S. The threadcount is 10 x 40 per cm.
The fragment consists of 3 bands (each 6 cm wide) stitched together (with 2S cotton yarn). The bands have selvedges on all sides. On two of the bands the warp selvedges are still present, and so the measurement stated above is probably the original complete textile. Top and bottom edge is embroidered (cotton 2S, three strands) – top cross knit loop stitch edging, and at bottom with a 0,5 cm stripe of stem stitches.

Museum number: V 9.007

Item: Fragment
Style: Central coast
Size: 14 x 27 cm
Material/technique: The technique is tapestry with the warp in 3S cotton and the weft 2S camelid fiber. The threadcount is 12 x 70 per cm.

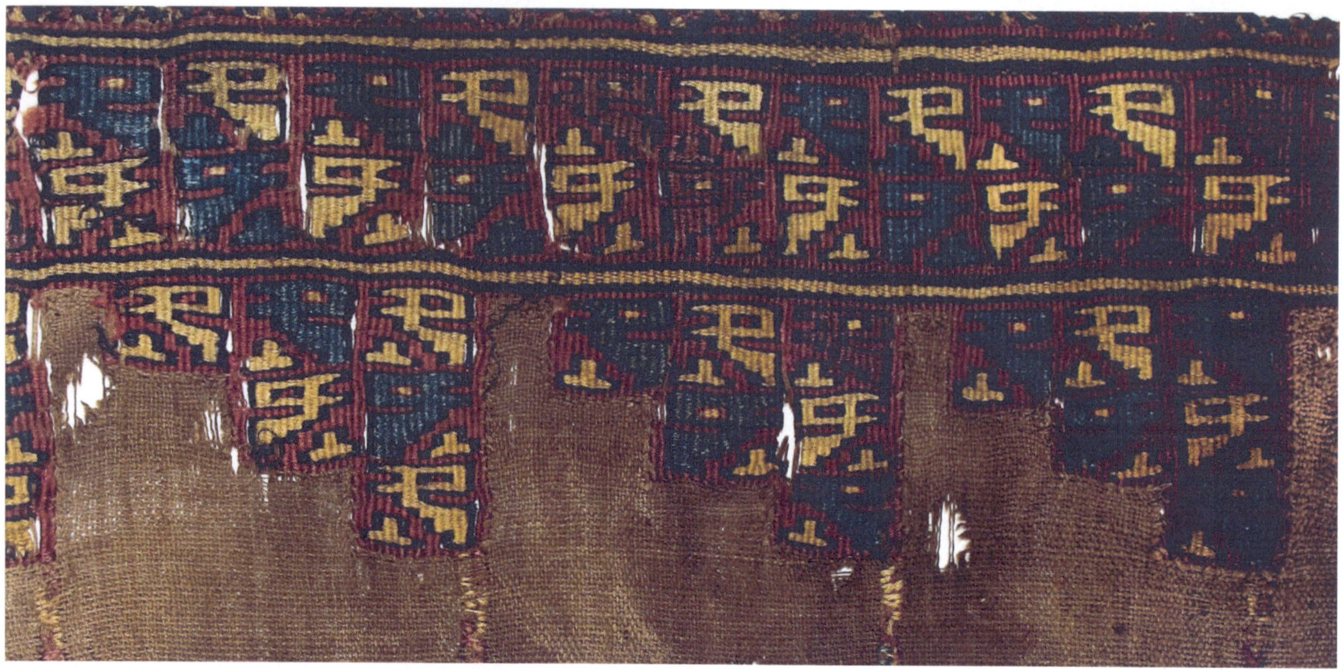

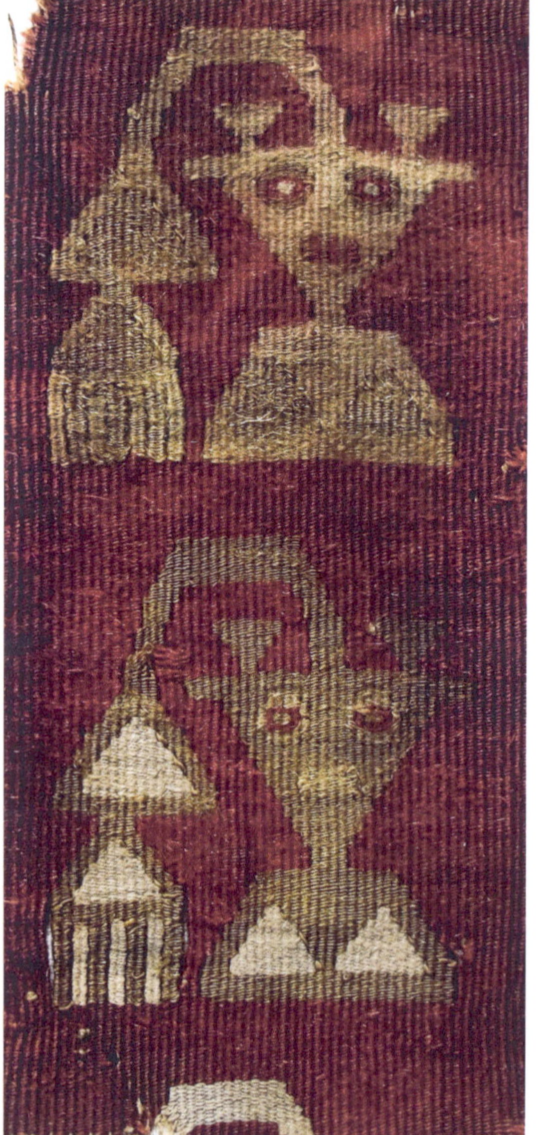

Museum number: V 9.014

Item: Fragment
Style: Central coast
Size: 16,5 x 31 cm
Material/technique:

1. Foundation textile is in plain weave cotton 2S (both warp and weft) and the threadcount is 11 x 11 per cm.
2. The patterning is in slit tapestry with paired warps from the foundation plain weave and wefts in camelid fiber 2S. The threadcount of the wefts are 48 per cm.
3. At the top is a warp selvedge with loop stitch embroidery.

Museum number: V 9.020

Item: Fragment of band
Style: Central coast
Size: 19 x 7,5 cm
Material/technique: The band is woven in slit tapestry with warps in cotton 2S and wefts in camelid fiber 2S. The threadcount is 8 x 46 per cm.

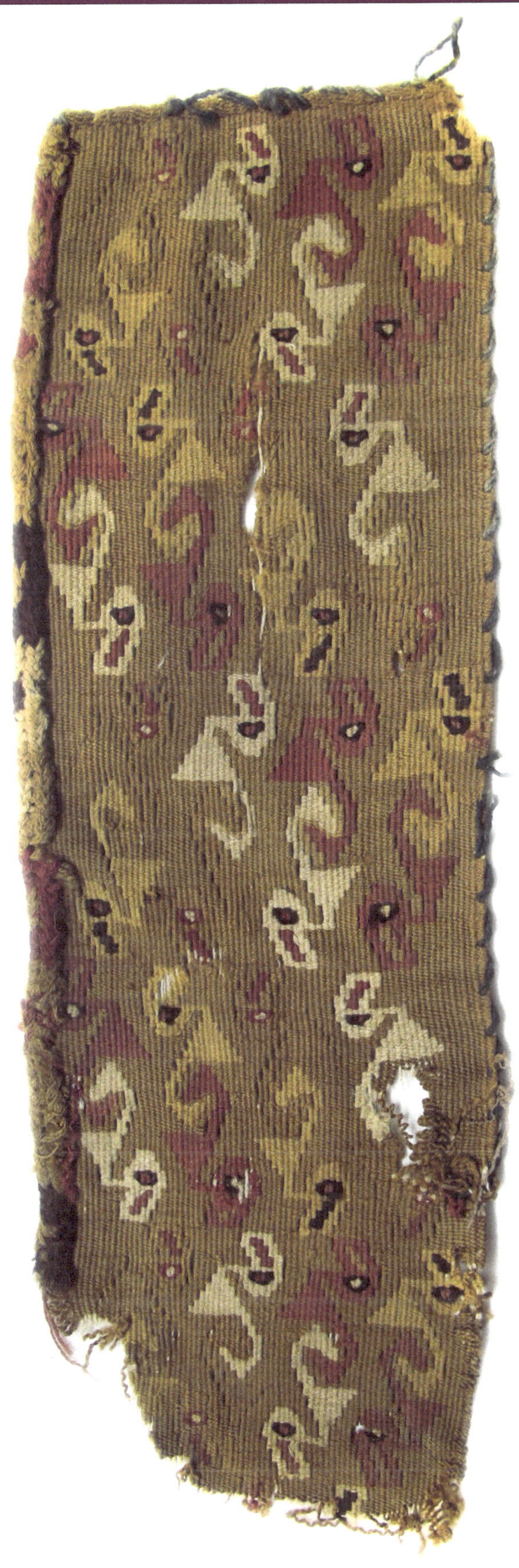

Museum number: V 9.022

Item: Fragment of a band
Style: Central coast
Size: 26 x 9 cm
Material/technique: Tapestry woven band with 3 selvedges in camelid fiber 2S. At one side selvedge the band has a loop stitch embroiderey. Along the other side selvedge and along the warp selvedge are fragments of a stitching with a blue yarn.

Museum number: V 9.023

Item: Fragment, probably of a bag
Style: Central Coast, Ychsma
Size: 22 x 12 cm
Material/technique: The textile is woven in tapestry and has cotton warp, 3S and camelid fiber wefts, 2S. The threadcount is 9 x 50 per cm.
The fragment has warp selvedge and one side selvedge. Attatched to the side selvedge is a loop stitch embroidery.

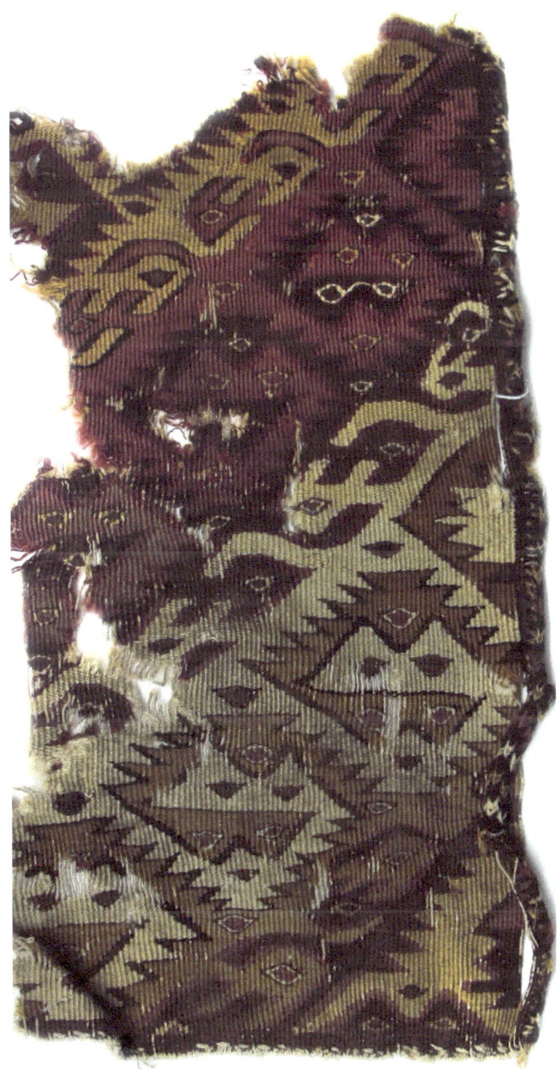

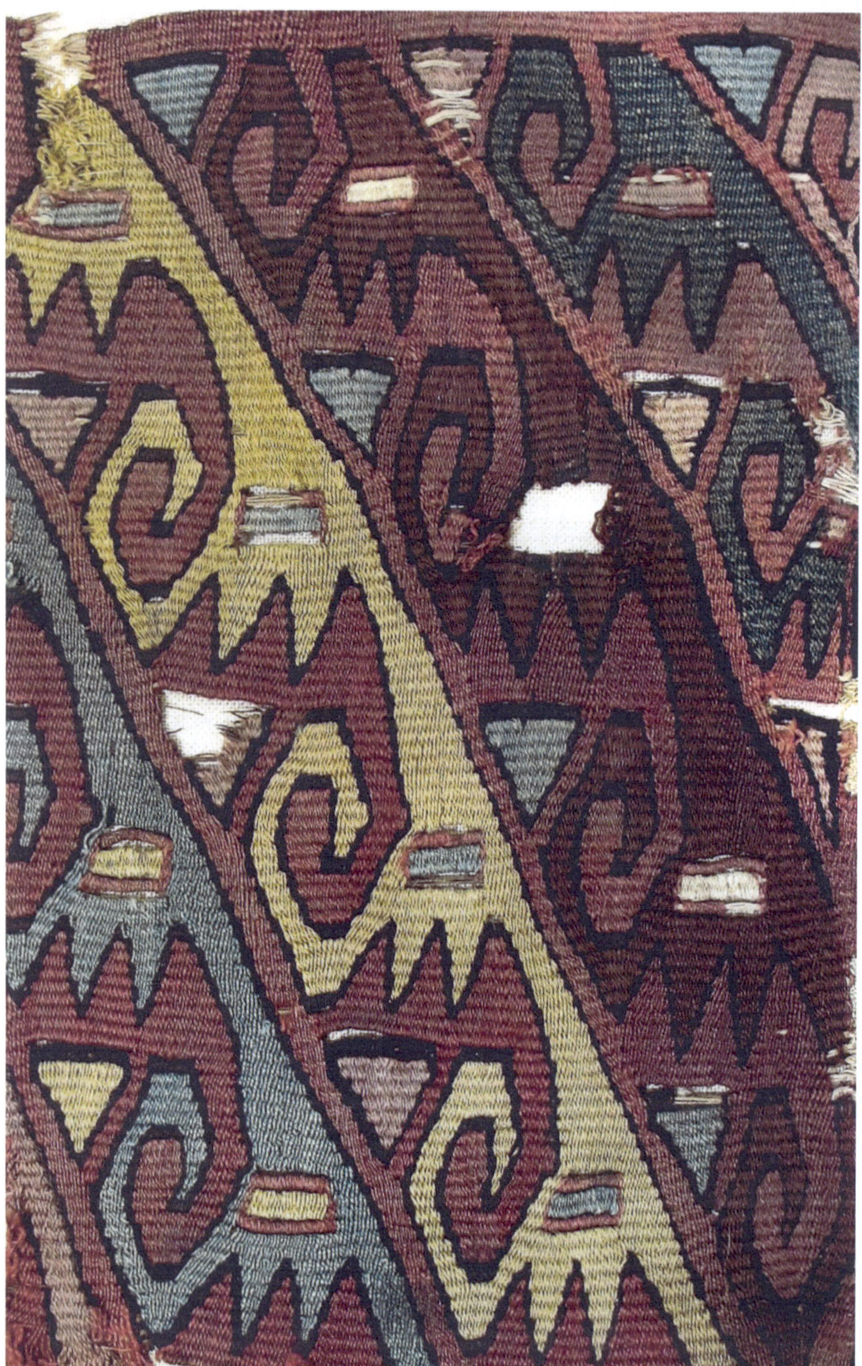

Museum number: V 9.052

Item: Fragment
Style: Central coast
Size: 15 x 18 cm
Material/technique: The textile is woven in plain weave and slit tapestry. The plain weave has cotton 2S in both warp and weft. The threadcount is 38 x 15 per cm.
In the tapestry the warp is 4 warps of the plain weave in each shed and the weft is camelid fiber 2S. The threadcount in the tapestry is 7 x 40 per cm.
Further description: At bottom is a 2,5 cm wide woven fringe – partly tapestry, partly plain weave.

Museum number: V 9.081

Item: Band
Style: Central coast
Size: 17 x 17 cm
Material/technique: The textile is woven in tapestry with the warp in cotton 2S and the weft in camelid fiber 2S. The threadcount is 8 x 26 per cm
The textile has two side-selvedges.

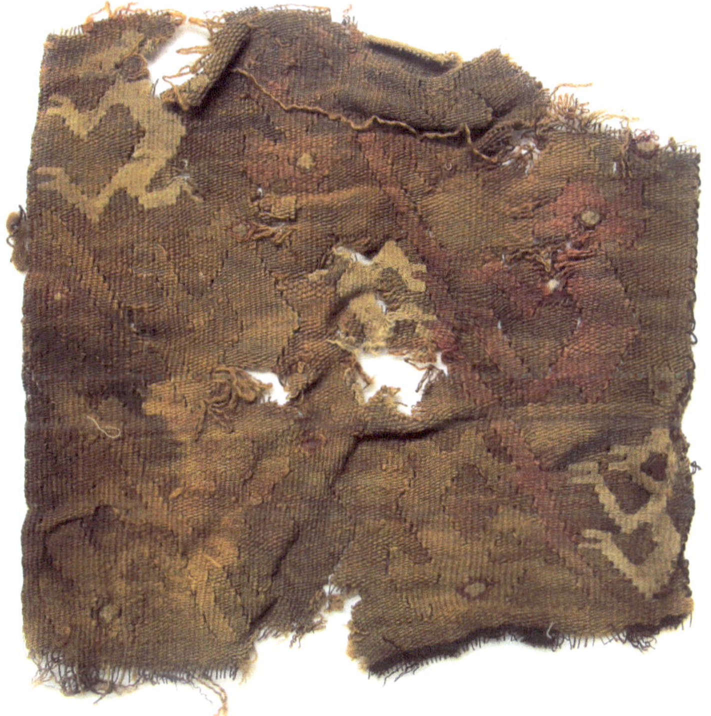

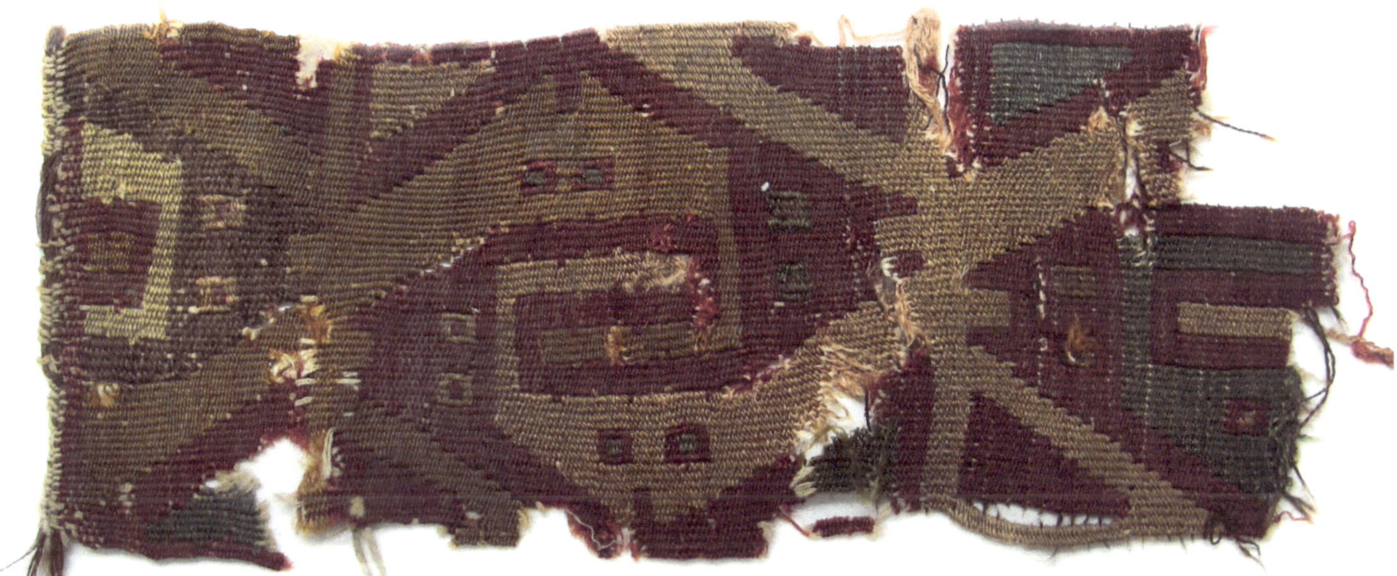

Museum number: V 9.083

Item: Fragment
Style: Central Coast
Size: 16 x 6 cm
Material/technique: The weaving is tapestry with the warp in paired camelid fiber 2S. The weft is also camelid fiber 2S. The threadcount is 10 x 28 per cm.
One warp selvedge.
Further description: the part of the textile closest to the warp selvedge has its vertical lines interlinked as dovetailed tapestry. The lower part, however, has every 5 wefts an extra dark weft going from edge to edge, which is invisible but keeping the vertical tapestry lines together without being interlinked.

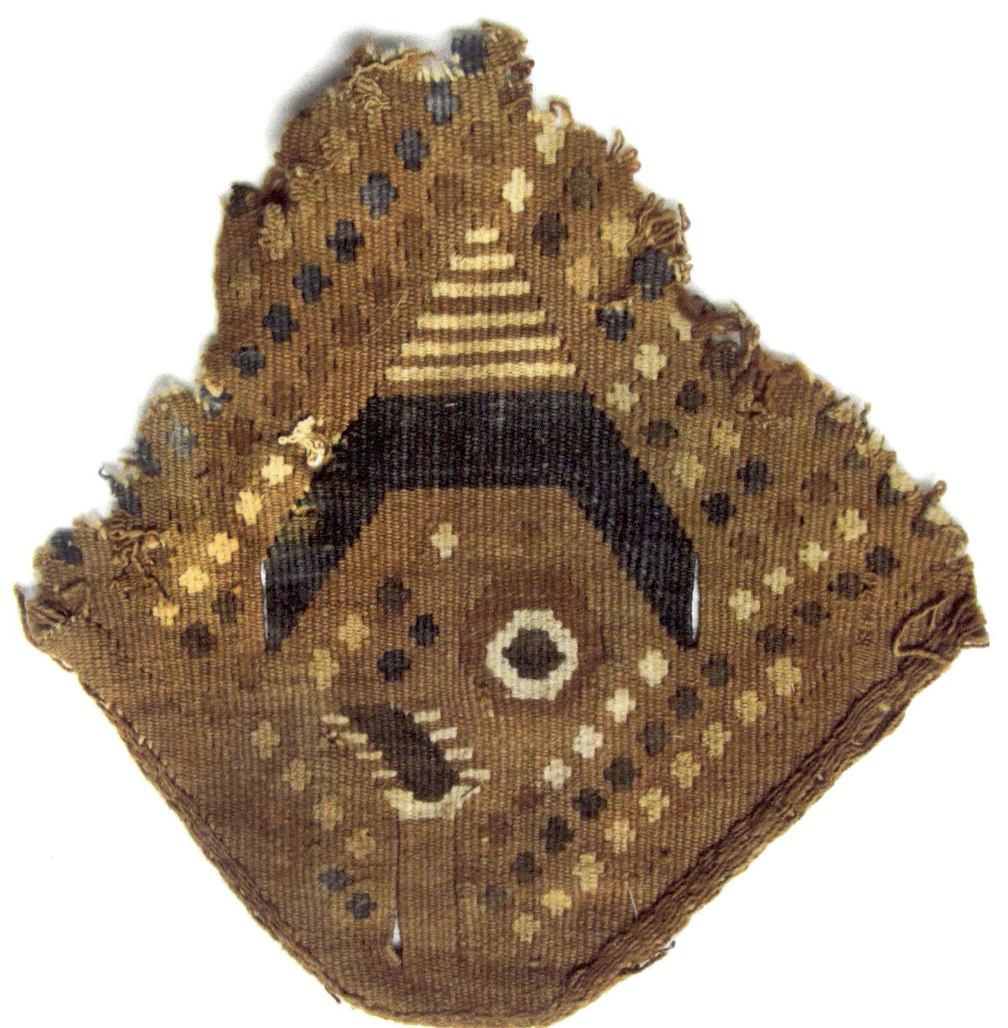

Museum number: V 9.090

Item: Fragment
Style: Central Coast, Ychsma
Size: 15 x 15 cm
Material/technique: The textile is in slit tapestry with all yarns in cotton 2S. The threadcount is 8 x 46 per cm.
The fragment is probably a patch from a shroud. It is cut as a diamond with the warp diagonal and edged with 0,5 cm wide running stitch embroidery.

Museum number: V 9.101

Item: Fragment
Style: Central Coast
Size: 57 x 4,5 cm
Material/technique: The textile yarns are all cotton 2S and the technique is plain weave and complementary warp weave. The threadcount is 20 x 13 per cm.
There is one warp selvedge and one weft selvedge.

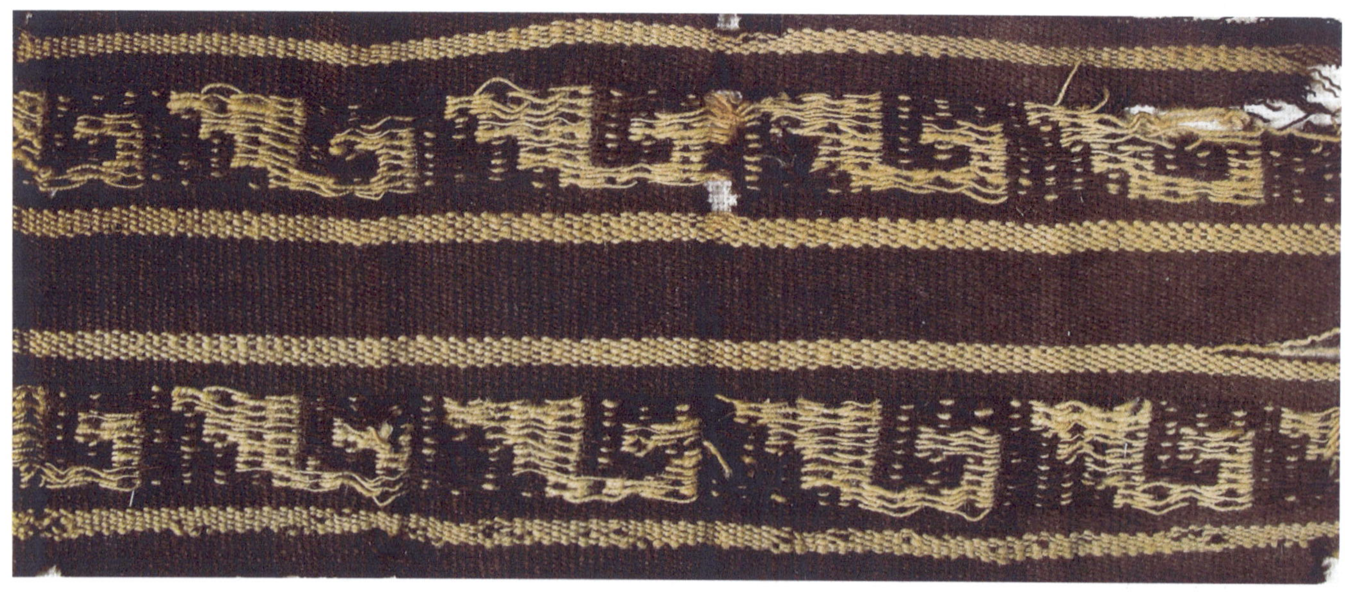

Museum number: V 9.139, and V 9.310

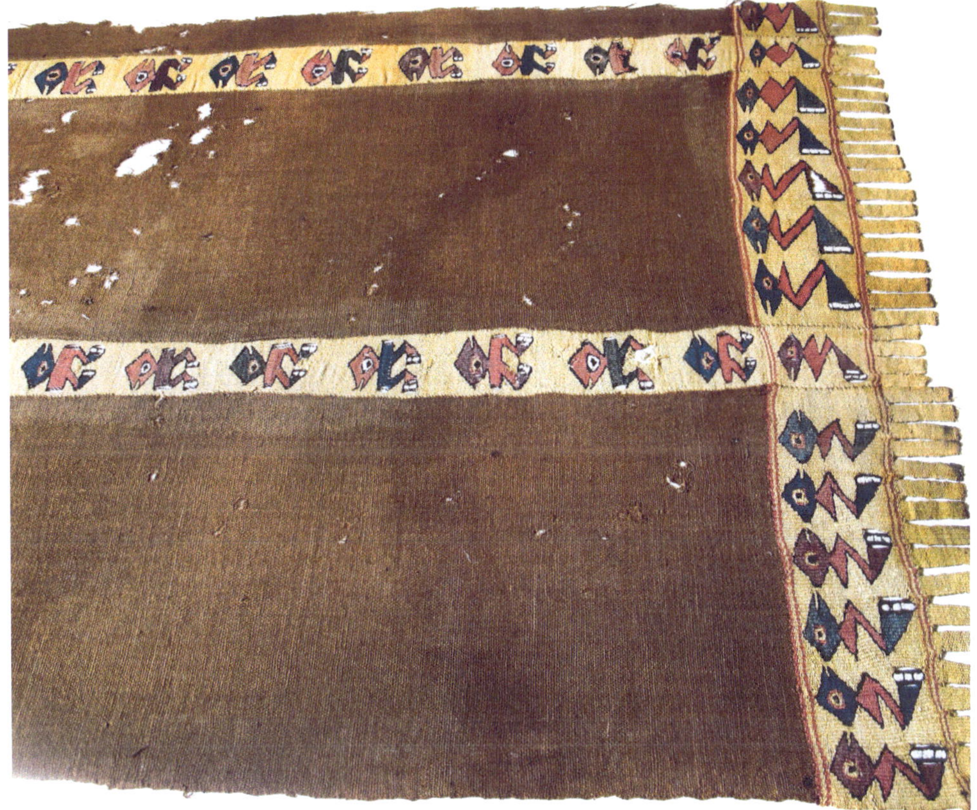

Item: Fragments of mantle
Style: Central Coast
Size: V9.139: 95 x 55 cm,
V9.318: 192 x 160 cm,
V9.310: 22 x 33 cm
Material/technique: The mantle consists of 5 panels woven in plain weave with both warp and weft in camelid 2S. The threadcount is 11 x 11 per cm. Between the monocrome panels separately woven are 4,5 cm wide tapestry bands with abstract antropomorphic motives. These bands are stitched between the plain weave panels. At either end of the mantle is 10 cm tapestry (with the same patterns as the inserted bands) with 4 x 1 cm woven fringes.

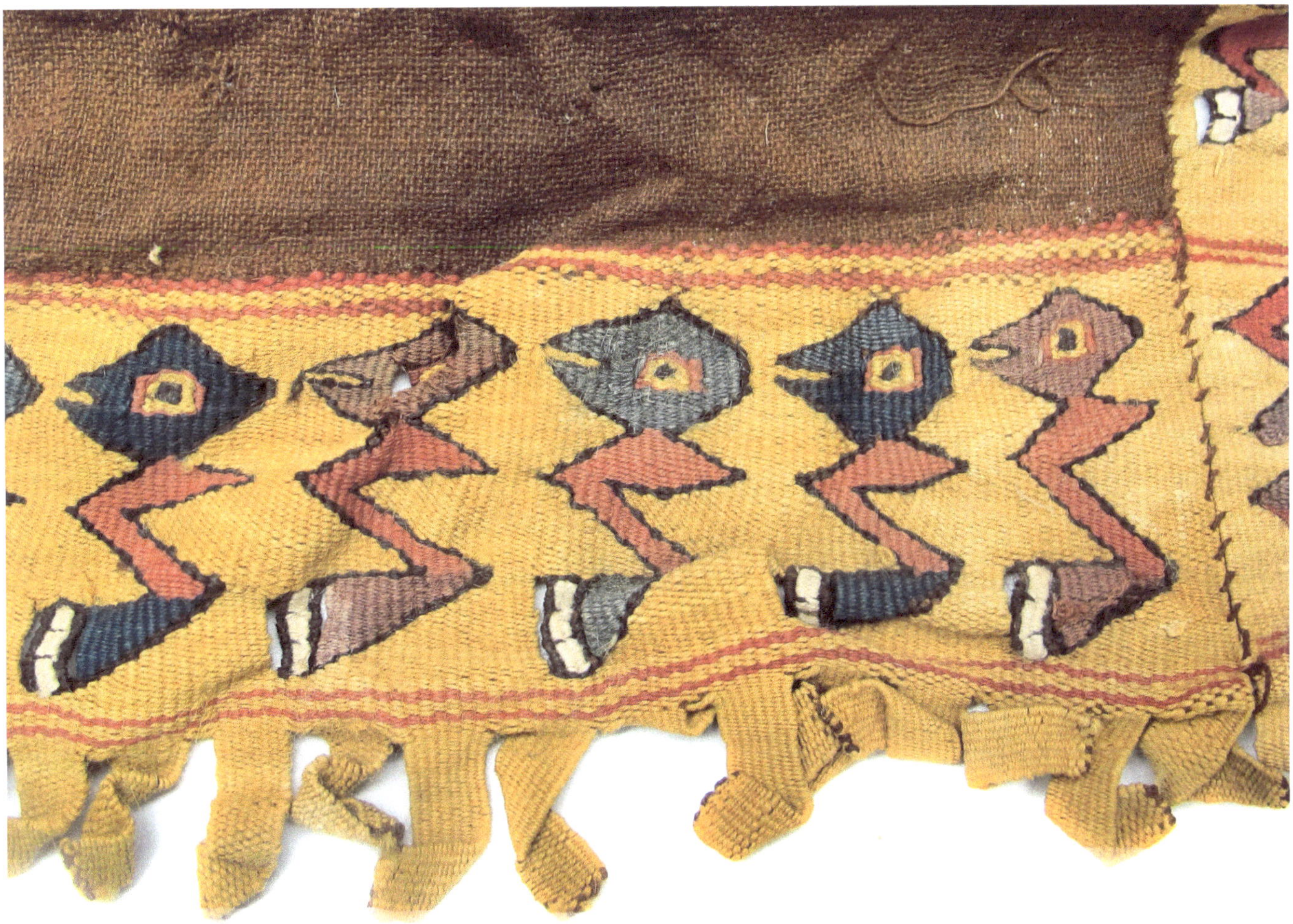

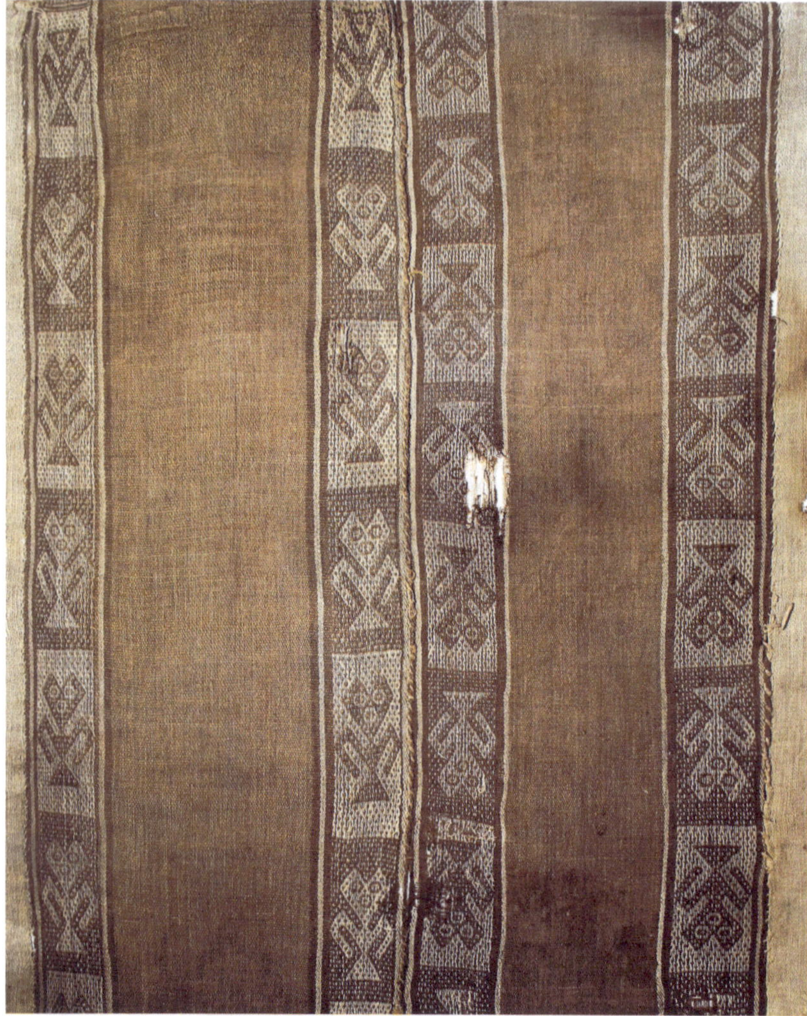

Museum number: V 9.142

Item: Fragment
Style: Central Coast
Size: 65 x 47 cm
Material/technique:

1. A cotton (2S warp - Z weft) textile of 41 cm width with complimentary warp patterning in stripes. This textile has one warp selvedge and two weft selvedges. The threadcount in the plain weave is 14 x 8 per cm.
2. On both sides the textile is sewn to 3 cm wide fragments of plain weave cotton textiles – which has one warp selvedge at bottom and one side selvedge towards the seam and is cut at the other side. This warp is 2S and the weft Z. The threadcount is 10 x 10 per cm.

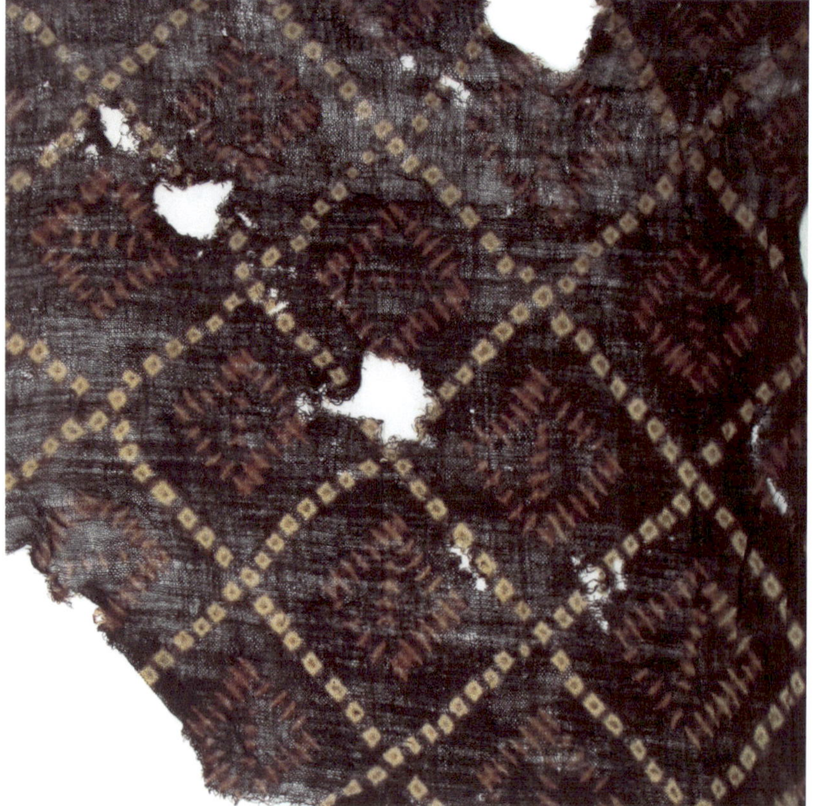

Museum number: V 9.158

Item: Fragment of scarf/shawl
Style: Central coast
Size: 78 x 50
Material/technique: Plain weave in cotton Z. Threadcount 12 x 10 per cm.
The textile was originally of at least 2 panels – (48 cm wide) - a small fragment (2x3 cm) of the second panel is still in place.
The large panel has warp selvedge, and fragments of two side-selvedges.
The patterning technique is tie dye. With 4 colors - dyed 3 times (dark brown, reddish, light braun).

Museum number: V 9.172

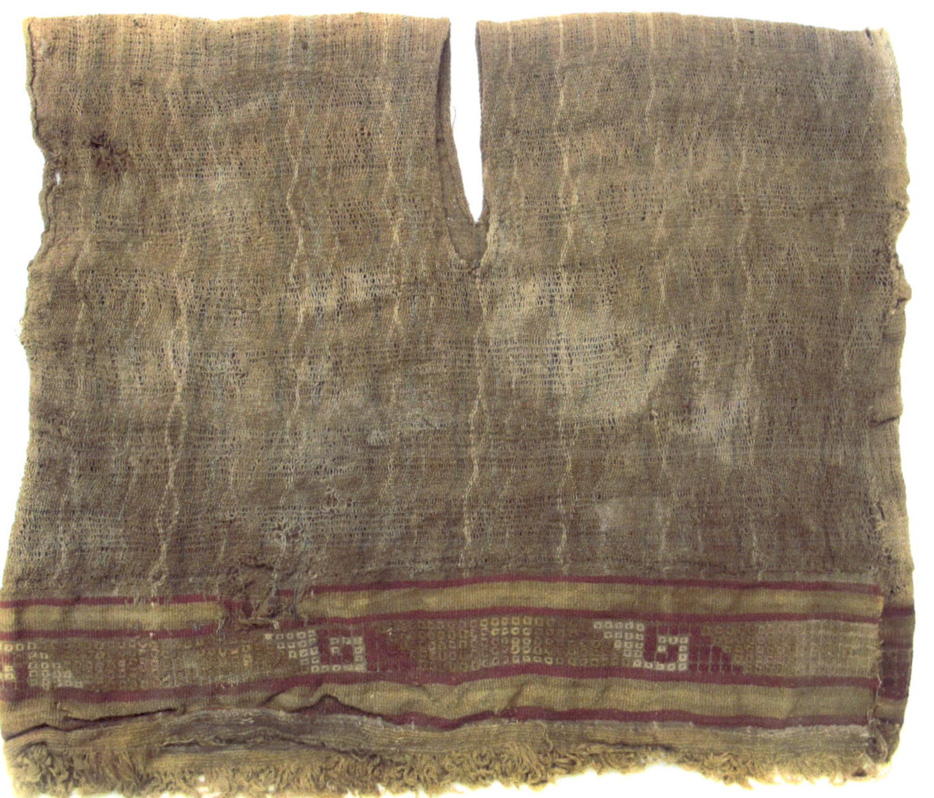

Item: mini (or child's?) tunic.
Style: Central Coast, Ychsma
Size: 33 x 40
Material/technique: The complete tunic has cotton S warp. One panel with cut vertical 19 cm long neck hole! The cut edge is rolled and sewn down. The threadcount is in the warp 16 per cm, in the gauze weave the weft varies. At the bottom of the warp is a 6,5 cm wide pattern with camelid fiber weft - in the center (2 cm wide) with a pattern in complementary-weft weave with discontinous-weft substitution. At either side of this is 2 cm wide weft face plain weave with 2 warps in each shed. This weft is camelid fiber 2S.
The rest of the tunic is gauze weave. One side a simple gauze all over – on the other side a more complicated and varied gauze.
At bottom is a 3 cm wide weft fringe band – 1,5 cm woven, 1,5 cm looped fringe (typical Ychsma). The warp of this band is S cotton and the weft is camelid fiber 2S.

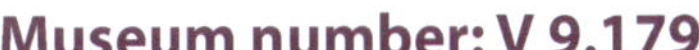

Museum number: V 9.179

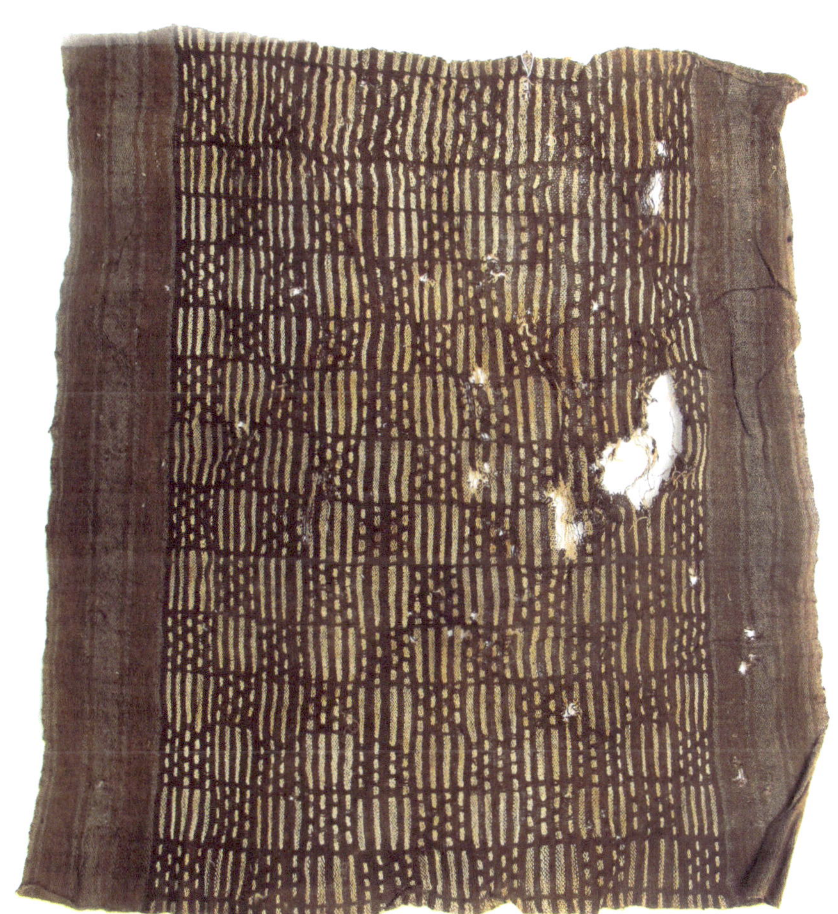

Item: Complete textile with 4 selvedges.
Style: Central coast
Size: 4 x 40 cm
Material/technique: The textile is plain weave in cotton, 2S, with warp supplementary patterning. The threadcount is 14 x 12 per cm.

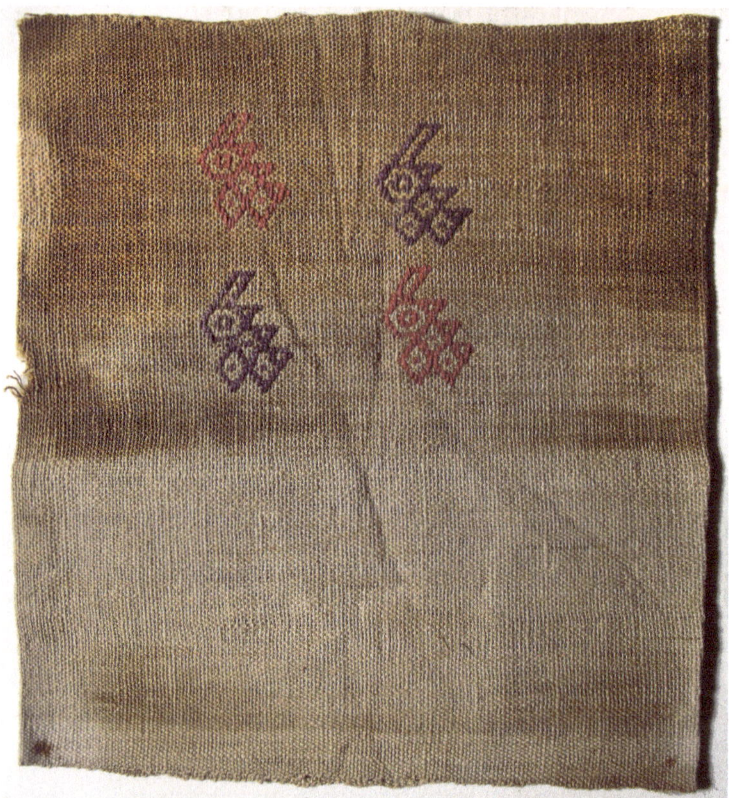

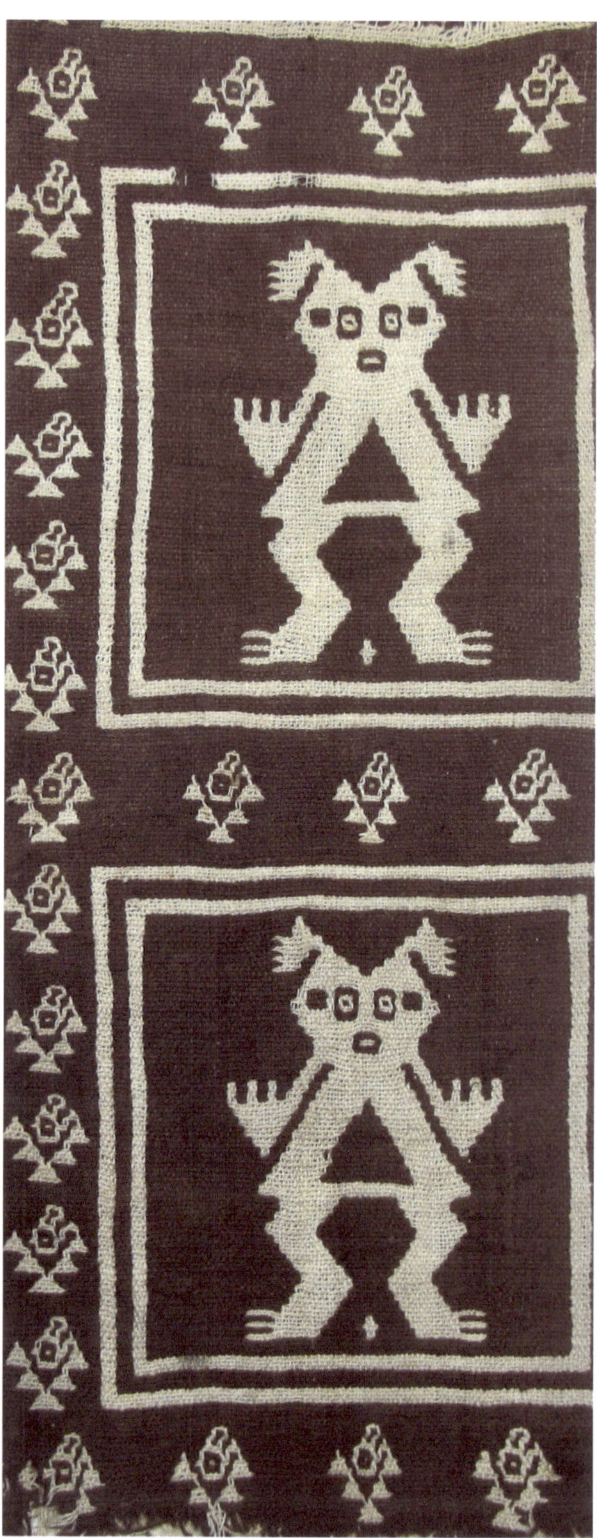

Museum number: V 9.189

Item: Complete mini woman's dress
Style: Central coast
Size: 28 x 29 cm
Material/technique: Plain weave cotton 2S in both warp and weft. Warp horizontal when "worn". The threadcount is 10 x 6 per cm.
4 brocaded birds in 2S camelid fiber.
Further description: The complete warp is 56 cm (four selvedges), folded sideways (warp horizontal) and sewn together as a tube.

Museum number: V 9.204

Item: Fragment
Style: Central coast
Size: 33 x 13,5 cm
Material/technique: The textile is woven in double weave, cotton 2S (both warp and weft). The threadcount is 14 x 11 per cm. There is one side selvedge.

Museum number: V 9.205

Item: Fragment
Style: Central coast
Size: 19 x 30 cm
Material/technique: A double weave textile in cotton 2S for both warp and weft. The threadcount is 16 x 10 per cm, and the textile has two side selvedges.

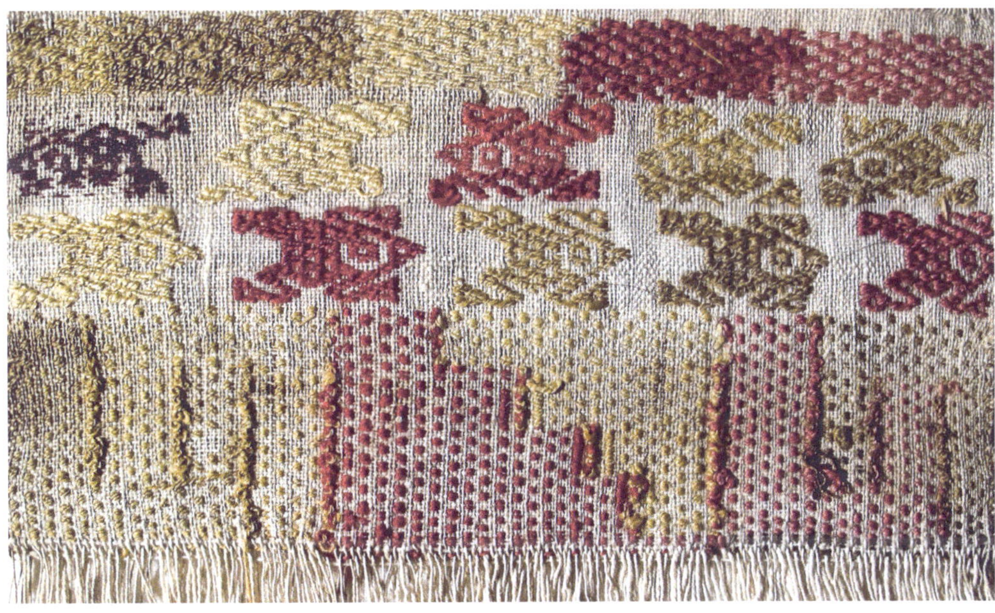

Museum number: V 9.216

Item: Fragment
Style: Central coast
Size: 14 x 21 cm
Material/technique: The technique is brocade on plain weave.
The plain weave has cotton 2S for both warp and weft. The brocade pattern wefts are camelid fiber 2S.

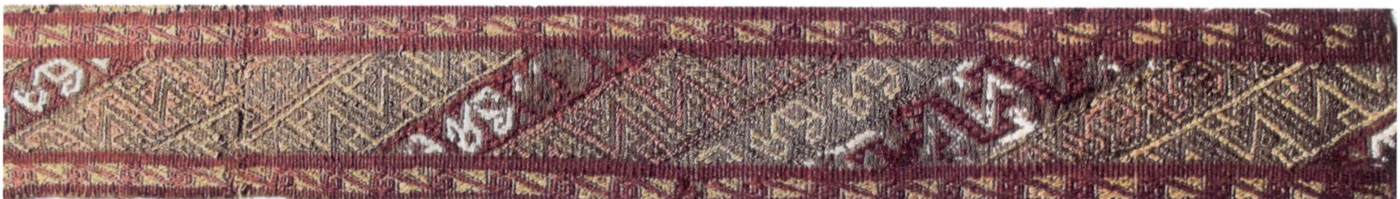

Museum number: V 9.224

Item: Fragment
Style: Central Coast, Ychsma
Size: 7 x 47 cm
Material/technique: The textile is the bottom edge of a cotton tunic – warp and weft are 2S. The pattern is in supplementary weft (lancée) in camelid fiber 2S. The warp selvedge is intact. At the warp selvedge a fragment of a 1 cm wide looped weft fringe is stitched on - 0,5 cm weaving (4 warps) and has 0,5 cm looped loose wefts.

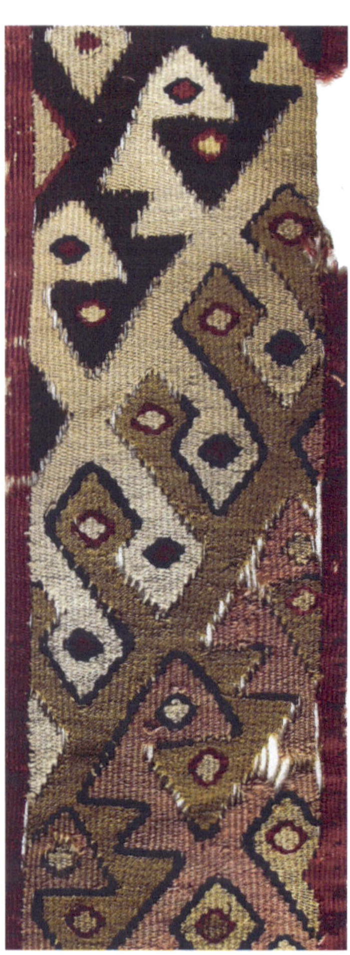

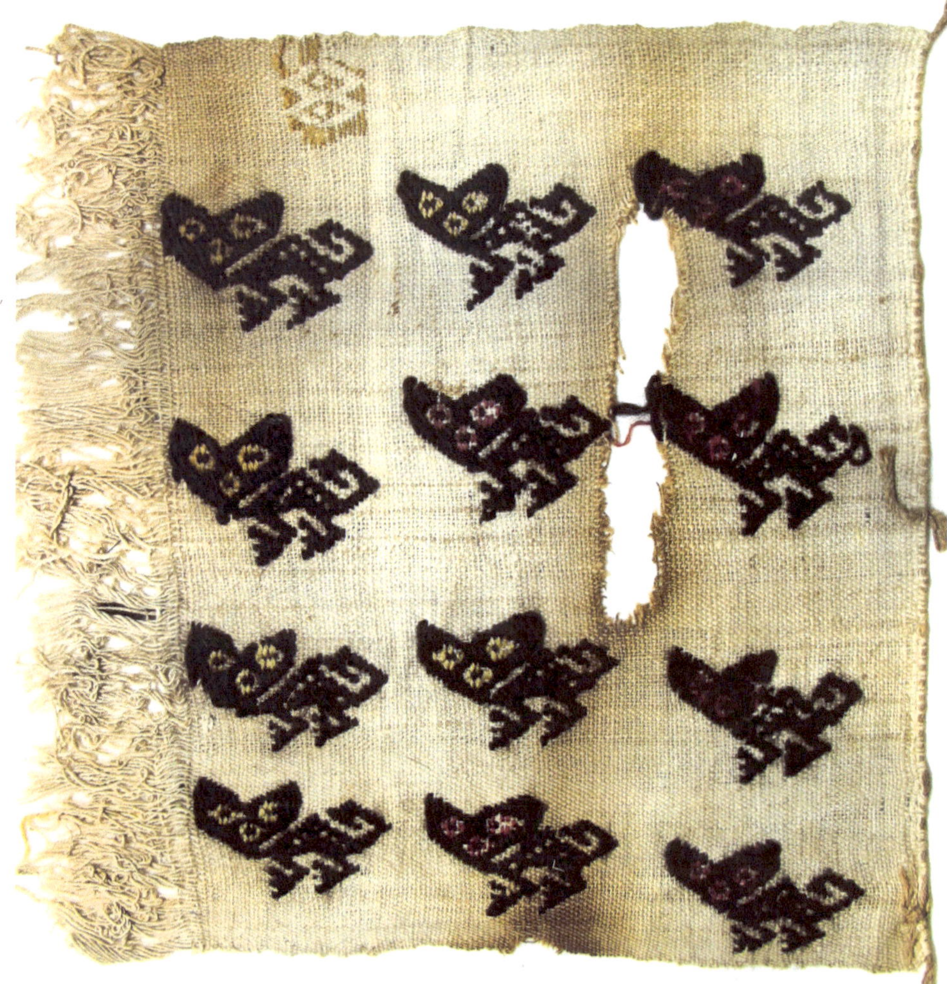

Museum number: V 9.232

Item: Fragment of a band
Style: Central coast
Size: 6 x 26 cm
Material/technique: The band has two side selvedges and no warp selvedge.
It is tapestry weaving. The warp is cotton 2S. The weft is camelid fiber 2S and cotton S. The threadcount is 8 x 34 per cm.

Museum number: V 9.234

Item: Fragment
Style: Central coast
Size: 19 x 20 cm
Material/ technique: Cotton textile with 3 selvedges woven in plain weave. Both warp and weft are 2S. The threadcount 16 x 10 per cm.
The patterns are brocaded animals (cats) in 2S camelid fiber. At one end there is 4 cm warp fringe.

Museum number: V 9.235

Item: Fragment
Style: Central Coast, Ychsma
Size: 38 x 35 cm
Material/technique: The upper part of the fragment (15 cm) is in slit tapestry. The warp is cotton 2S, the weft is camelid fiber 2S. The threadcount is 6 x 36 per cm. The textile has warp selvedge at the left side and weft selvedge at top and bottom.
At bottom is a 19 cm weft fringe (1,5 cm woven (7 warps), 17 cm looped wefts) with warps in 2S cotton and wefts in 2S camelid fiber.

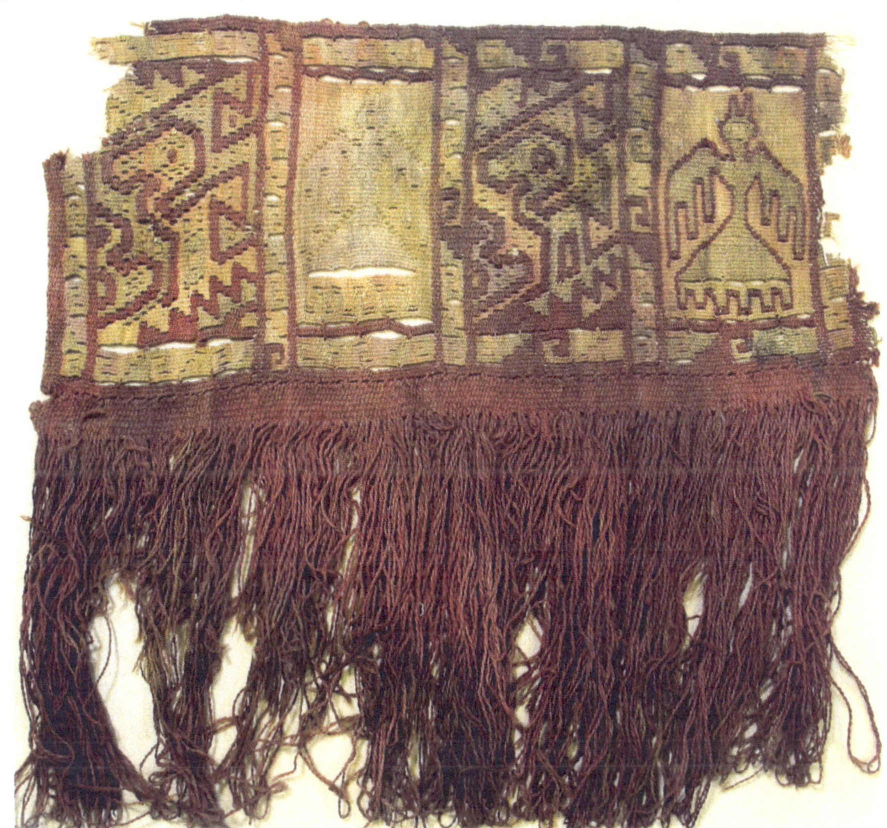

Museum number: V 9.241

Item: Fragment
Style: Central Coast, Chancay
Size: 25 x 27 cm
Material/technique: The fragment consists of a 17 cm wide slit tapestry with warp in cotton 2S and weft in camelid fiber 2S. The threadcount is 11 x 30 per cm. The fragment has two warp selvedges and one weft selvedge (right in photo).
At bottom is a 10 cm weft fringe in camelid fiber 2S (1 cm woven (5 warps, cotton S) – 9 cm loose wefts (cut at bottom).

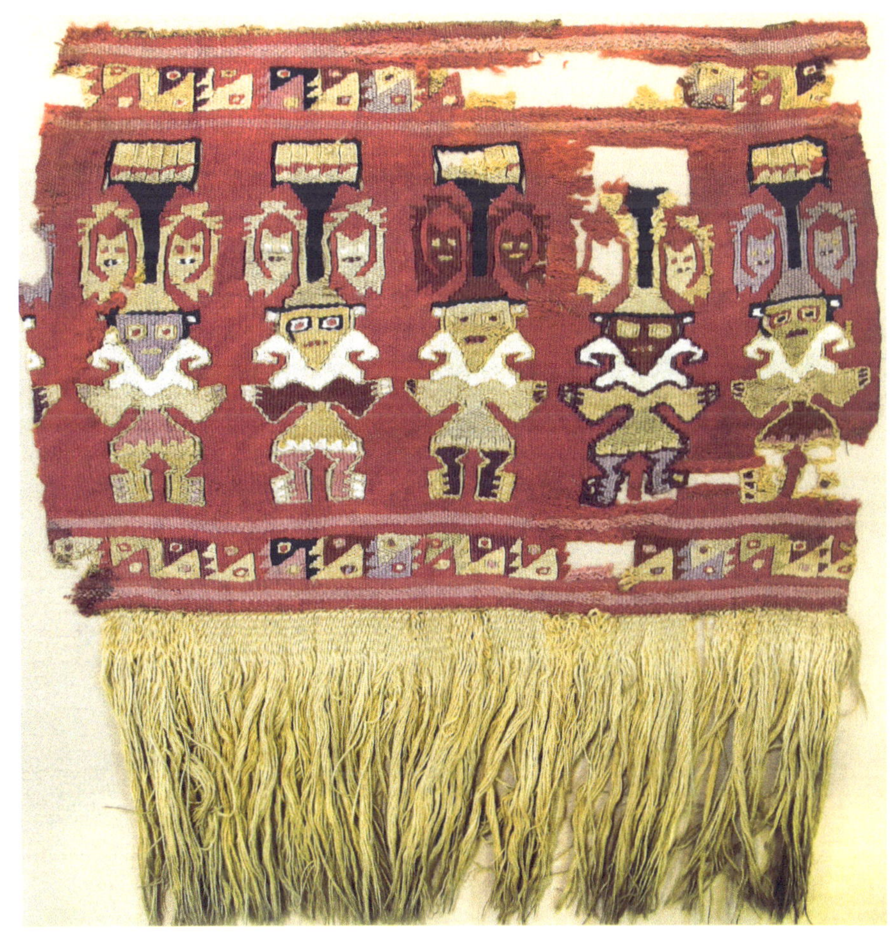

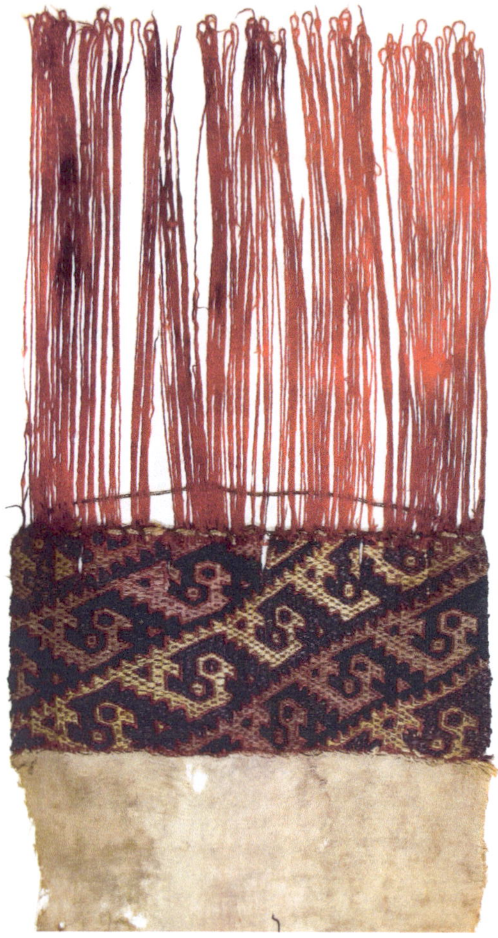

Museum number: V 9.260

Item: One side of a bag?
Style: Central Coast, Ychsma
Size: 42 x 21 cm
Material/technique:

1. Top: 10 x 20 cm plain weave in cotton S with a threadcount of 15 x 15 per cm. On all sides are complete or fragments of selvedges.
2. Center part: Complimentary weft weave with wefts in camelid fiber 2S and warps in cotton 2S.
3. Looped fringe – 23 cm, in camelid fiber 2S.

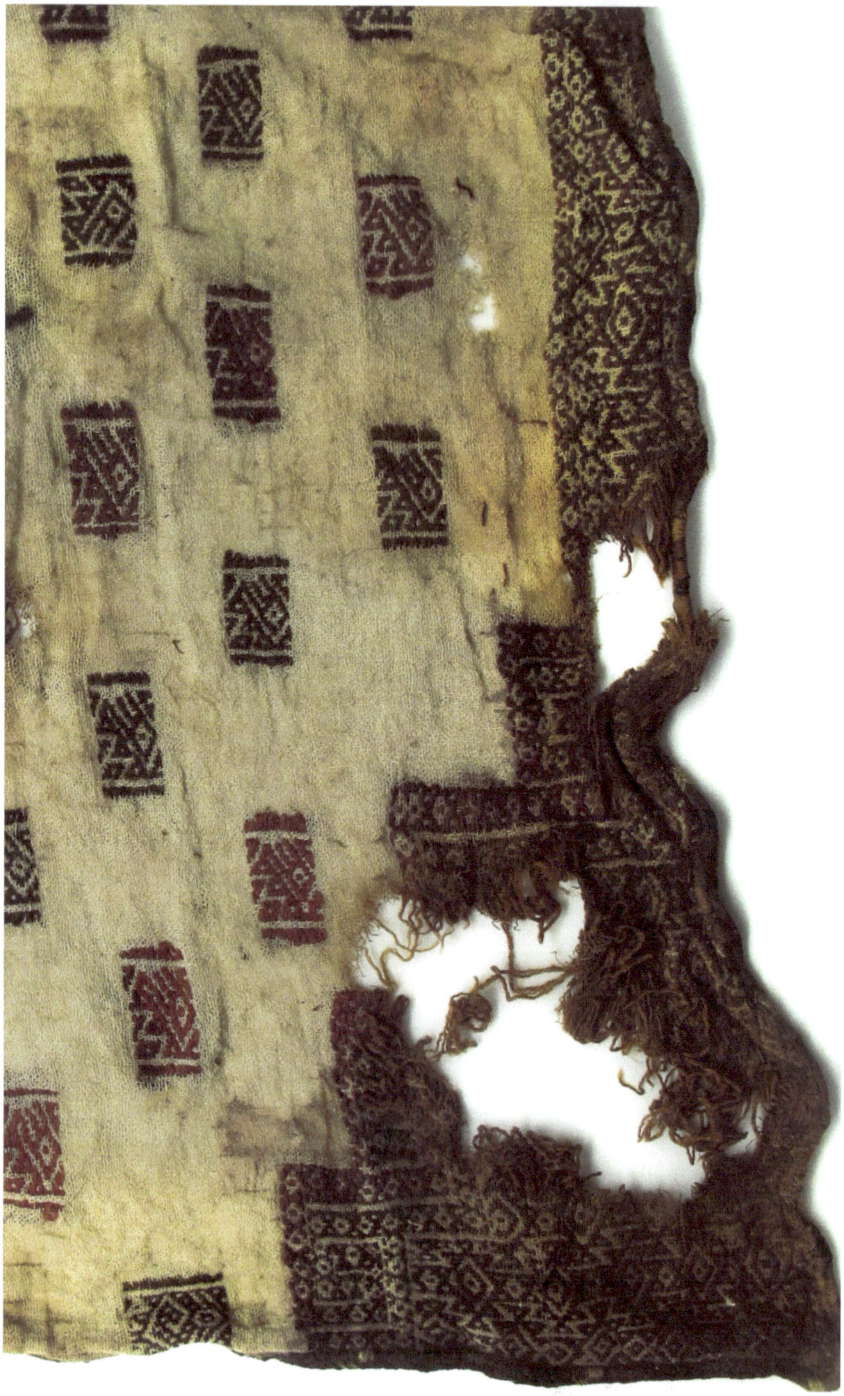

Museum number: V 9.264

Item: Fragment of a mantle
Style: Central coast (south coast?)
Size: 26 x 30 cm
Material/technique: Corner of a mantle.
The textile is in plain weave cotton S (both warp and weft). The threadcount is 20 x 15 per cm.
The designs are in negative brocade in camelid fiber 2S. The textile is edged with cross loop embroidery also in camelid fiber 2S.

Museum number: V 9.271

Item: Fragment of band
Style: Central coast
Size: 49 x 5 cm
Material/technique: The band has one warp selvedge and two weft selvedges. The warp is lengthwise.
The techniques are complementary warp weave and warp rep.
Both warp and weft are cotton 2S. The threadcount is 34 x10 per cm.

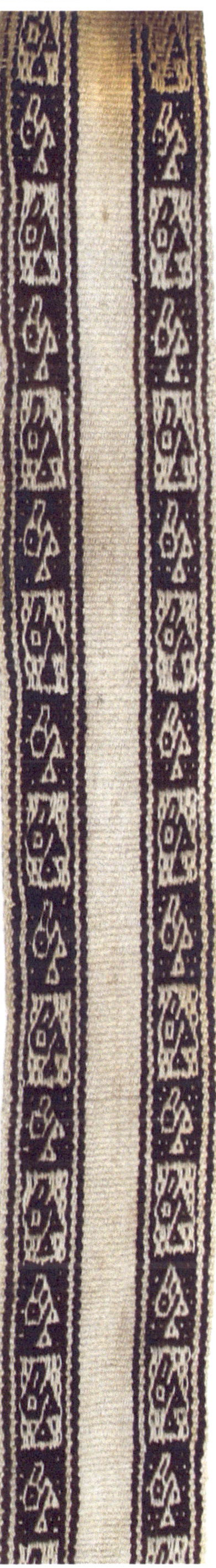

Museum number: V 9.277

Item: Fragment
Style: Central Coast, Ychsma
Size: 14 x 38 cm
Material/technique:

1. 11 cm plain weave with brocaded designs. The pattern wefts are in 2S camelid fiber. The foundation textile is in plain weave cotton - the warp is 2S and the weft S. The threadcount is 15 x 16 per cm. There is a warp selvedge at the bottom, where the fringe-band is attatched.
2. 2 cm wide weft fringe-band – 1 cm is woven, 1 cm is looped wefts.

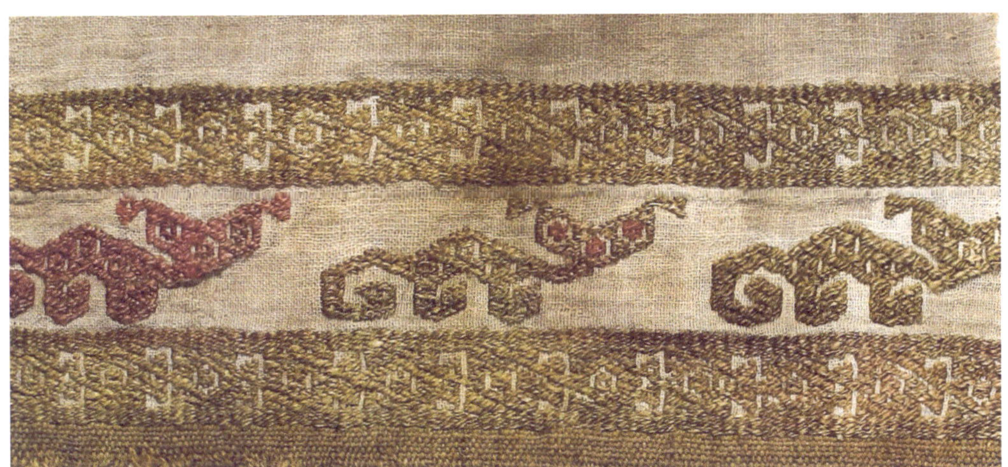

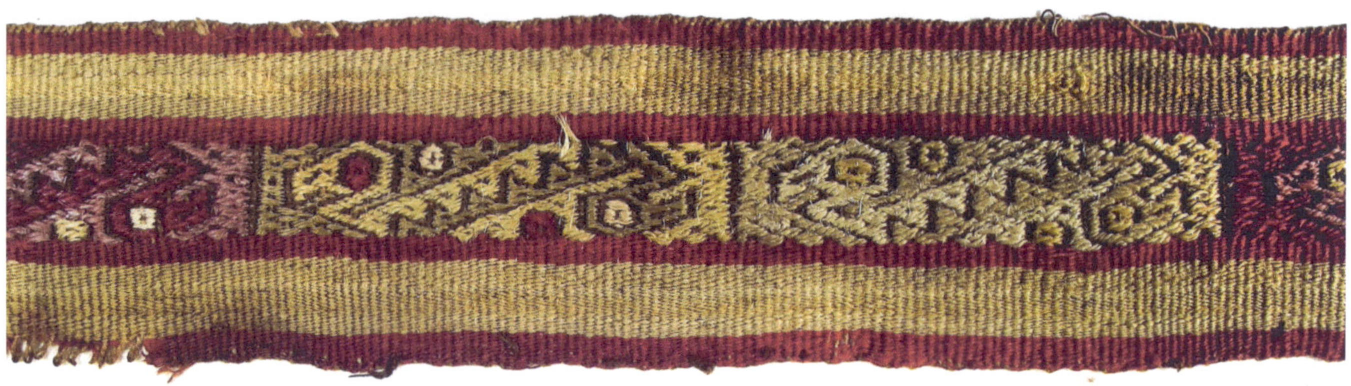

Museum number: V 9.282

Item: Fragment of a band
Style: Central Coast
Size: 5 x 30 cm
Material/technique: The textile is in weft rep and supplimentary weft weave. The warp is on the short side. The warp is cotton 2S and the weft camelid fiber 2S. The threadcount is 8 x 46 per cm.

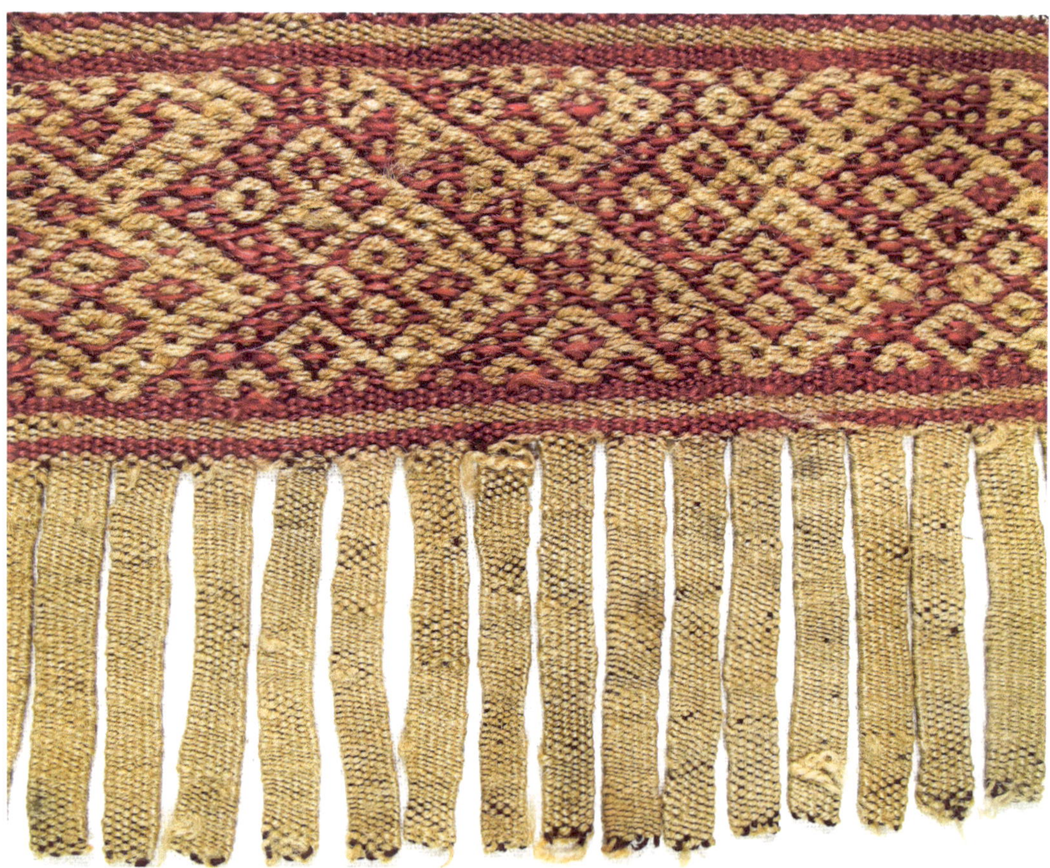

Museum number: V 9.305

Item: Fragment
Style: Central coast
Size: 9 x 29 cm
Material/technique: The textile is in 3 panels: 6, 16, 7 cm wide – all with weft selvedges and at fringe-bottom one warp-selvedge. Upper 5 cm: complementary weft weave (lancée); lower part 5 cm woven fringes, 0,6 mm wide.
Warp cotton 2S, weft camelid fiber 2S.

Museum number: V 9.324

Item: Closed bag
Style: Central Coast
Size: 15 x59 cm (bag 15 x 15 cm, fringe 45 cm)
Material/ technique: Plain weave in cotton 2S. The threadcount is 5 x 5 per cm. The straps are two 3-braided bands of 15 cm each, sewn to the upper corners of the bag and tied to each other.

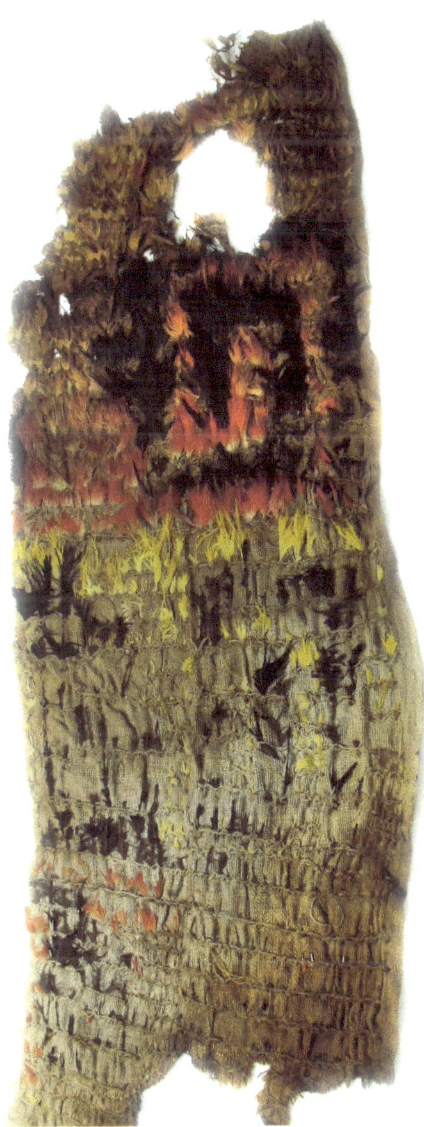

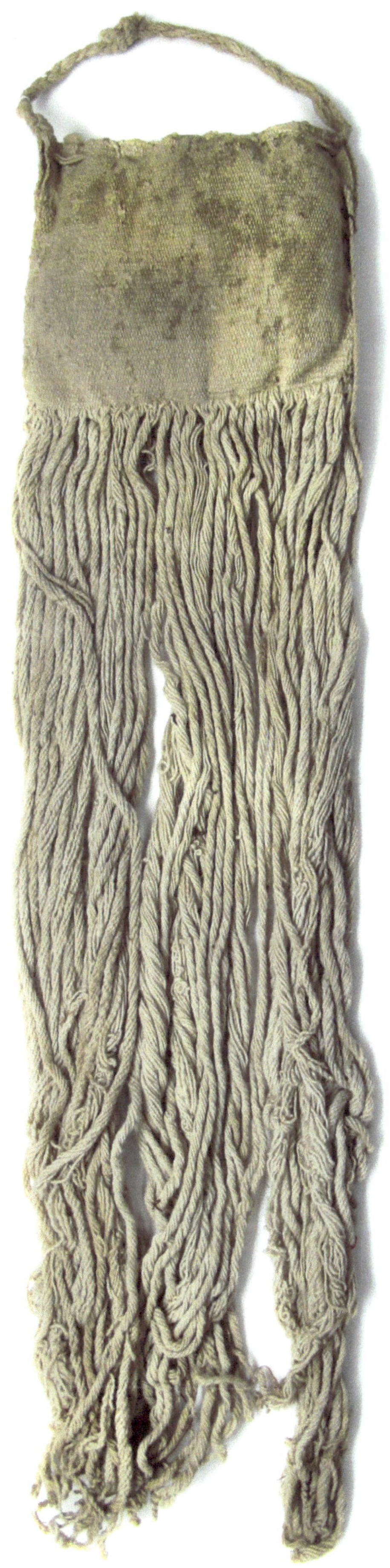

Museum number: V 9.326

Item: Feather textile, Maybe back piece for hat???
Style: Central Coast
Size: 73 x 29 cm
Material/ technique: Plain weave in cotton with warp in 2S and weft in Z. The threadcount is 9 x 9 per cm. There are two side selvedges.
Rows of feather fringes are stitched on every 2 cm. The sewing thread is cotton 2S.
V 9.325 is a fragment of the same textile.

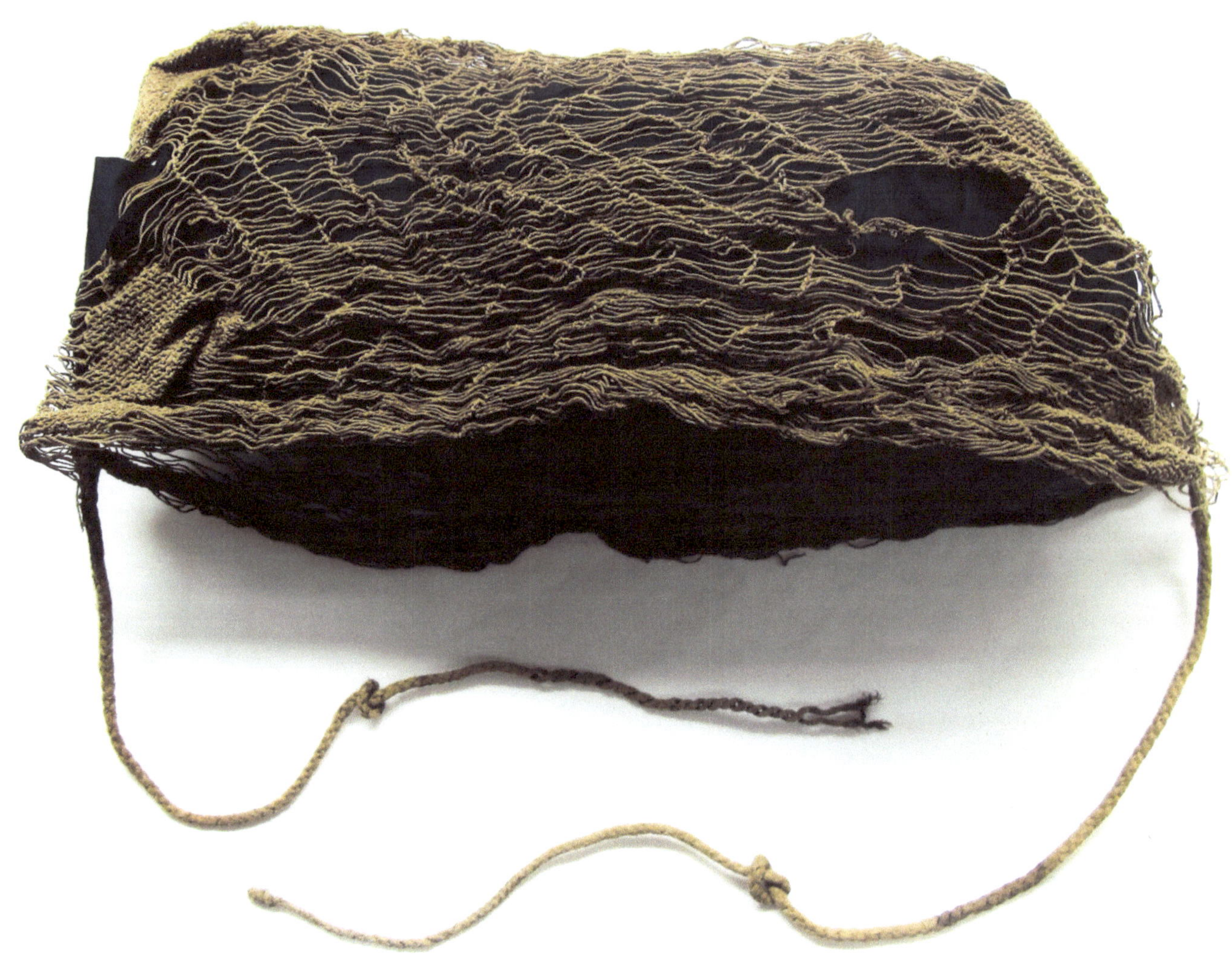

Museum number: V 9.342

Item: Hairnet
Style: Central Coast
Size: 21 x 10 cm
Material/technique: Knotted hairnet (lark's knots) with 4-8 strands braided tying bands. Material is plantfiber (*Fourcraea andina*).
Bibliography: Pre-Columbian Hairnets in the Museum of Ethnology in Berlin, *Baessler-Archiv*, 2010, Vol. 58, p39-51. 13p.
Lena Bjerregaard, *Pre-Columbian Textiles in the Ethnological Museum in Berlin,* 2017, https://digitalcommons.unl.edu/zeabook/52/ , pp. 157-159.

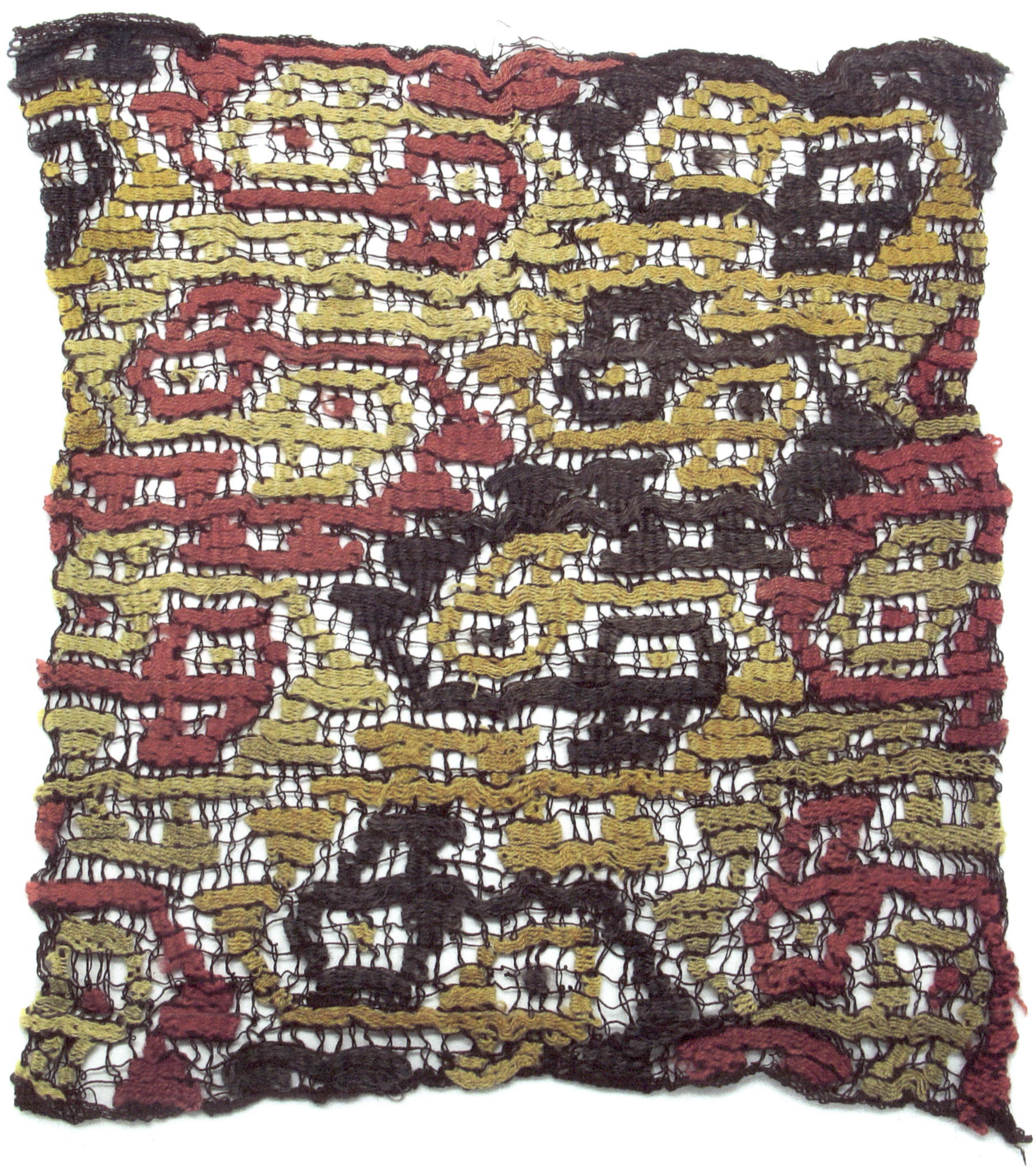

Museum number: V 9.600

Item: Complete textile
Style: Central coast
Size: 32 x 32 cm
Material/technique: The textile is complete with 4 selvedges. It is woven in gauze weave with brocaded patterns. All yarns are camelid fiber 2S.

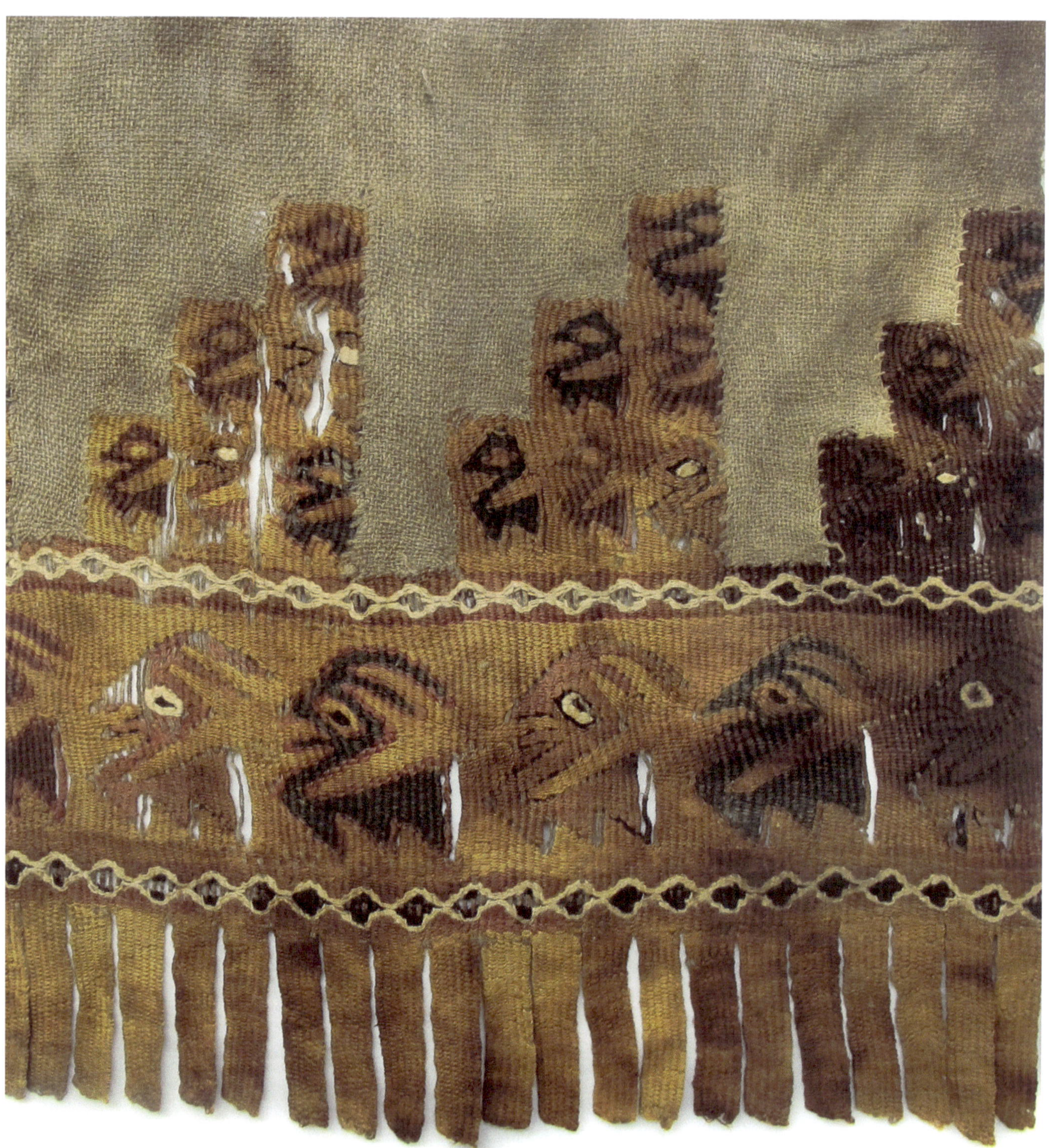

Museum number: V 10.187

Item: Fragment (of a tunic)
Style: Central coast
Size: 22 x 57 cm
Material/technique: The textile is the lower edge of a tunic. The textile has warp selvedge at bottom and at both sides weft selvedges. It has at bottom 0,8 cm wide woven fringes.
The basic material is plain weave cotton. Both warp and weft are 2S. The threadcount is 16 x 14 per cm.
The lower part has slit tapestry over two plain weave cotton warps and with 2S 4-camelid fiber wefts per cm.

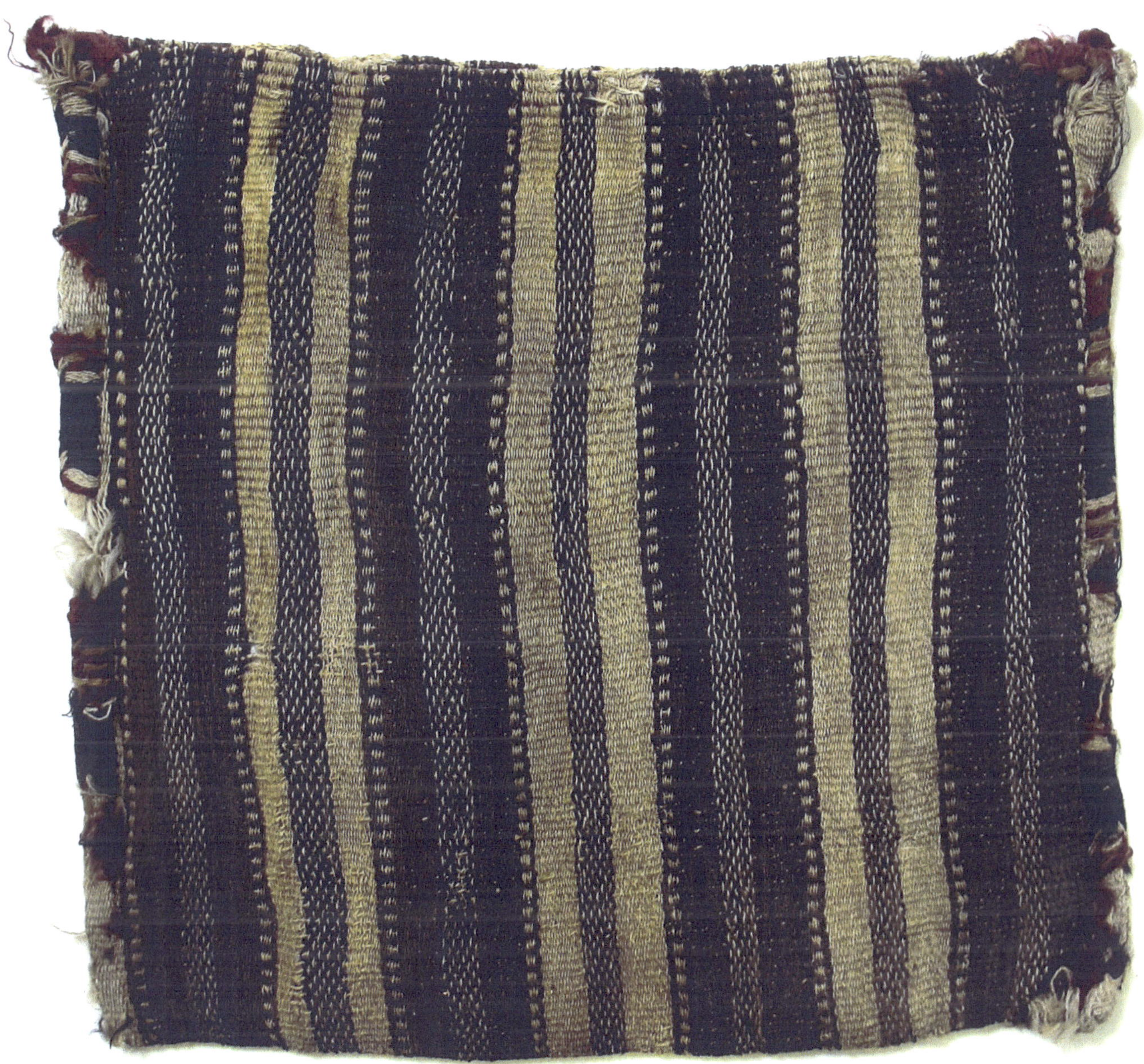

Museum number: V 11.261

Item: Bag
Style: Central coast
Size: 18 x 20 cm
Material/technique: The bag is warp faced plain weave with camelid fiber 2S in both warp and weft. The threadcount is 36 x 6 per cm. At the weft edges the two layers of the bag are connected with a multicolor striped loopstitch embroidery.

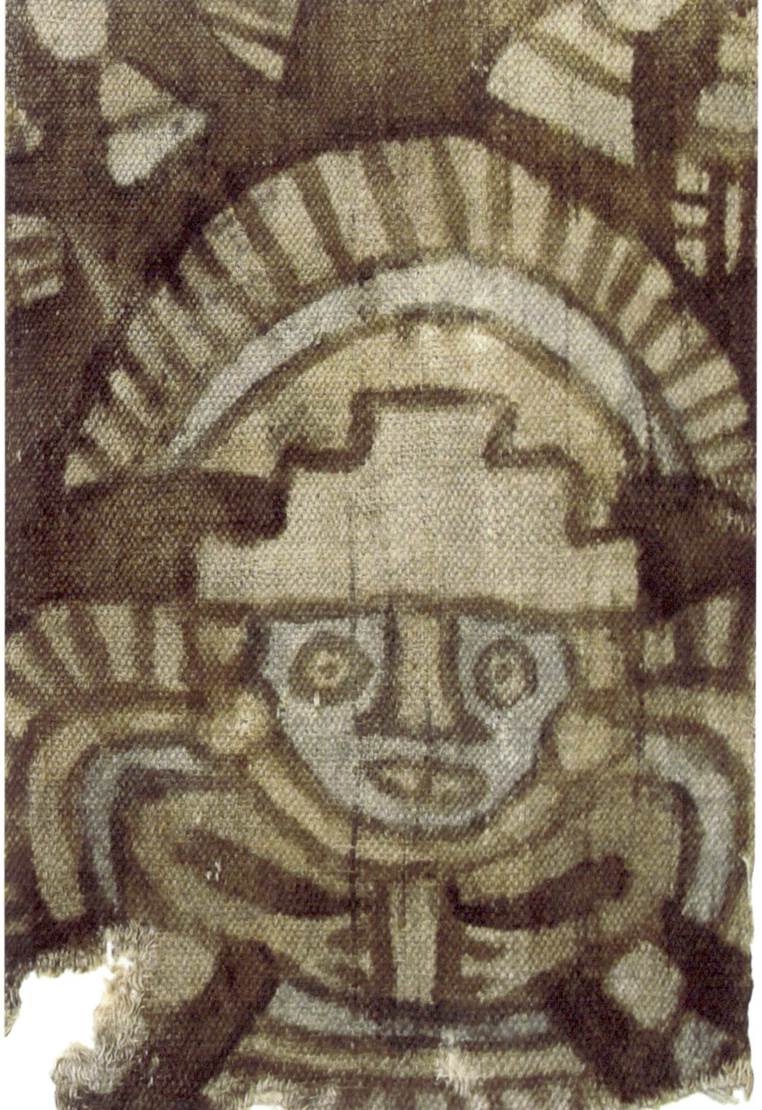

Museum number: V 8.955

Item: Fragment
Style: North Coast
Size: 26 x 38 cm
Material/technique: Plain weave, painted (nothing on back side) textile fragment. All yarns are cotton S. Warp is paired and the weft is single. The threadcount is 11 (paired) x 9 per cm.

Museum number: V 8.960

Item: Fragment
Style: North coast
Size: 32 x 43 cm
Material/technique: Plain weave cotton with the warp S and the weft Z. The threadcount is 9 x 9 per cm. The textile is painted and has two side selvedges.

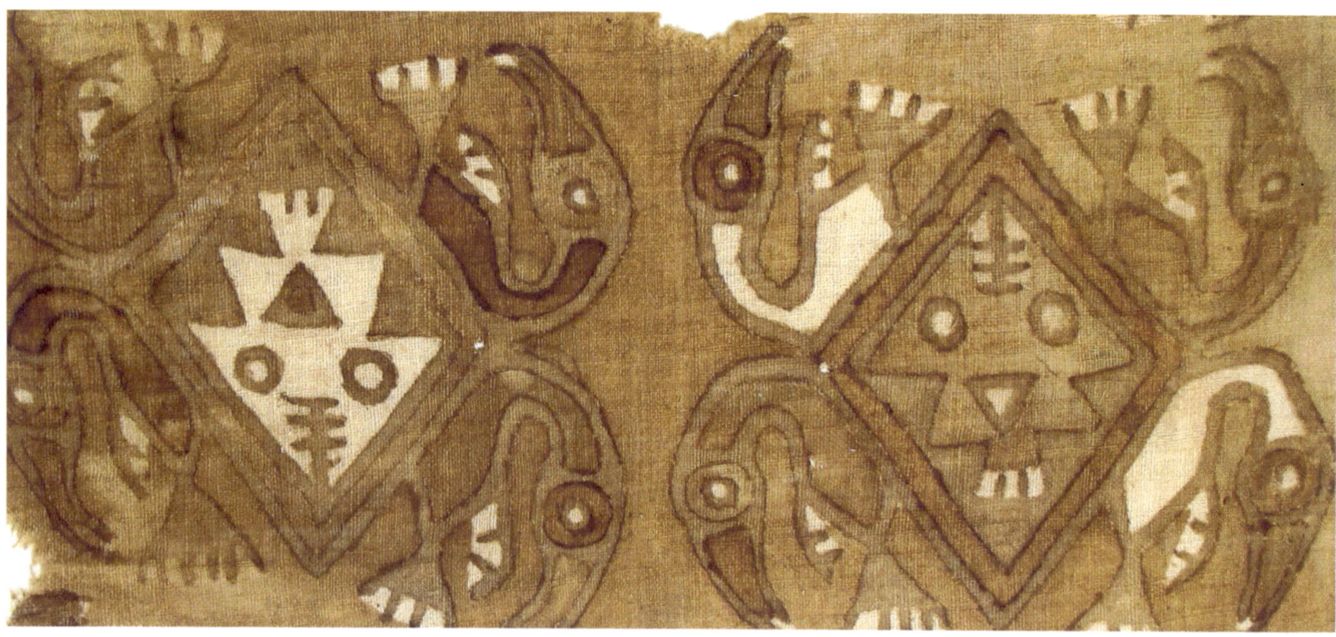

Museum number: V 8.973

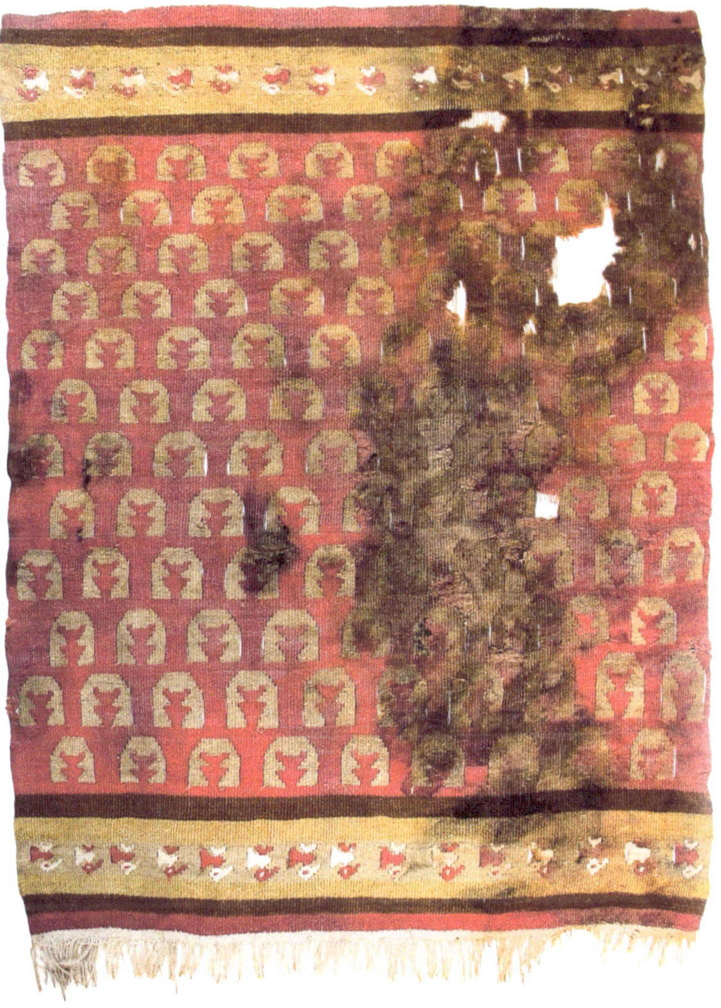

Item: Textile (complete)
Style: North Coast
Size: 59 x 43 cm
Material/technique: The textile is woven in slit tapestry. The warp is cotton 2Z and the weft camelid fiber 2S. The threadcount is 6 x 28 per cm. The textile has two side selvedges and one warp selvedge. It has loose warps (fringe) at the other end.

Museum number: V 8.959

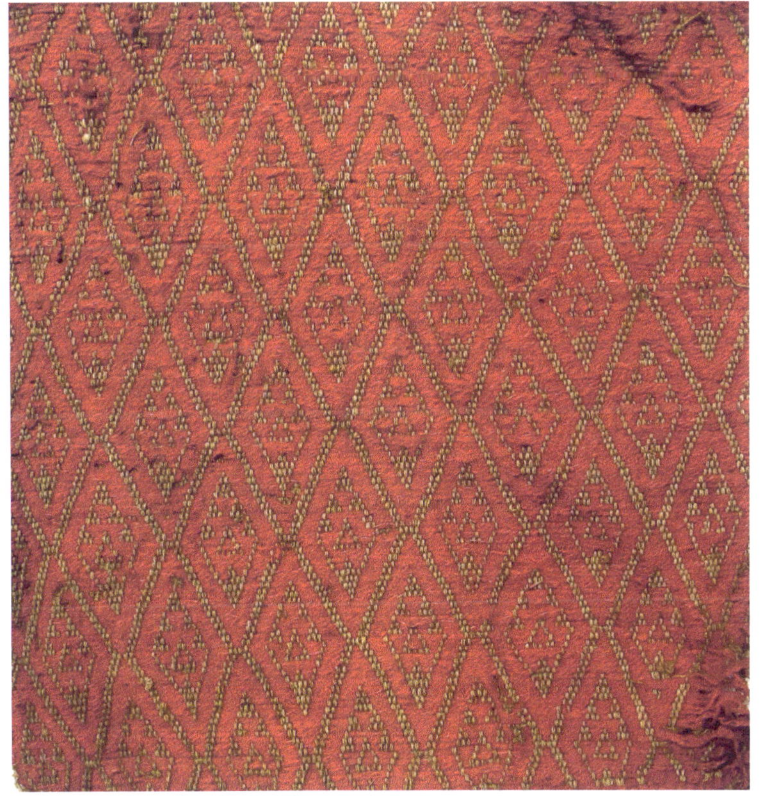

Item: Bag
Style: North Coast
Size: 19 x 19 cm
Material/technique: The textile has supplementary weft patterning (lancée). Warp and weft are paired cotton S and the pattern-weft is 2S camelid fiber. The threadcount is 14 x 9 (both paired) per cm. The bag has four selvedges. It is folded along the warp and the two side selvedges are sewn together.

Museum number: V 8.981

Item: Fragment
Style: Central Coast
Size: 21 x 20 cm
Material/technique: Dovetailed tapestry weave with warps and wefts in cotton 2S. The warps are replied in Z from two different colored 2S yarns. The threadcount is 7 x 40 per cm.
Further description: At the bottom of the fragment is a warp selvedge, and at top (over the upper stripe) the warps are loose (not being woven). The image is of high status (feather crown) lobster or scorpion.

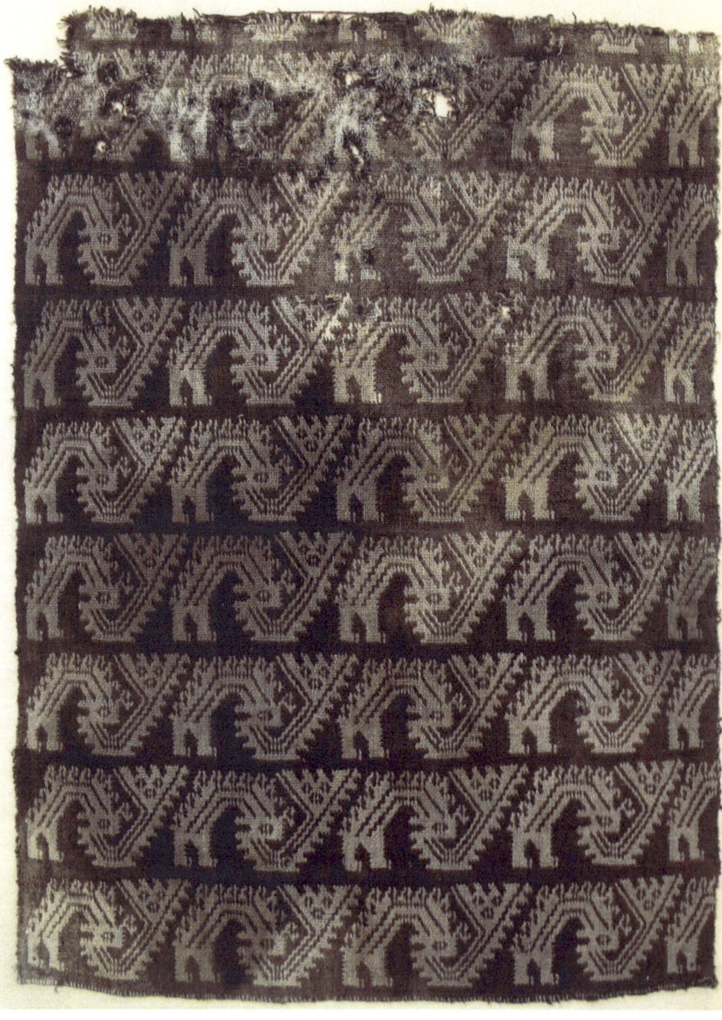

Museum number: V 9.001

Item: Fragment
Style: North Coast
Size: 30 x 40 cm
Material/technique: The textile is woven in doubleweave. It has cotton Z warp and S weft. The threadcount is (in every layer) 12 x 10 per cm.
There are two weft selvedges and one warp selvedge.

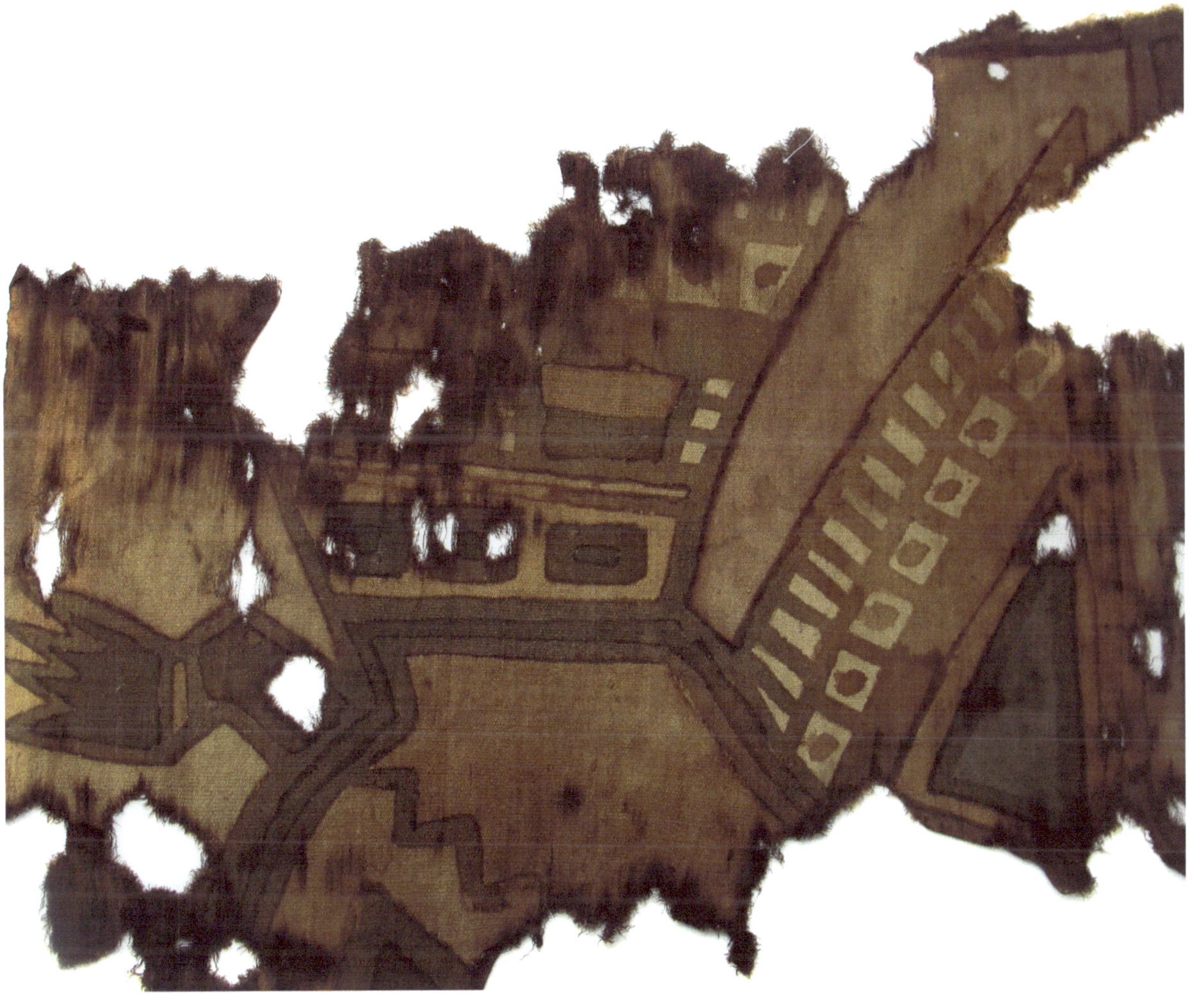

Museum number: V 9.003 + V 9.126

Item: 2 fragment of the same textile.
Style: North Coast
Size: V 9.003: 45 x 55 cm, V 9.126: 53 x 53 cm
Material/technique: The textile is woven in plain weave. It has cotton S, paired warps and paired wefts. The threadcount is 28 x 9 per cm.
The textile is painted. Both textiles have fragments of weft selvedges.

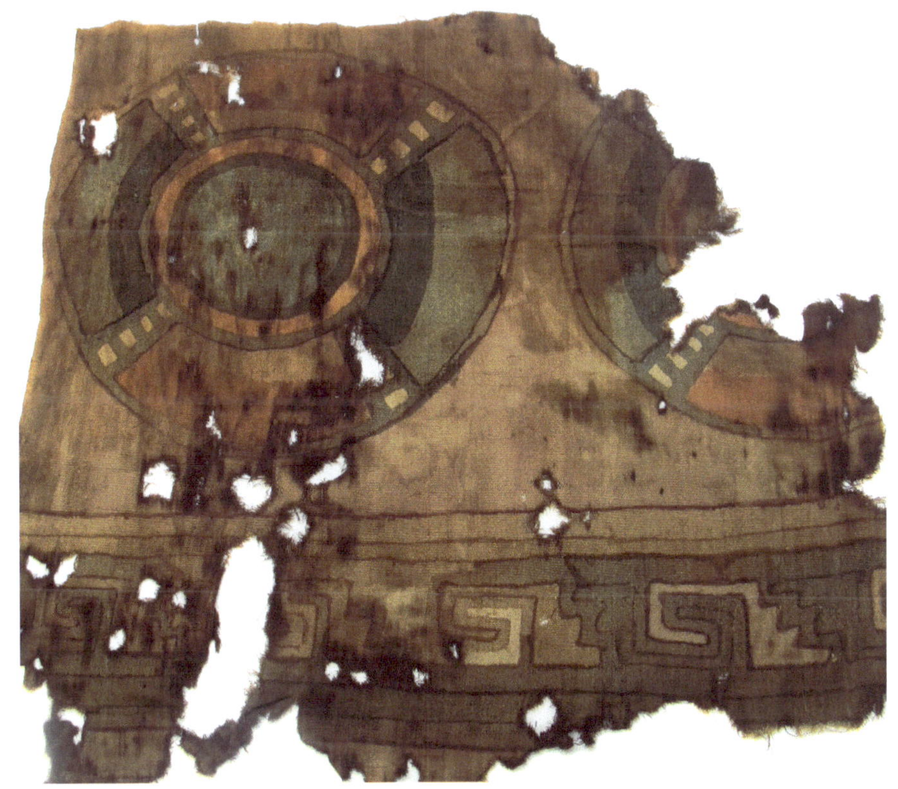

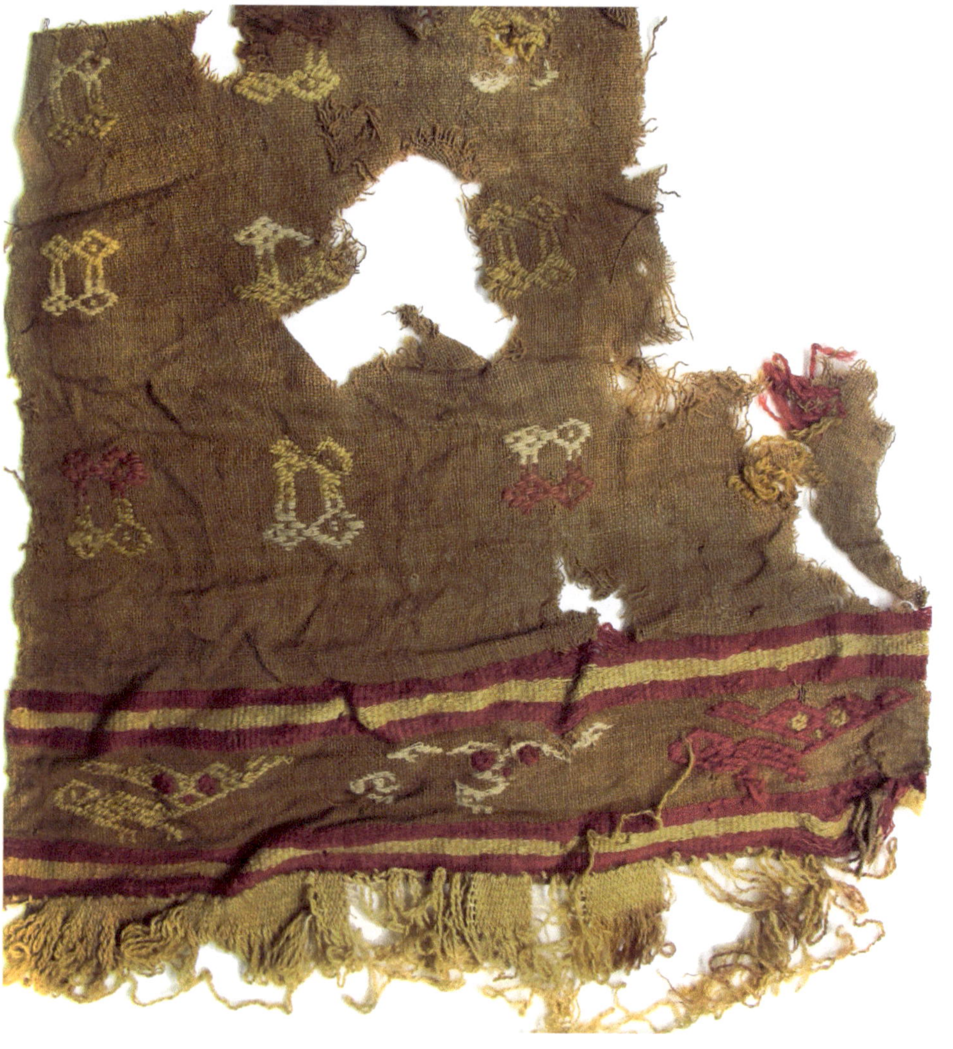

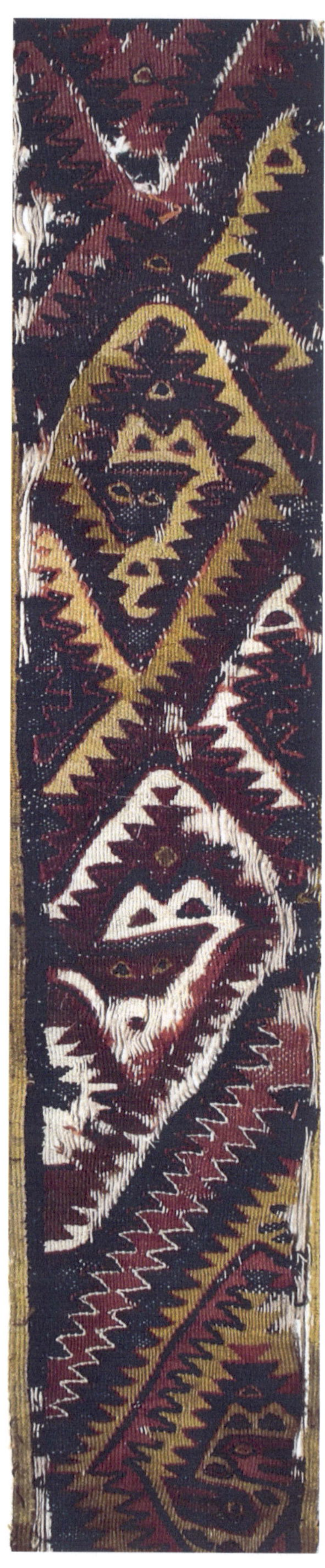

Museum number: V 9.004

Item: Fragment of a mantle or tunic
Style: North Coast
Size: 26 x 25 cm
Material/technique: The textile is woven in plain weave, cotton S with a threadcount of 16 x 14 per cm (varying some). The patterning is brocade in 2S camelid fiber yarns.
The textile has weft selvedge on one side, and there are fragments of a stitching, indicating that another panel was sewn on here.
At bottom is a separately woven 3 cm wide band of 2S camelid fiber yarns. It is half woven/ half loose weft fringe.

Museum number: V 9.009

Item: Fragment of band
Style: South or North Coast
Size: 40 x 8,5 cm
Material/technique: The warp is cotton 3Z and the weft camelid fiber 2S. Along the sides of the band is a narrow yellow stripe – it is attached as dovetailed tapestry.

Museum number: V 9.021

Item: Fragment
Style: North coast
Size: 17,5 x 12 cm
Material/technique: A textile woven in tapestry with warp cotton 3Z and weft 2S camelid fiber. The threadcount is 8 x 40 per cm.

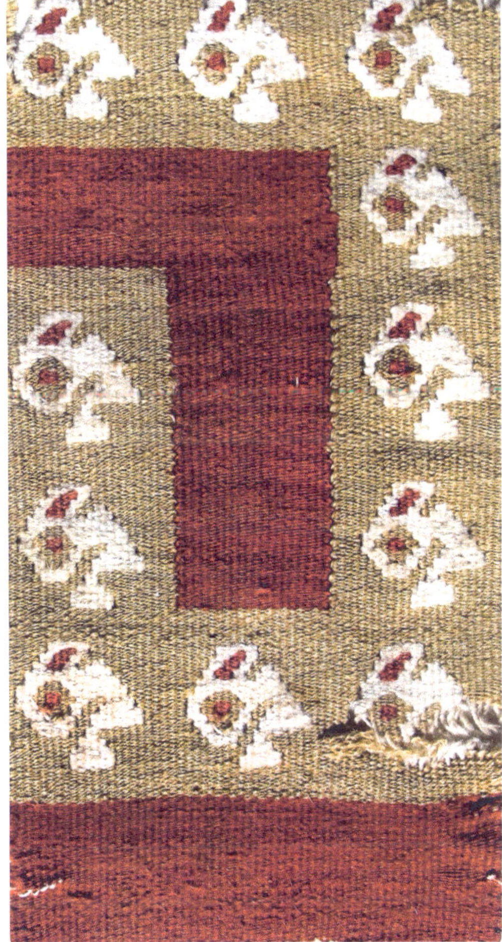

Museum number: V 9.035 and V 9.230

Item: Two fragments
Style: North Coast
Size: V 9.230: 20 x 23 cm, V 9.035: 19 x 17 cm
Material/technique: A textile woven in tapestry with warp cotton S and weft camelid fiber 2S. The threadcount is 9 x 32 per cm.
Both fragments are cut on all sides (no selvedges).

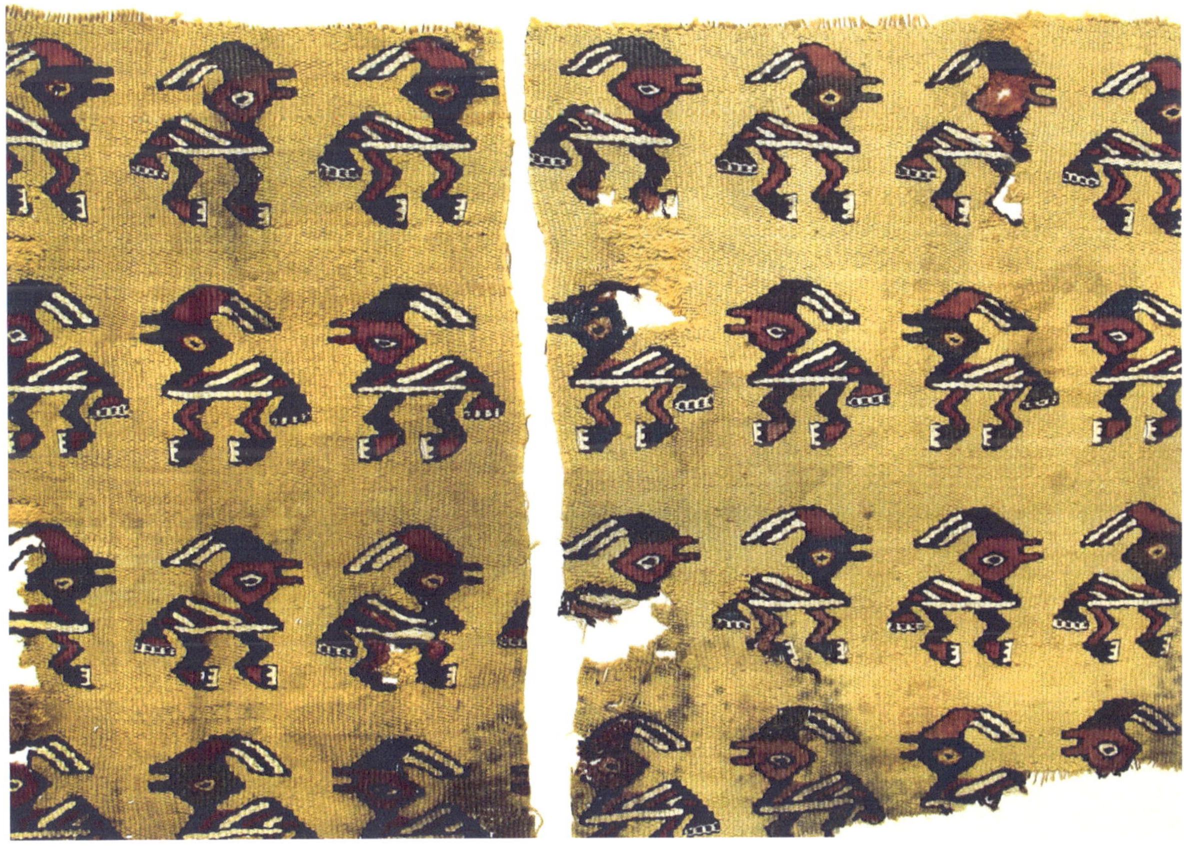

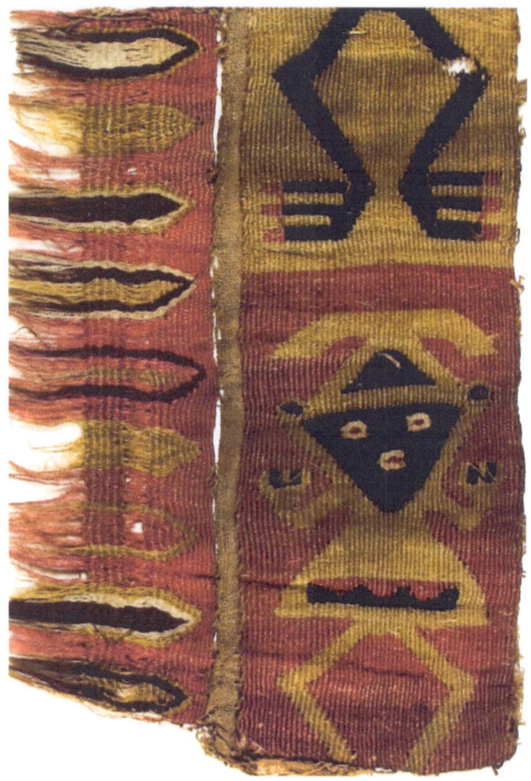

Museum number: V 9.068

Item: Fragment
Style: Central/ North Coast
Size: 21 x 13 cm
Material/technique: Bottom edge of a tunic.

1. At bottom is a 5 cm wide weft-fringe band with tapestry and cut fringe. The warp is 2Z cotton and the weft is 2S camelid fiber.
2. A 7 cm wide tapestry band with 2Z cotton warp and 2S camelid fiber weft. The band has two weft selvedges.
3. On the backside of this tapestry is a plain weave textile in cotton S (both warp and weft) - threadcount 15 x 12 per cm - which was probably the foundation material of the tunic. This cloth has warp selvedge at bottom.

Museum number: V 9.074

Item: Fragment
Style: North coast
Size: 13 x 17 cm
Material/technique: The textile is in plain weave cotton S. The threadcount is 14 x 20 per cm. The patterning is in brocade with 2S camelid fiber wefts.

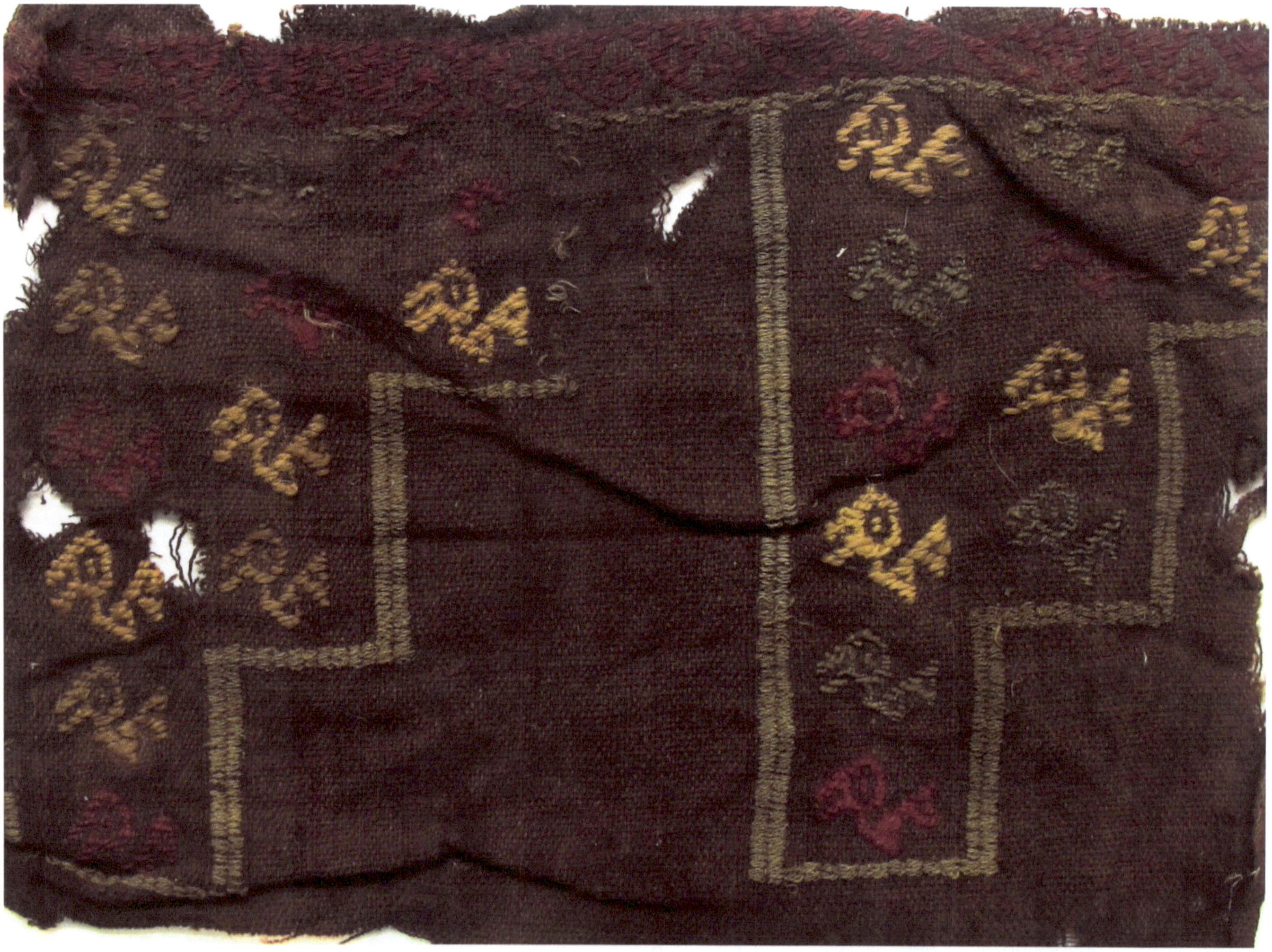

Museum number: V 9.075

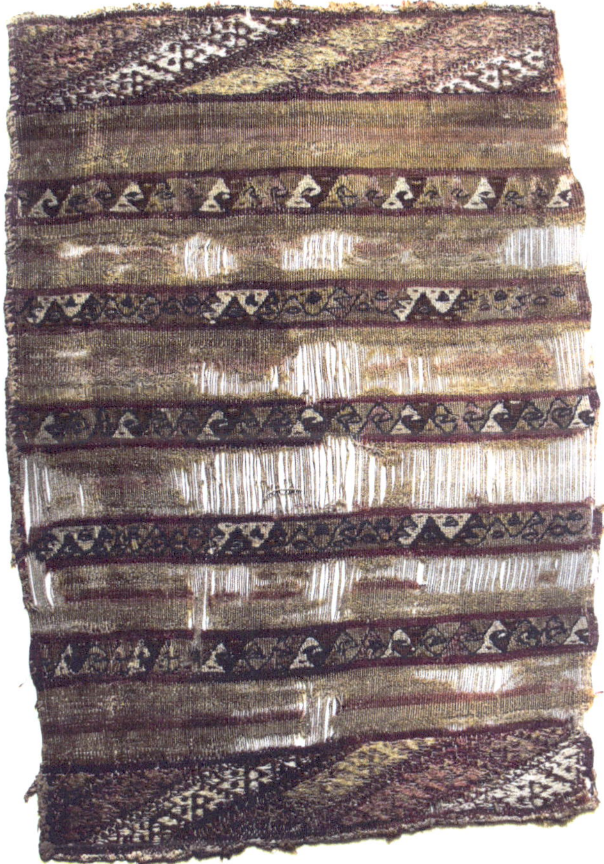

Item: Complete textile
Culture: South or Central Coast
Size: 42 x 29 cm
Material/technique: The textile has four selvedges. The warp is 2S cotton and the wefts are camelid fiber 2S.
The techniques are brocade, tapestry and weft rep. The threadcount is 9 x 36 per cm (in weft-rep).
At warp ends are fragments of loopstitch embroidery.
Along one weft selvedge are fragments of a plain weave cotton material stitched on.

Museum number: V 9.132

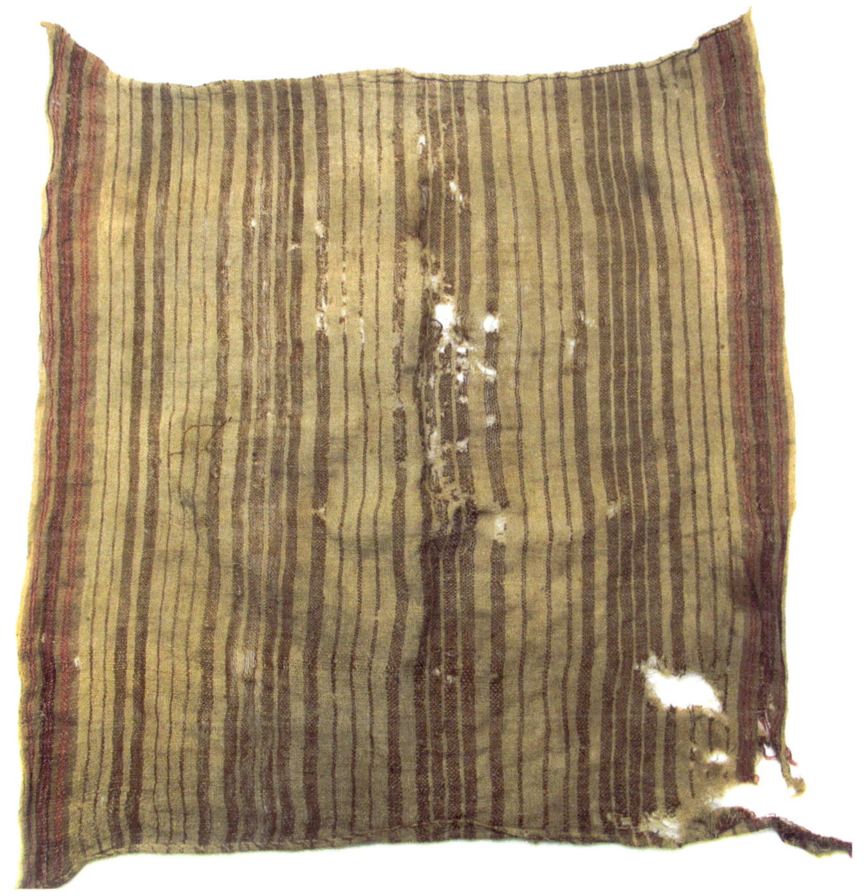

Item: Complete textile
Culture: Central/North-coast
Size: 48 x 45 cm
Material/technique: Complete textile with 4 selvedges woven in plain weave. Both weft and warp are cotton S. The warp is in some places paired and in some places single.
At the sides are red/brown warps of 2S camelid fiber.
The textile is complete with 4 selvedges.

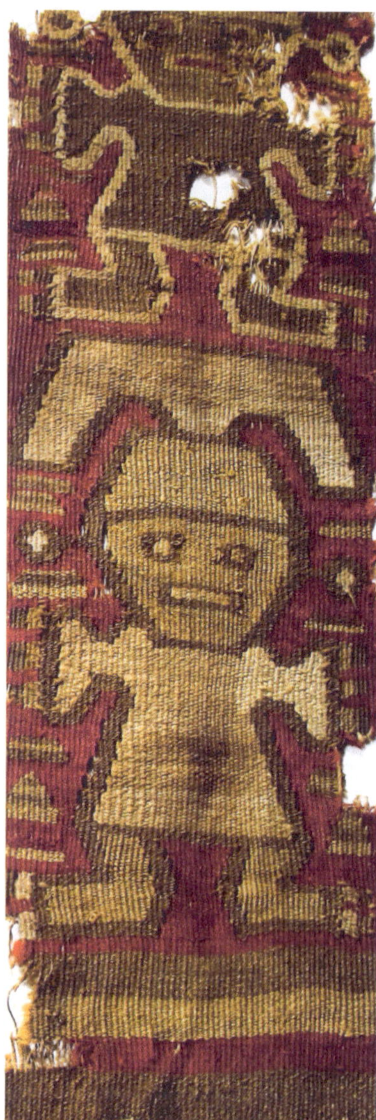

Museum number: V 9.122

Item: Fragment of a band.
Style: North Coast, Chimu
Size: 35 x 10 cm
Material/technique: The band has weft selvedges and no warp selvedges.
It is woven in slit tapestry. The warp is cotton 2Z and the weft is camelid fiber 2S and paired cotton Z. The threadcount is 8 x 36 per cm.

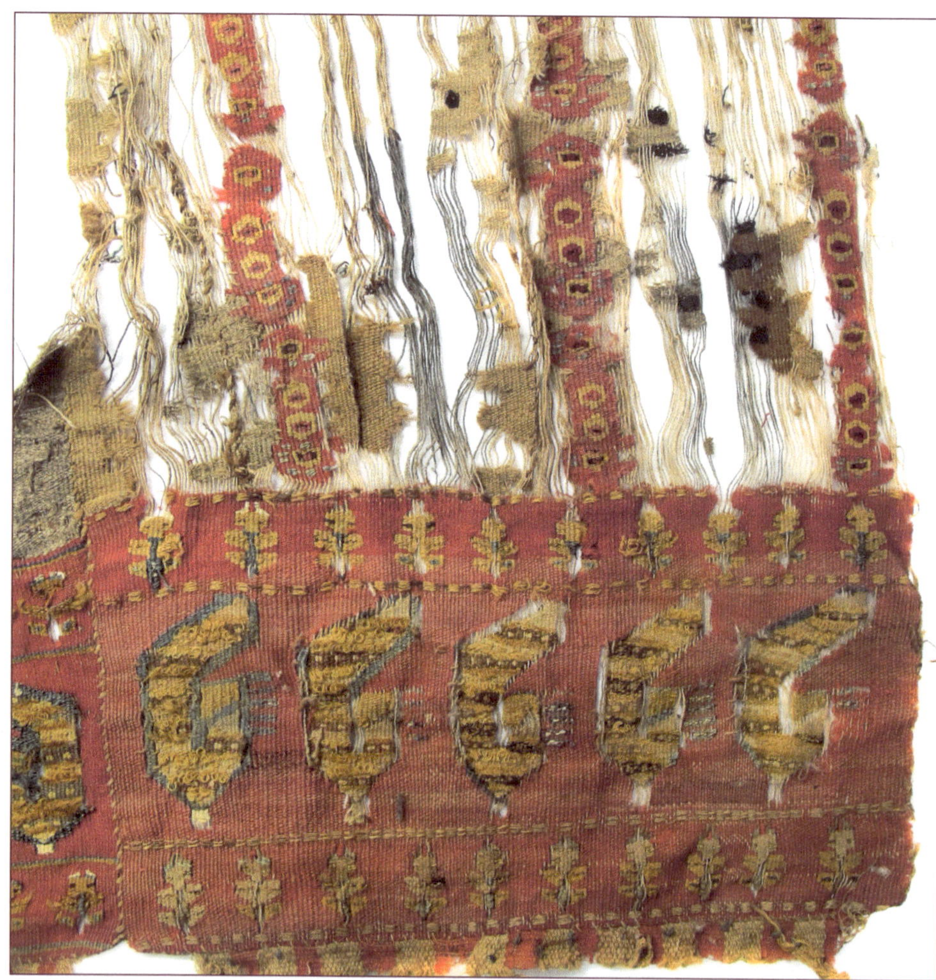

Museum number: V 9.141

Item: Fragment of a tunic (?)
Style: North coast
Size: 90 x 66 cm
Materia/technique: Dove tailed tapestry, warp cotton 2Z, weft camelid fiber 2S. Part of the pattern has looped floss.
The textile consist of 3 panels – each 27 cm wide. All 3 panels have at bottom warp-selvedge, and 2 weft-selvedges.
At bottom a 3 cm wide band with looped weft fringe - warp lengthwise cotton S, weft camelid fiber 2S. The band has 2 cm woven, 1 cm looped wefts.
This band is stitched on to the textile after the panels have been sewn together – it stretches over the whole textile.
The images with looped floss are maybe cashew nuts?

Museum number: V 9.143

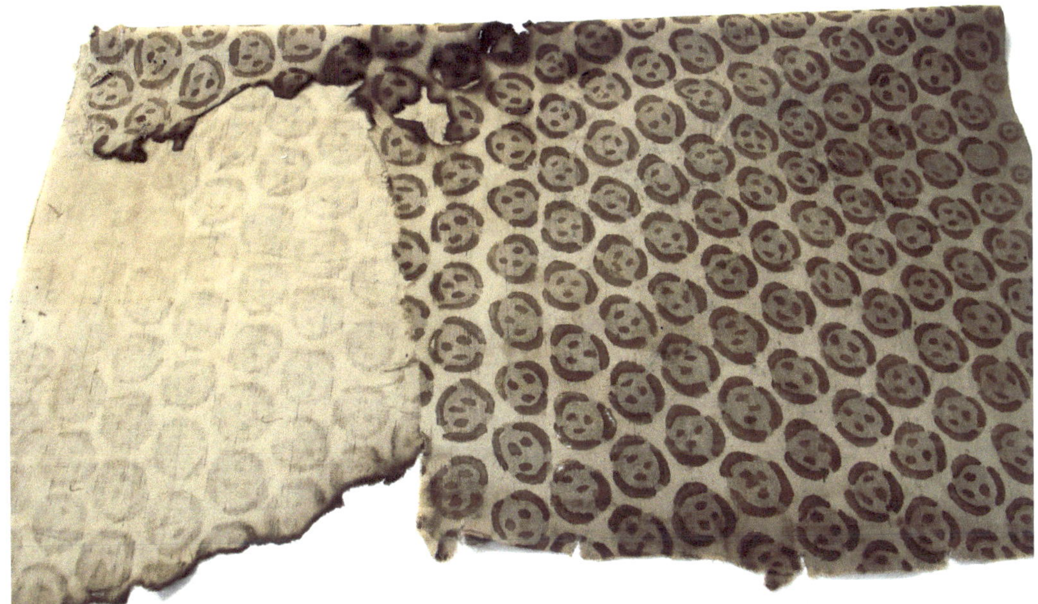

Item: Fragments of a large textile
Style: North Coast
Size: 93 x 72 cm
Material/technique: The textile is in plain weave and is woven in cotton S, paired warps and paired wefts. The threadcount is 28 x 14 (paired) per cm.
There are fragments of another panel sewn along one weft-selvedge. The textile is very similar to V 9.148, but has a different threadcount.
The pattern is painted or printed, and is only at the front side of the textile.

Museum number: V 9.148

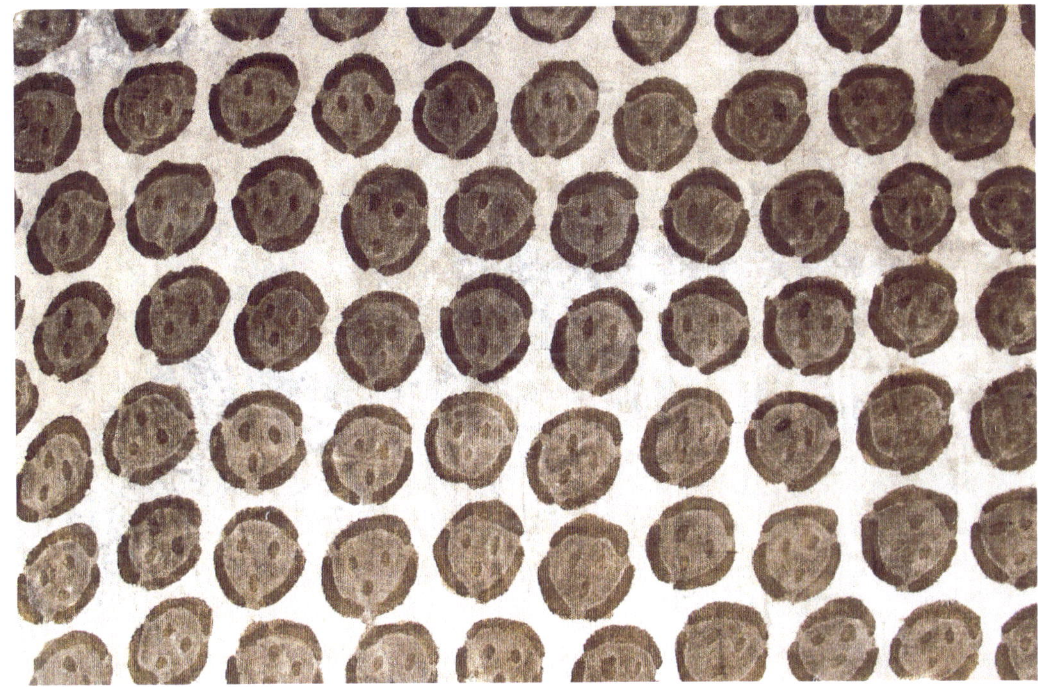

Item: fragment
Style: North coast
Size: 97 x 48 cm
Material/technique: The textile is in full warp length with two warp-selvedges. A fragment of a second panel is sewn on. It is woven in warp faced plain weave. The threadcount is 18 x 15 per cm. It has paired wefts Z and paired warps Z. It is printed or painted. The textile is very similar to V9143 – it has the same painted/printed pattern, but has a different threadcount, so it is not from the same textile.

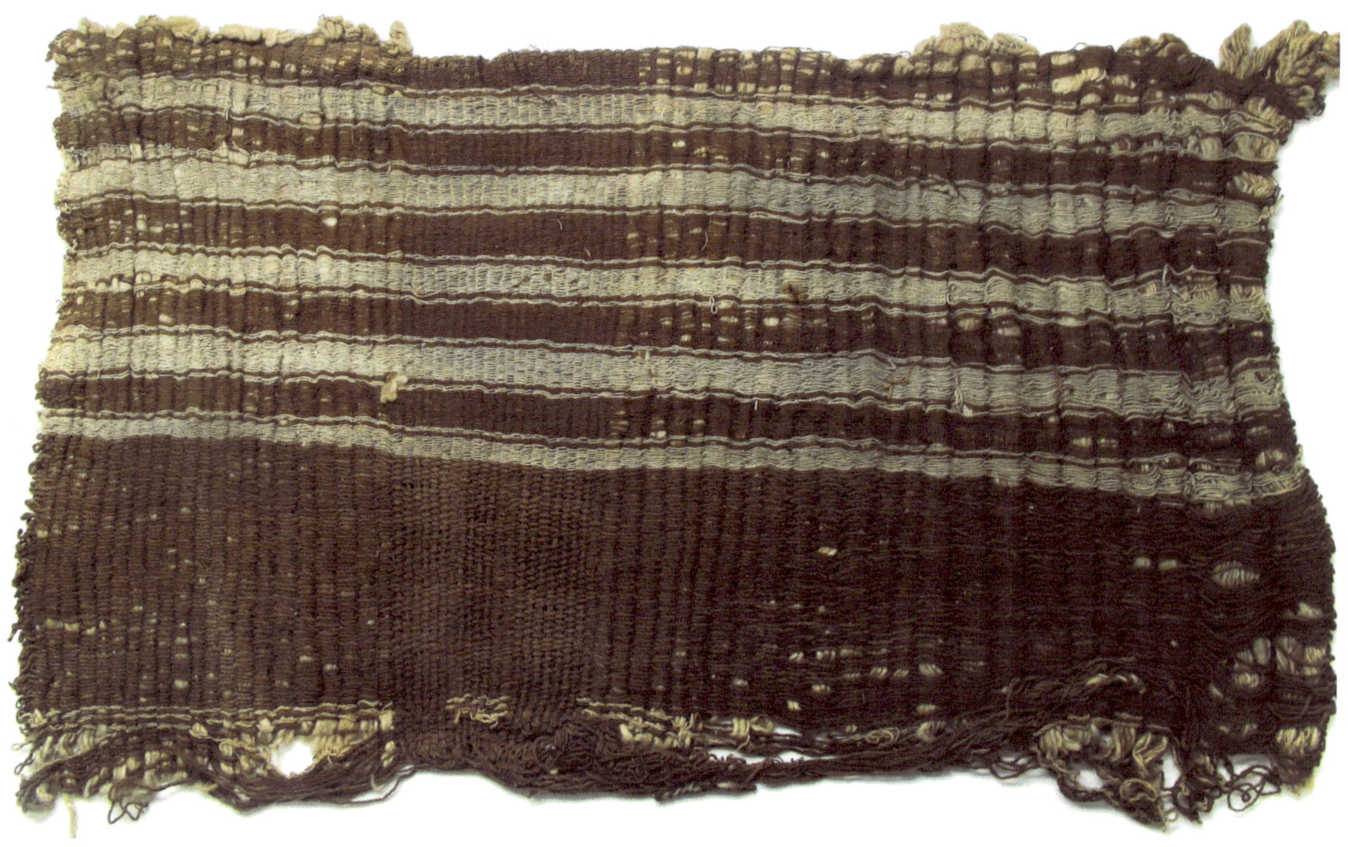

Museum number: V 9.144

Item: Complete textile
Style: North coast
Size: 57 x 35 cm
Material/technique: A very coarse textile with 4 selvedges. It is woven in warp faced plain weave – cotton 2S replyed Z with three yarns. The wefts are paired and tripled Z and 2S cotton. The tripled wefts are very thick, maybe the item was a mat to sit on. The threadcount is 3 x 20 per cm.

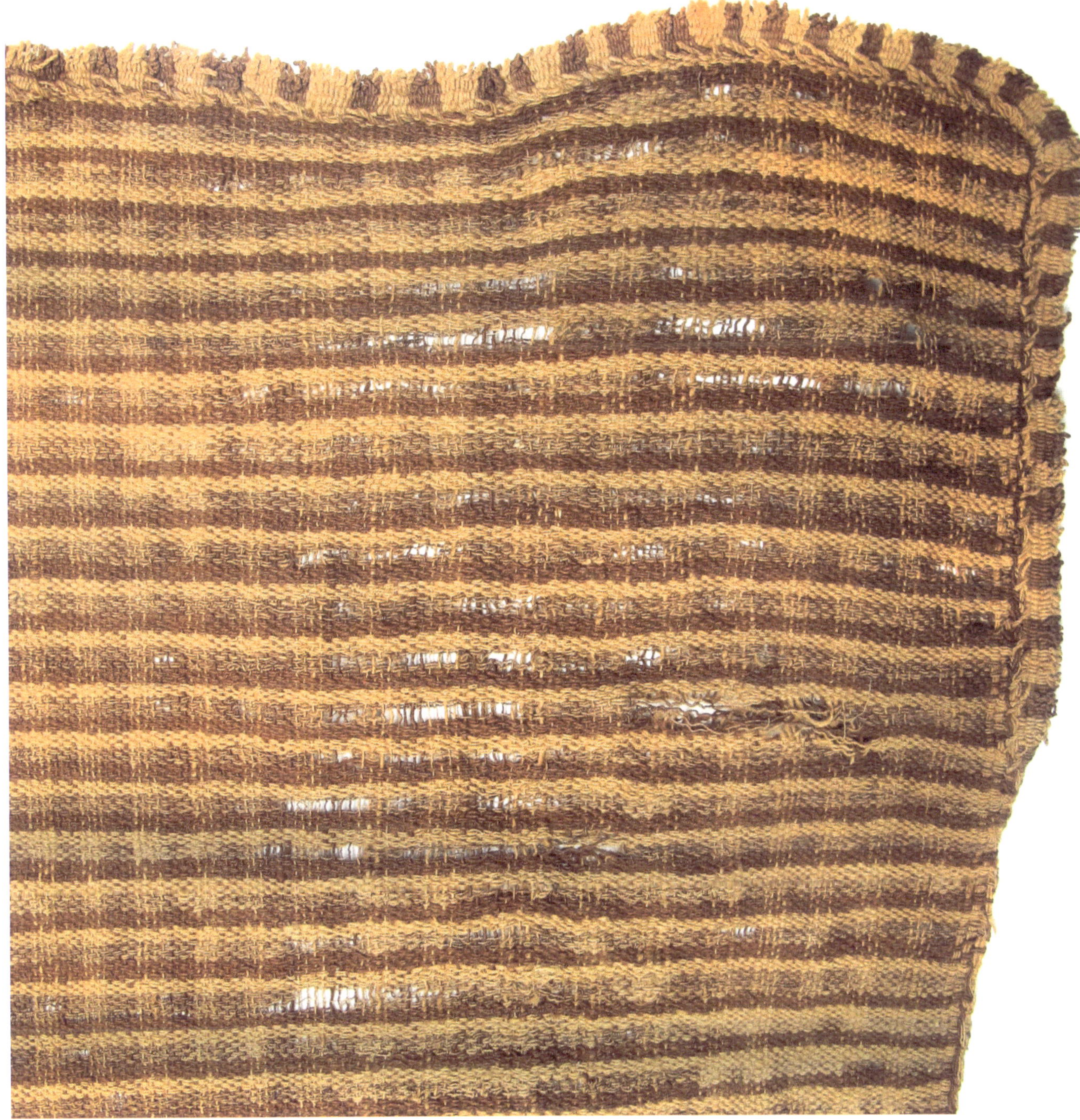

Museum number: V 9.153

Item: Mantle
Style: North coast
Size: 140 x 171 cm
Material/ technique: the textile has 3 panels – each one is 57 cm wide. It is woven in plain weave cotton S, with paired warps and single wefts. The threadcount is 18 (paired) x 10 per cm.
The outer weft-sides of the mantle have a woven band attached going just around the corners of the warp-selvedge. This band is 6 mm wide – it has 3 warps and a tiny (1mm) looped weftfringe towards the outside.

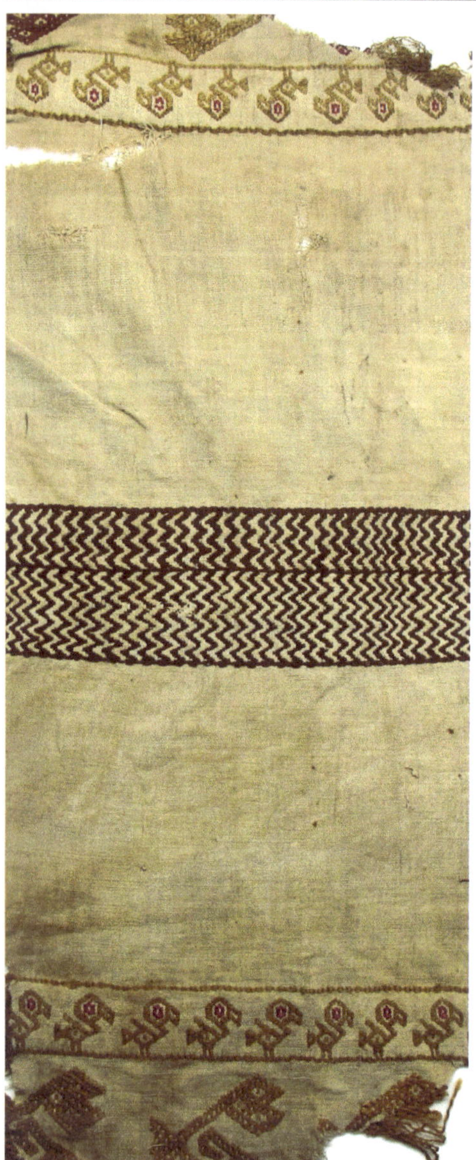

Museum number: V 9.154

Item: Fragment from tunic.
Style: North coast
Size: 52 x 30 cm
Material/technique: Shoulderpiece of a tunic. The zigzag stripes are the center shoulderpiece (the side selvedge on the left is either vertical neck opening or left arm hole). The brocaded patterns are oriented opposite each other indicating front and back side and thus it is a shoulder piece.
The textile is woven in plain weave cotton S (both warp and weft) and the threadcount is 17 x 15 per cm.
The brocaded patterns are made with camelid fiber 2S yarns.

Museum number: V 9.161

Item: Textile, scarf.
Style: North coast
Size: 77 x 90 cm
Material/technique: The textile is woven in cotton S (both warp and weft) in plain weave with a threadcount of 10 x 8. The pattern is made in tie-dye. There are 4 selvedges (one weft-selvedge is fragmented but exists).

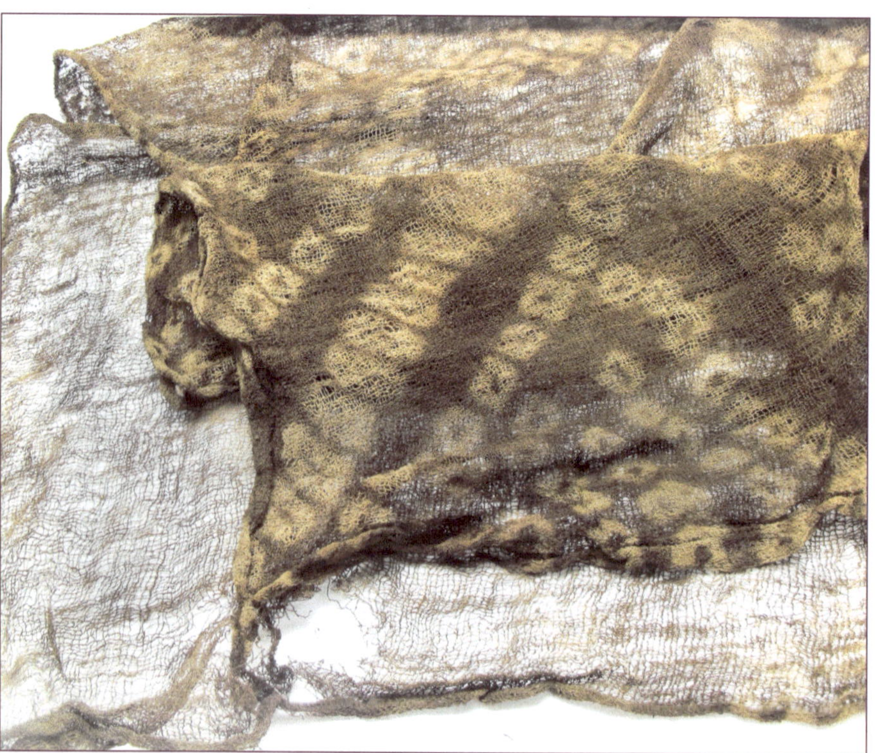

Museum number: V 9.162

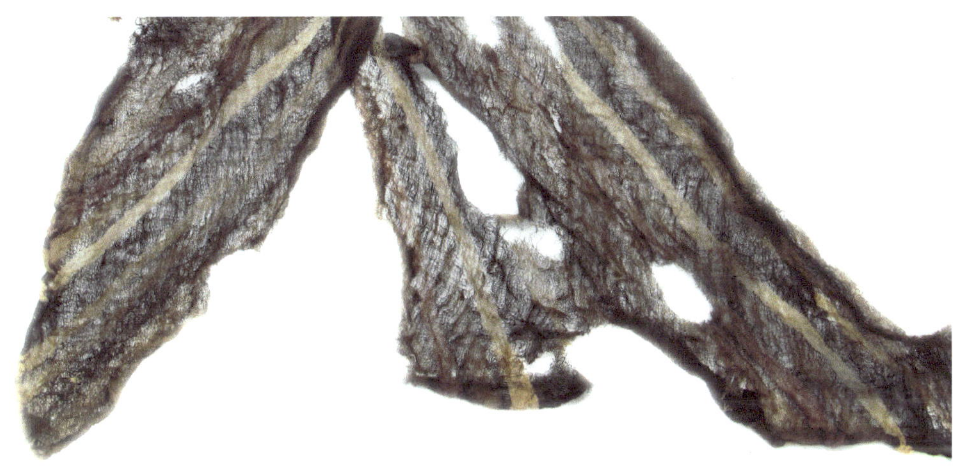

Item: Fragment of a large textile
Style: North coast
Size: Original complete size was around 100 x 100. The fragment is a diagonal stripe about 40 cm wide.
Material/technique: The textile is woven in loose woven plain weave in cotton S. There are fragments of selvedges on all warp and weft sides.
The textile is painted in ca 1 – 2 cm diagonal stripes.

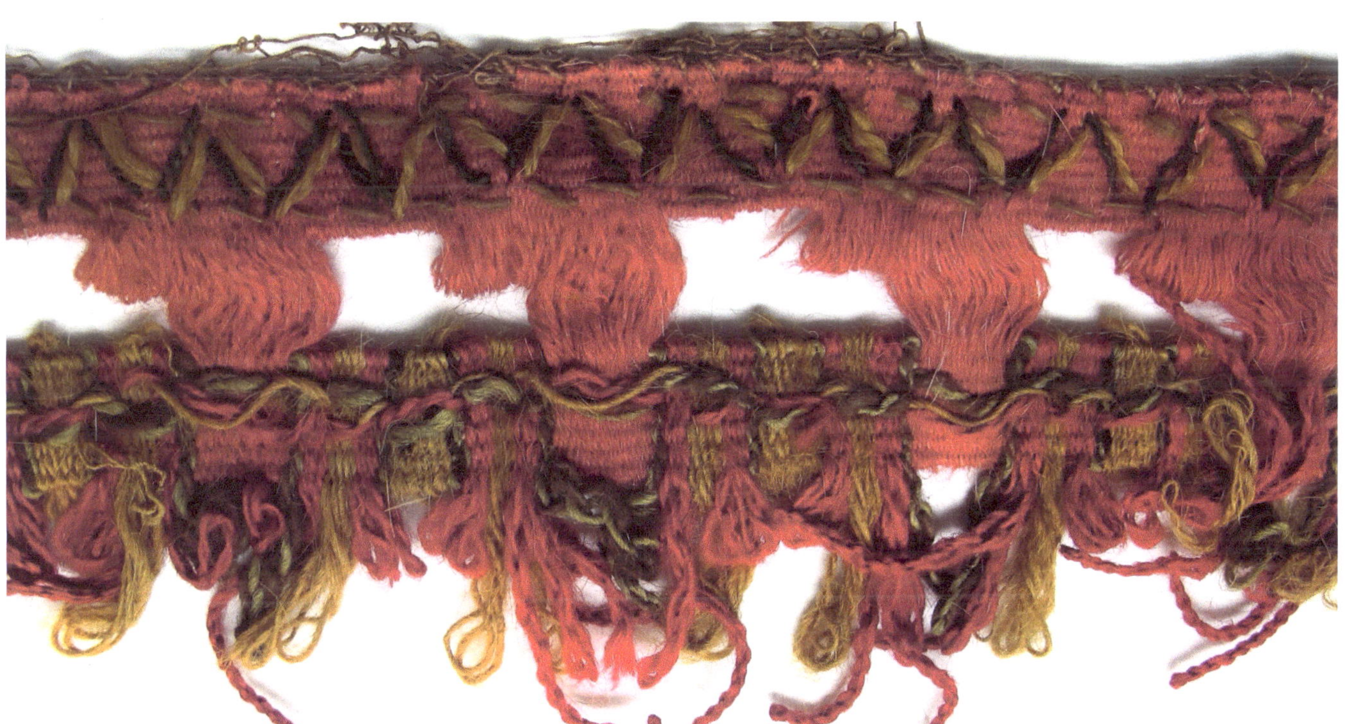

Museum number: V 9.176

Item: Fringe band from tunic
Style: North Coast, Chimu
Size: 180 x 5 cm
Material/technique: The textile has cotton 2Z warp and 2S camelid fiber wefts. The tapestry band has openwork and at bottom 1,5 cm weft fringe. At top is a zigzag embroidery (yellow/green on one side, red on other). At top fragments of a plain weave, loose cotton textile (warp and weft S).

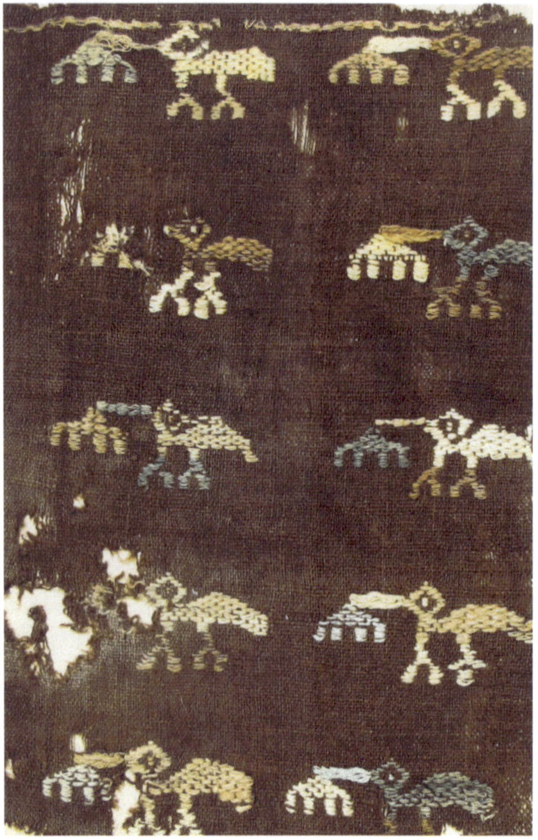

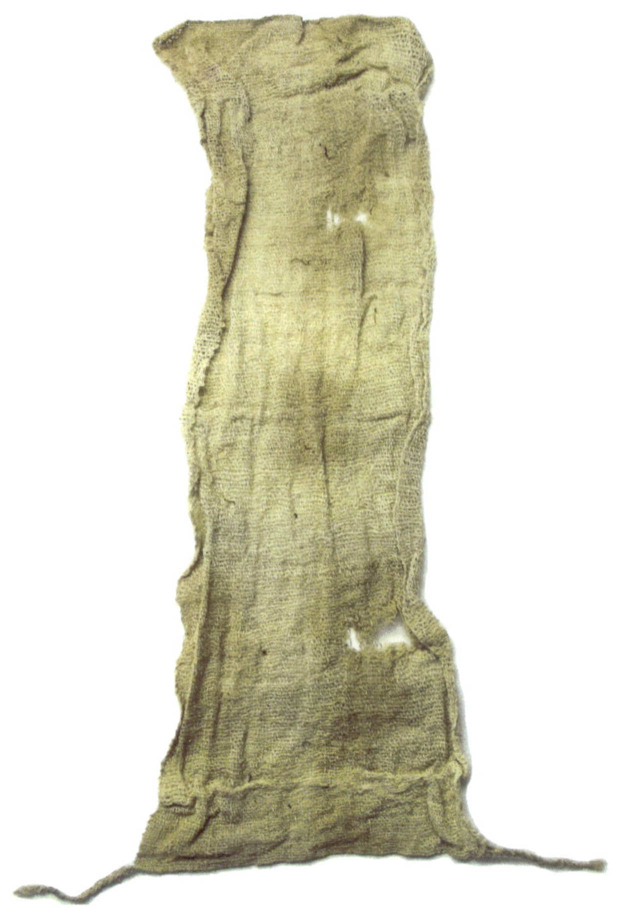

Museum number: V 9.184

Item: Fragment
Style: North coast
Size: 30 x 25 cm
Material/technique: The textile is in plain weave cotton with warp and weft S. The threadcount is 14 x11cm.
The pattern is brocated birds in paired cotton, S and Z varying.
The fragment has one side selvedge

Museum number: V 9.192

Item: Loincloth for children?
Style: North coast
Size: 38 x 15 cm
Material/technique: the textile is woven in cotton with warp 2S and 2Z and weft paired Z. It is plain weave with paired wefts and single warp. It has 4 selvedges. The threadcount is 9 x 9 per cm.

Museum number: V 9.194

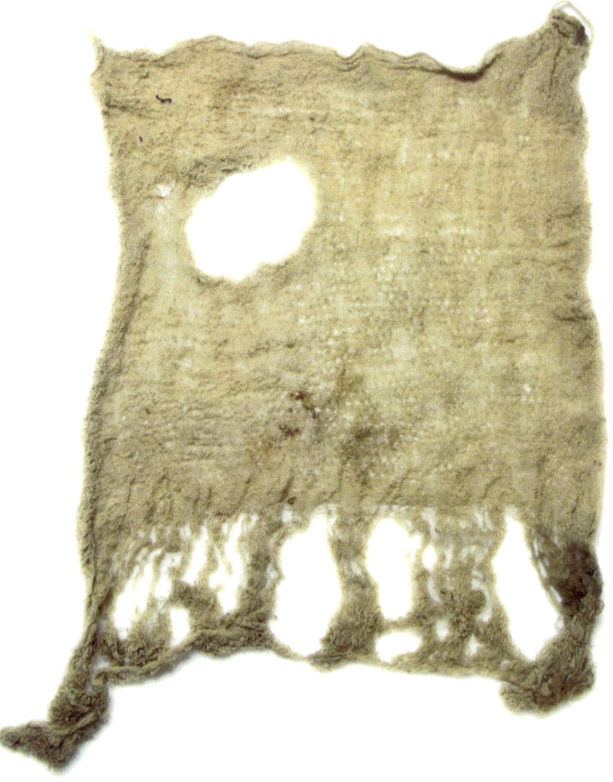

Item: Textile
Style: North coast
Size: 28 x 22 cm
Material/ technique: A complete textile with 4 selvedges in cotton S, gauze weave and plain weave. The threadcount is 11 x 11 per cm.

Museum number: V 9.213

Item: Fragment
Culture: North Coast
Size: 38 x 22 cm
Material/technique: The textile is in cotton S woven in discontinous warp and weft. The threadcount is 28-32 x 12 per cm.
The squares have after the "weaving" been taken apart, dyed individually and sewn back together. Each square is between 1,2 x 1,2 and 1,5 x 1,5 cm.

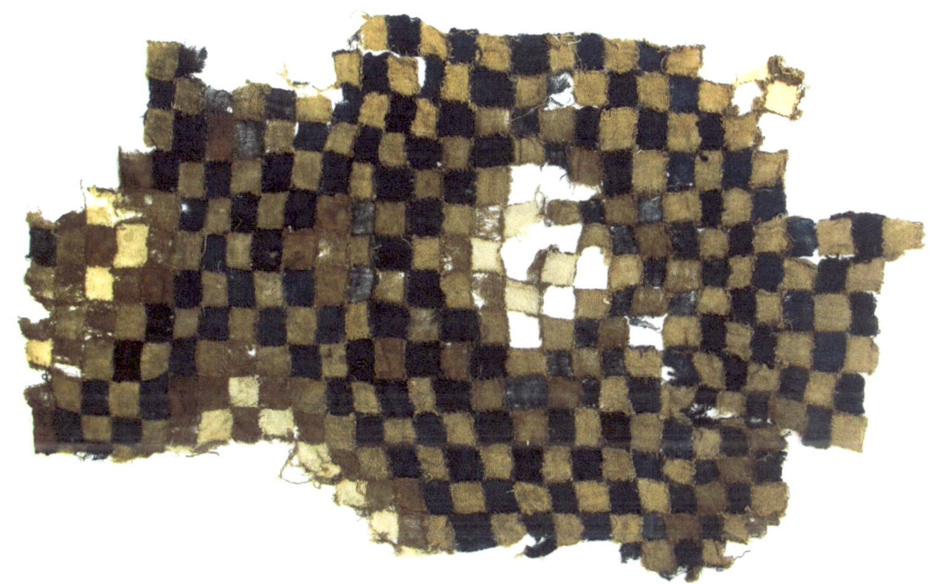

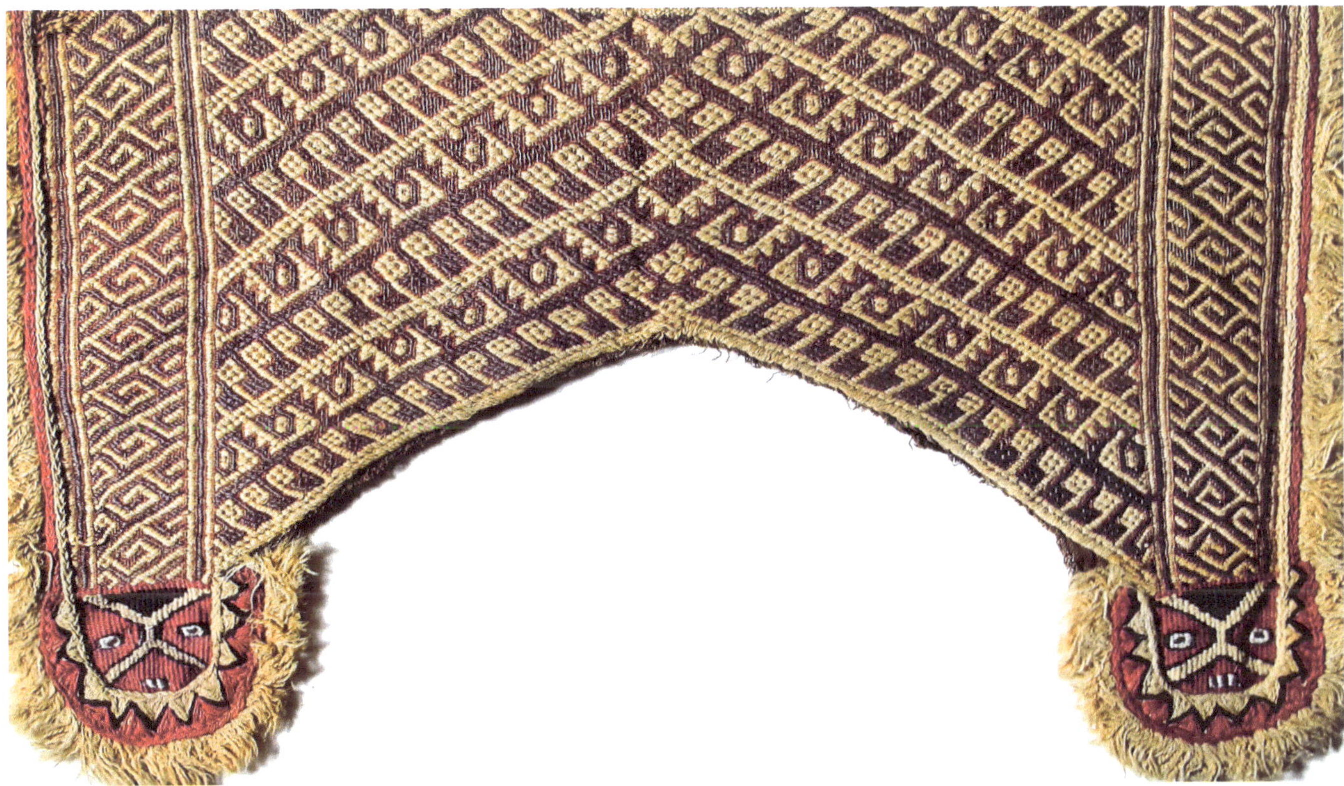

Museum number: V 9.222

Item: Fragment
Style: North Coast, Chimu
Size: 20 x 34 cm
Material/technique: A plain weave cotton textile (warp S and weft 2S) with camelid fiber 2S pattering in complementary weft weave (lancée). It has tapestry woven figures (heads) at bottom with a fringe in 2S camelid fiber. These tapestry heads are woven separately and stitched on. The threadcount is 17 x 30 per cm. The textile was sewn to a cotton fabric.
Bibliography: Reiss & Stübel, pl.61-62a.
D'Harcourt pl. 85

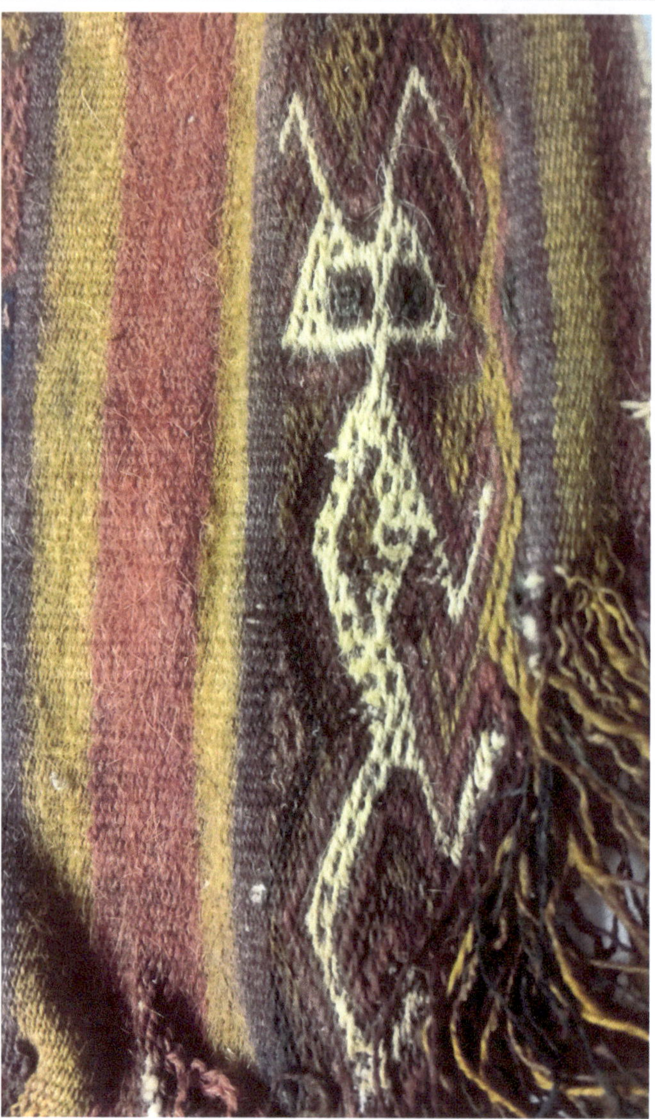

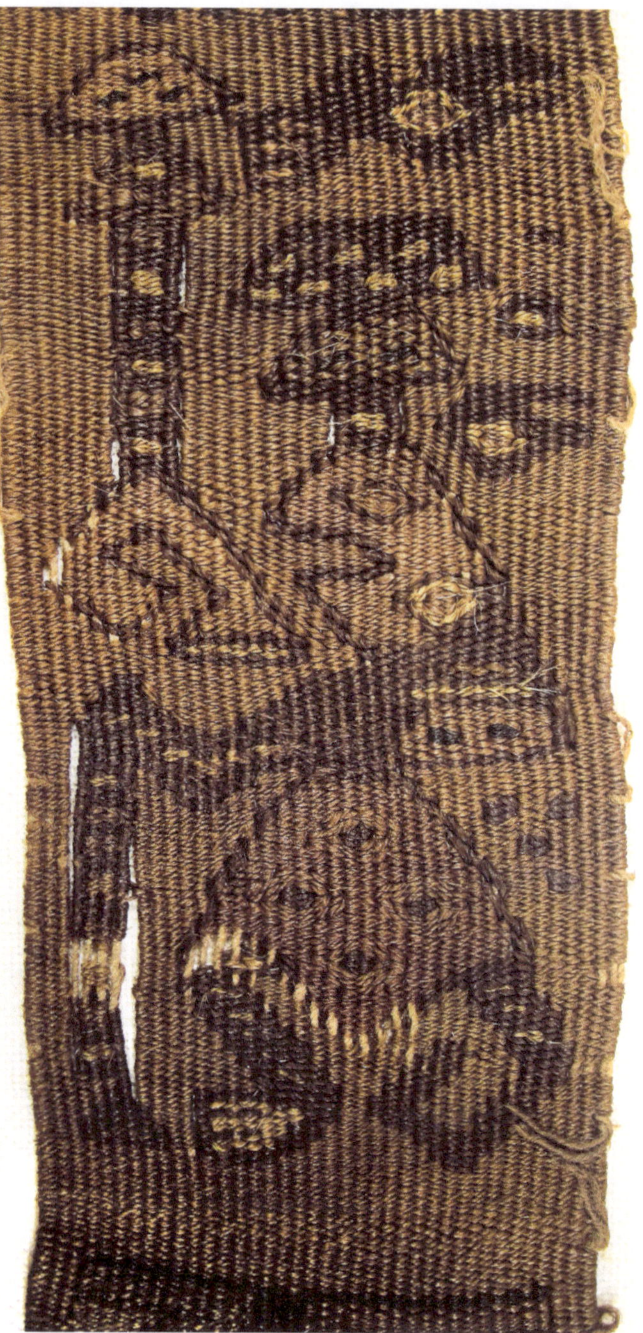

Museum number: V 9.281

Item: Fragment
Style: North coast
Size: 12,5 (+30 cm unwoven warp) x 30 cm
Material/technique: The textile is in complimentary weft weave and weft rep. The warp is cotton 3Z and the weft is camelid fiber 2S. The textile has one weft-selvedge and one warp-selvedge. The fragment has 30 cm unwoven warp – is probably unfinished.

Museum number: V 9.289

Item: Fragment of band
Style: North Coast, Chimu
Size: 50 x 4 cm
Material/technique: A tapestry band with one warp-selvedge and two weft-selvedges.
The warp is cotton 3Z and the weft is camelid fiber 2S. The threadcount is 11 x 60 per cm.

Museum number: V 9.316

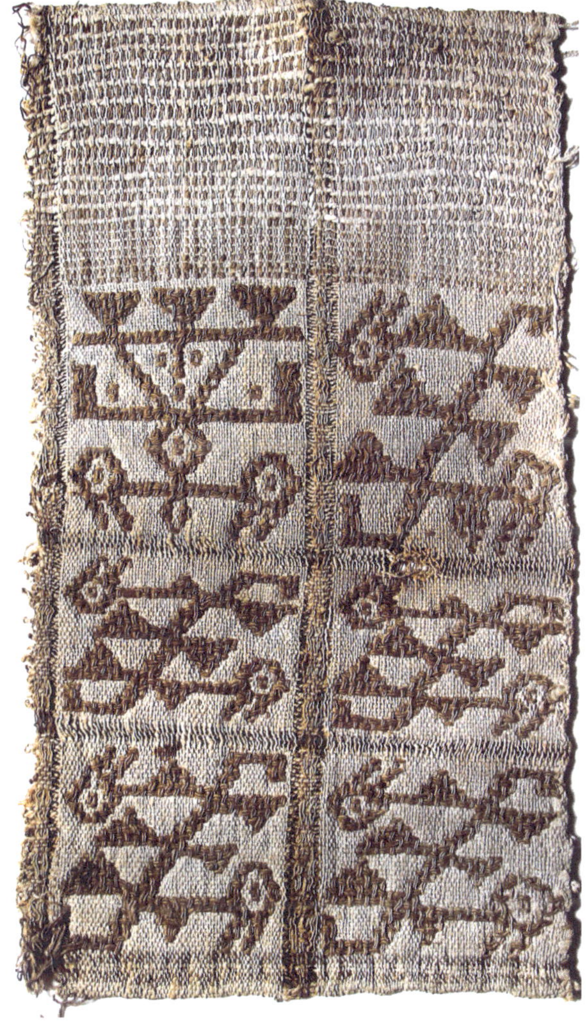

Item: Complete Textile
Style: North coast
Size: 33 x 18 cm
Material/technique: The textile has supplementary warp and weft patterning (or incomplete double weave). With floating warps and wefts at back. White warp and weft are cotton 2S, the brown warp and weft are cotton Z.
The textile has 4 selvedges.
Bibliography: Ann Rowe 1977 (Warp patterned weaves of the Andes) p. 46-48

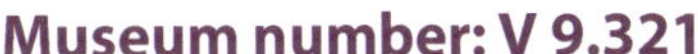

Museum number: V 9.321

Item: Loincloth
Style: North coast
Size: 57,5 x 130 cm. Belt 103 x 7 cm
Material/technique: The loincloth is woven in cotton S, plain weave with paired warp and single weft. The threadcount is 6 (paired) x 6 per cm.
At the end of the belt and of the loincloth is an attached tapestry band – 4 cm wide. The warp (lengthwise) is cotton 2S and the weft is 2S camelid fiber.
Added to this band is a small fringe-band 2,5 cm wide (1 cm woven, 1,5 cm looped fringe). It is in cotton Z with paired wefts and single warps.

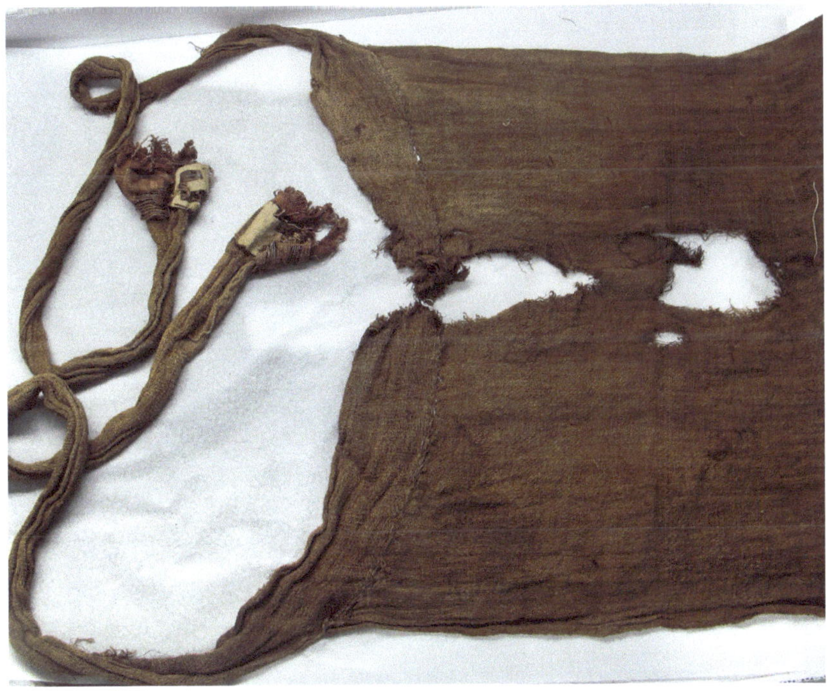

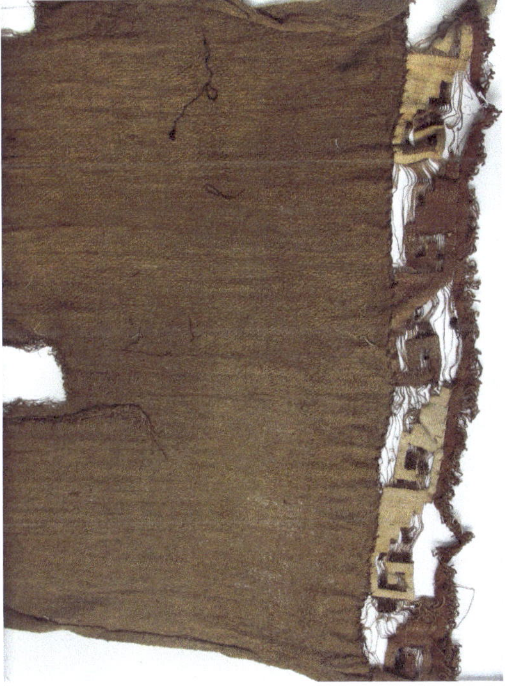

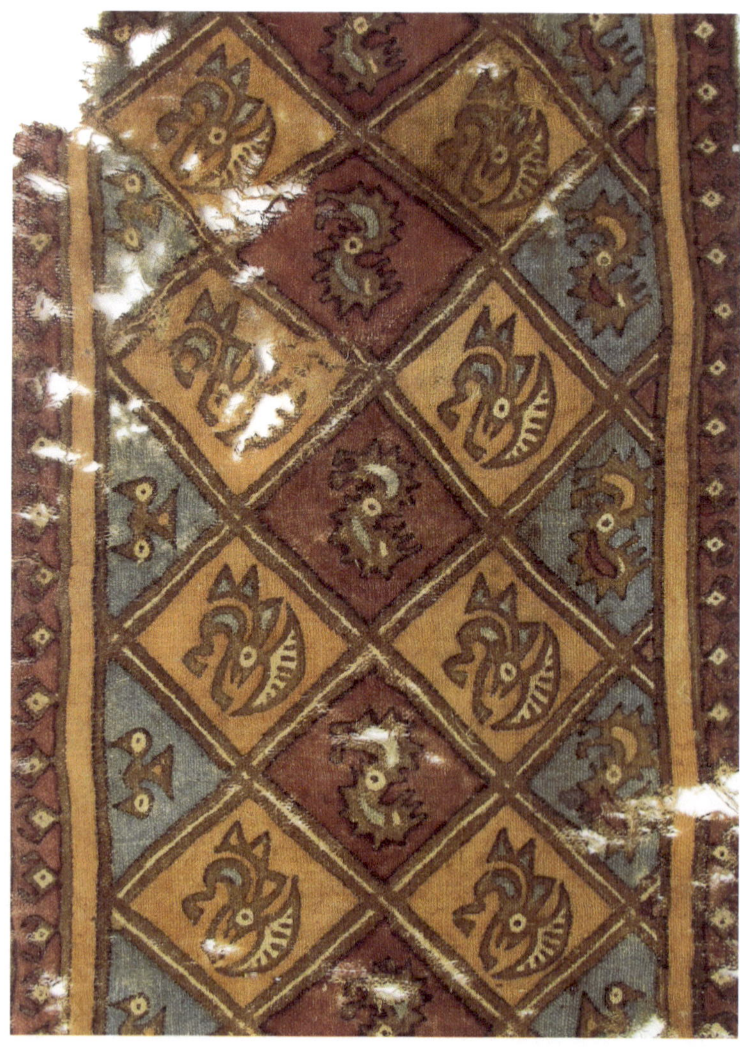

Museum number: V 9.352

Item: Head ornament
Style: North coast
Size: 45 x 22 cm. Bands: 1x 25 and 1 x 14 cm
Material/technique: The outer layer is in cotton 2S woven in plain weave with paired warps. The threadcount is 7 paired warps (lengthwise) x 6 single wefts per cm. The textile has selvedges at 3 sides (bottom, and two sides). The top part is cut off the textile.
Inside this is a textile in cotton S (slightly overspun), woven in plain weave. The threadcount is about 5 x 5 per cm.
The straps are cotton Z woven in plain weave. The threadcount is 13 warps x 6 wefts per cm.
Bibliography: Heiko Prümers, 1983, p. 92 (unpublished thesis)
Ann Rowe 1984 -110-133, fig. 70,75,88,89,126,127
Ann Rowe 1980 p. 105-6, fig 32-34,44

Museum number: V 10.188

Item: Fragment
Style: North coast
Size: 51 x 27 cm
Acquired: 1992
Material/technique: The textile is in plain weave cotton. It is woven in plain weave cotton with a warp in paired S and a weft in single S. The threadcount is 14 (paired) x 9 per cm. There are no selvedges.

Museum number: V 9.138

Item: Complete Scarf
Style: South coast
Size: 58 x 64 cm
Material/technique: The scarf consists of two panels sewn together. It is woven in dovetailed tapestry, sometimes with eccessive wefts. The warp is 2S cotton and the weft 2S cotton and camelid fiber. The threadcount is 8 x 24 – 28 per cm.

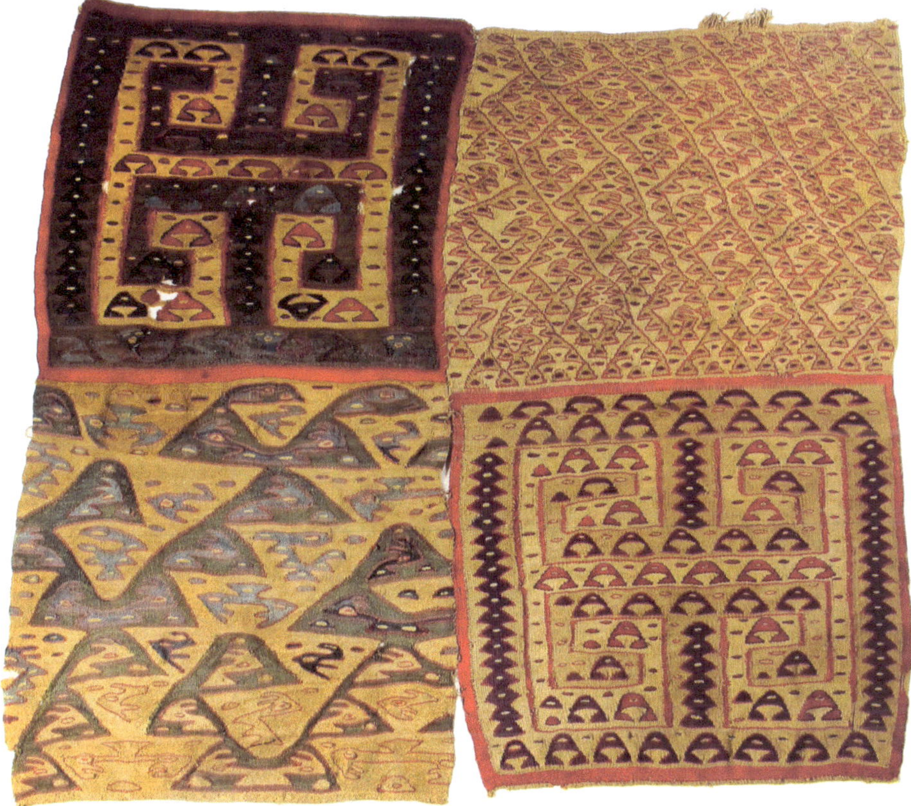

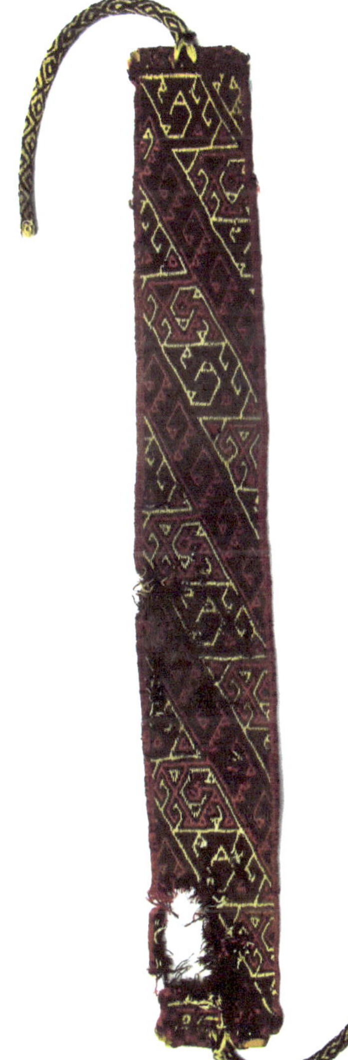

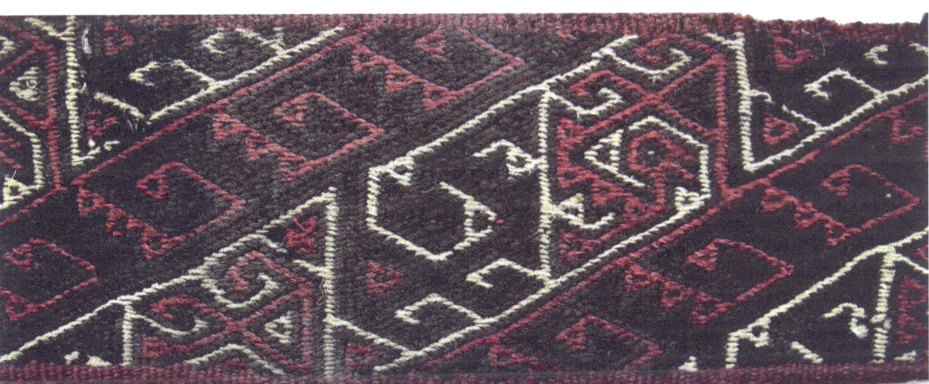

Museum number: VoNr 1827 / V 9.351

Item: Woman's belt
Style: South Coast
Size: Belt: 68 x 8,5 cm. Fragments of tying bands 25 and 18 cm.
Material/technique: The belt is woven in camelid fiber, 2S. The white yarns are Z twined from six 2S yarns, red and brown from three yarns.
The technique of the belt is tubular double woven complementary-warp weave with diagonal 2-span floats and warp substitution. The threadcount is 8 warps x 4 wefts per cm.
The tying cords are fist-braided with 2-span floats.
At both ends the belt warps are tied around cane sticks that are the same width as the belt.
Bibliography: Similar pieces in Uhle 1903:90-91, Pl. 19, Fig. 3 and in Wardle (1936:28, Pl. III) und Rowe (1977:97, Fig. 115).

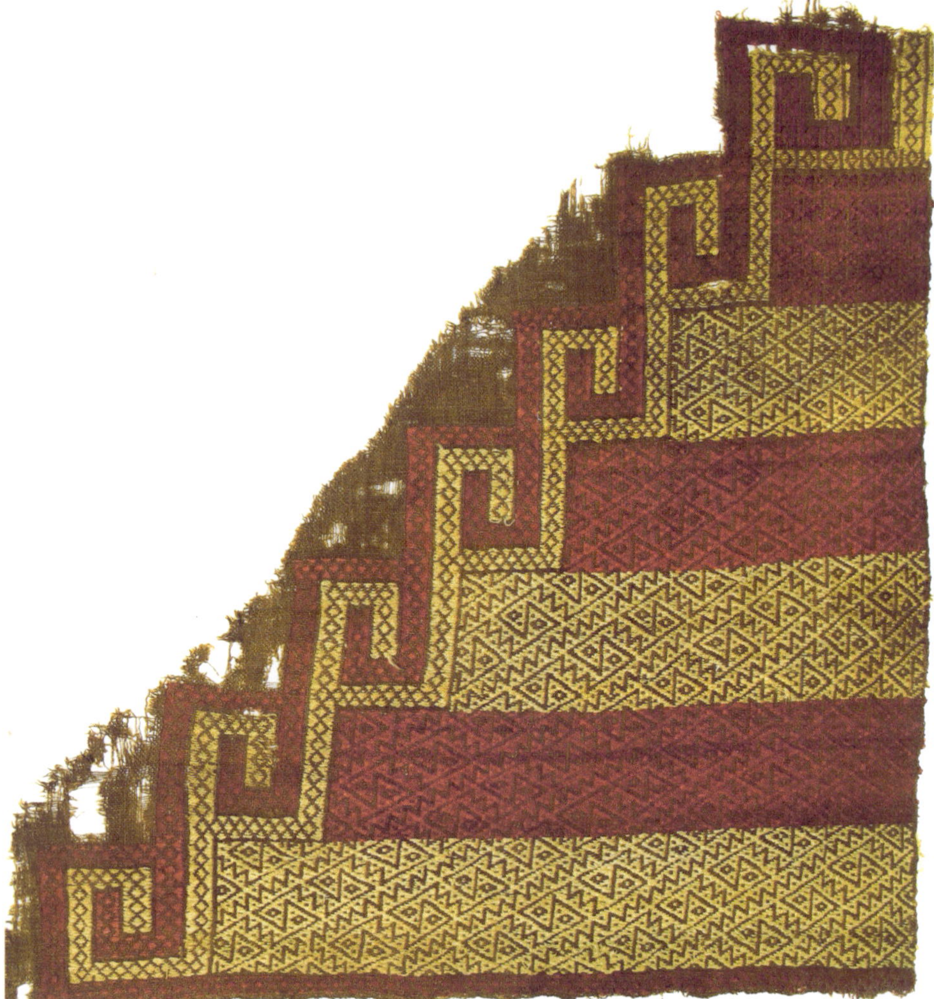

Museum number: V 9.127

Item: Fragment – probably from a mantle.
Style: South Coast
Size: 45 x 45 cm
Material/technique: The textile is a corner from a mantle. It has one warp and one weft selvedge.
The base material is cotton 2S. The threadcount is 10 x 10 per cm.
The patterning is camelid fiber 2S, lancée brocade (supplementary weft weave).

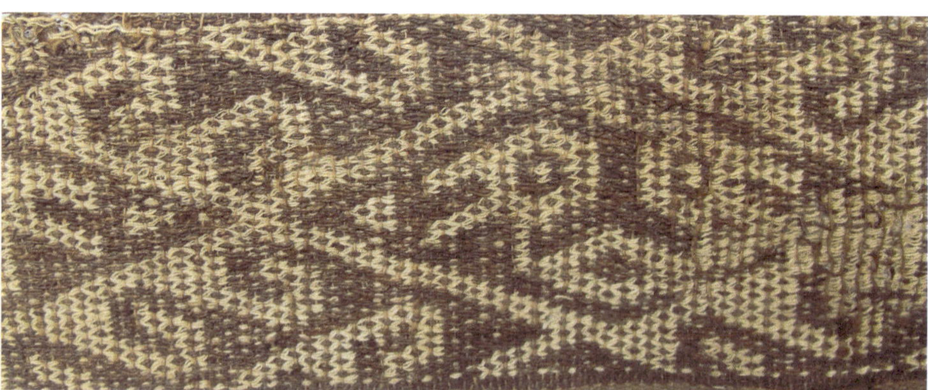

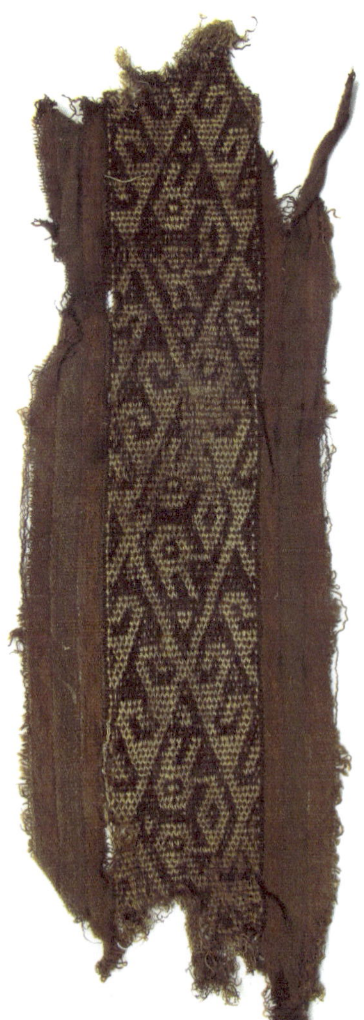

Museum number: V 9.182

Item: Fragment of a mantle
Style: South coast
Size: 14 x 48 cm
Material/technique: The textile is woven in plain weave and in the center has a warp patterning made with supplementary diverted warp pairs. It is in cotton and the threadcount is 8 x 22 cm.
Bibliography: Lena Bjerregaard, *PreColumbian Textiles in the Ethnological Museum in Berlin,* p. 174, 2017 , http://digitalcommons.unl.edu/zeabook 52/

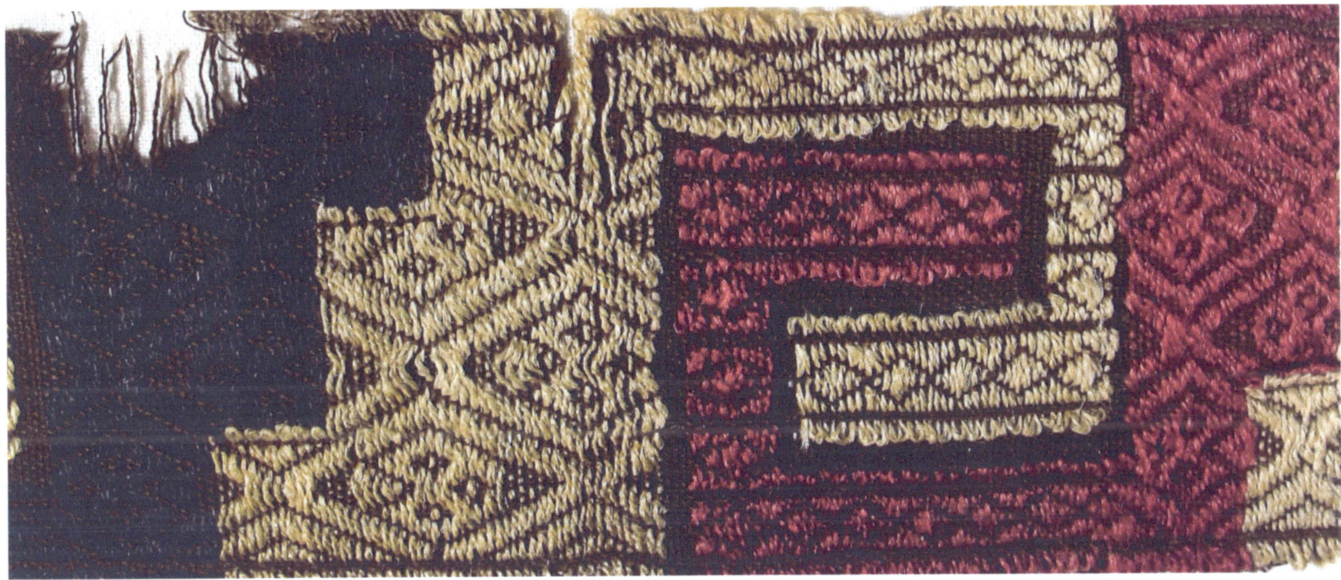

Museum number: V 9.223

Item: Fragment
Style: South coast
Size: 48 x 6 cm
Material/technique: Cotton cloth with camelid fiber 2S weft brocade. One long-side is a warp-selvedge. There are no other selvedges. The threadcount is 2o x 12 per cm.

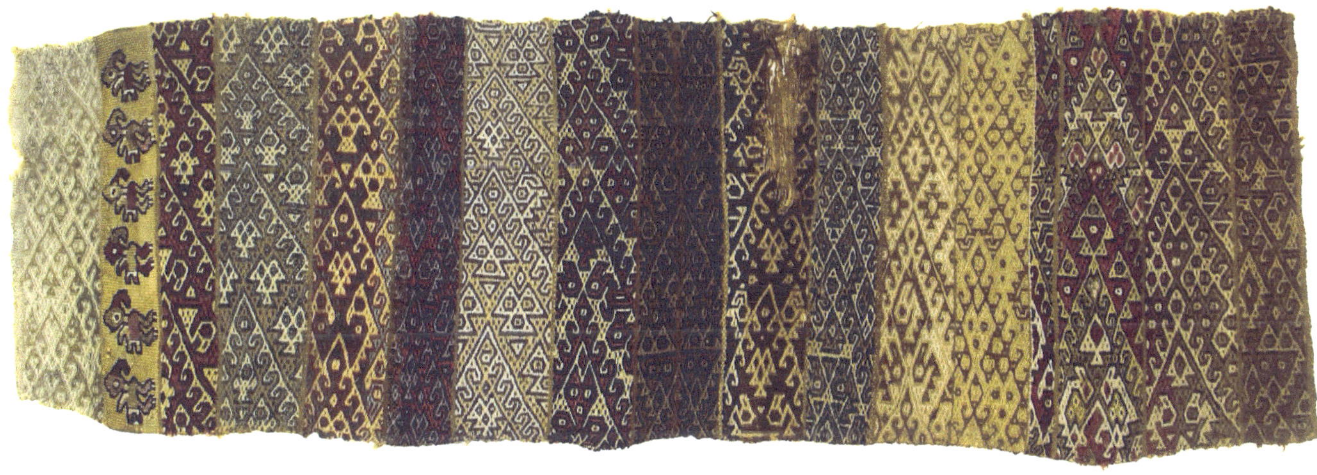

Museum number: V 9.225

Item: Complete textile
Style: South coast
Size: 50 x 17 cm
Material/technique: The textile has warp-selvedge at bottom and two side-selvedges. The upper edge has cut warps that have been doubled and sewn into the upper 0,3 mm wefts.
The base material is cotton 2S in both warp and weft. The patterns are in camelid fiber 2S, woven in supplimentary weft (lancée).
One pattern (2. From top) is tapestry (slit and eccentric).

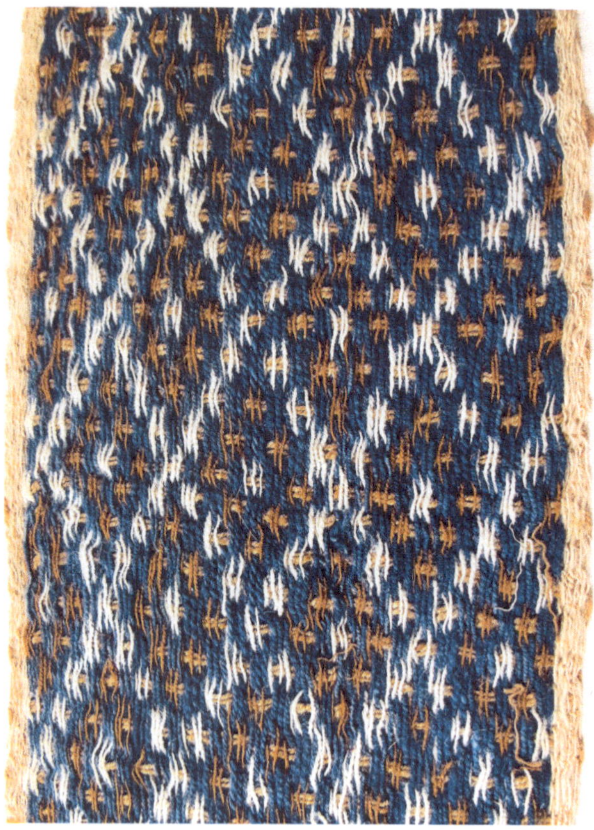

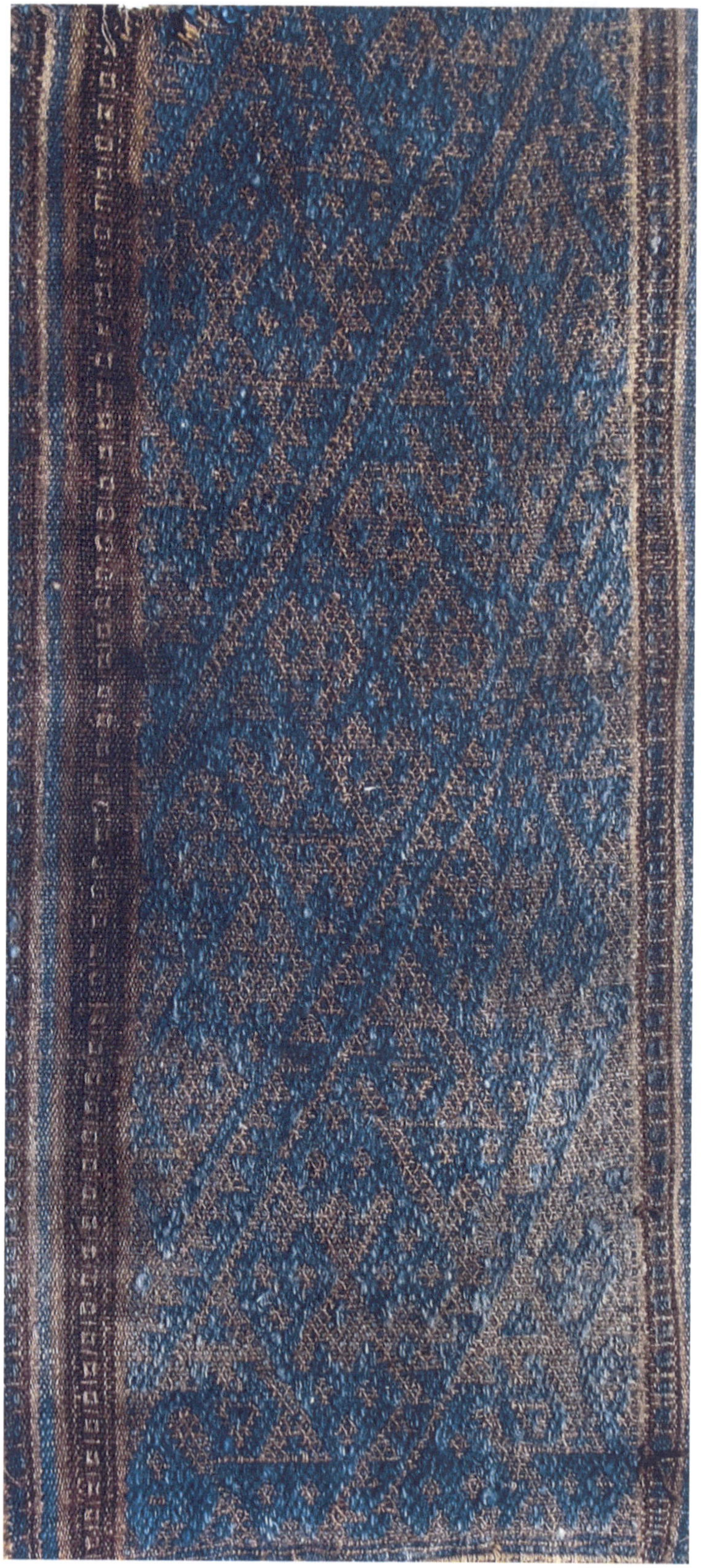

Museum number: V 9.273

Item: Fragment of band
Style: South or central coast
Size: 94 x 10 cm
Material/technique: The textile has warp in cotton and camelid fiber 2S and Z on the sides. The weft is paired cotton 2S. The threadcount is 8 x 2 per cm.
The band has weft-selvedges on both sides, and no warp selvedges.
It is woven in plain weave and supplementary warp weave.

Museum number: V 9.334

Item: Fragment
Style: South coast
Size: 26 x 12 cm
Material/technique: The textile is woven in plain weave and has warp patterning with diverted supplementary warps in pairs. All yarns are S cotton. The threadcount is 14 x 20 per cm. It is probably a fragment from a mantle. There is one warp selvedge and one weft selvedge.
This textile is very similar to V 9.335 – but the pattern is slightly different and the threadcount also.
Bibliography: Lena Bjerregaard, *PreColumbian Textiles in the Ethnological Museum in Berlin*, p. 174, 2017, http://digitalcommons.unl.edu/zeabook 52/

Museum number: V 9.335

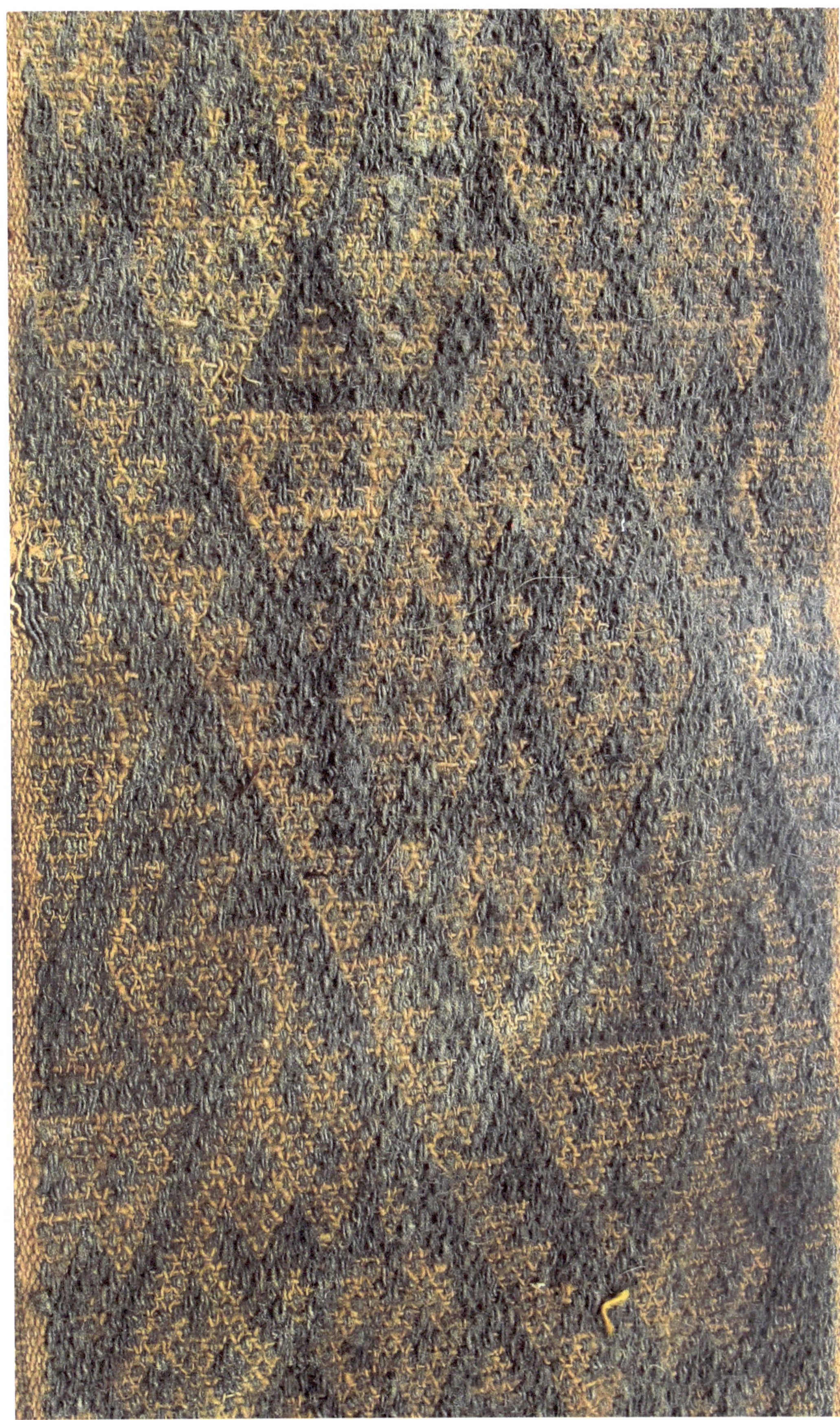

Item: Fragment.

Style: South coast
Size: 30 x 12 cm
Material/ technique: The textile is in cotton S (both warp and weft). It is woven in plain weave and supplementary warp patterning with diverted warps in pairs. There is one warp selvedge. The threadcount is 11 x 11 per cm (in edge plain weave).
This textile is very similar to V 9.334 – but the pattern is slightly different and the threadcount also.
Bibliography: Lena Bjerregaard, *PreColumbian Textiles in the Ethnological Museum in Berlin*, p. 174, 2017, https://digitalcommons.unl.edu/zeabook/52/

INKA – 1400-1550 AD

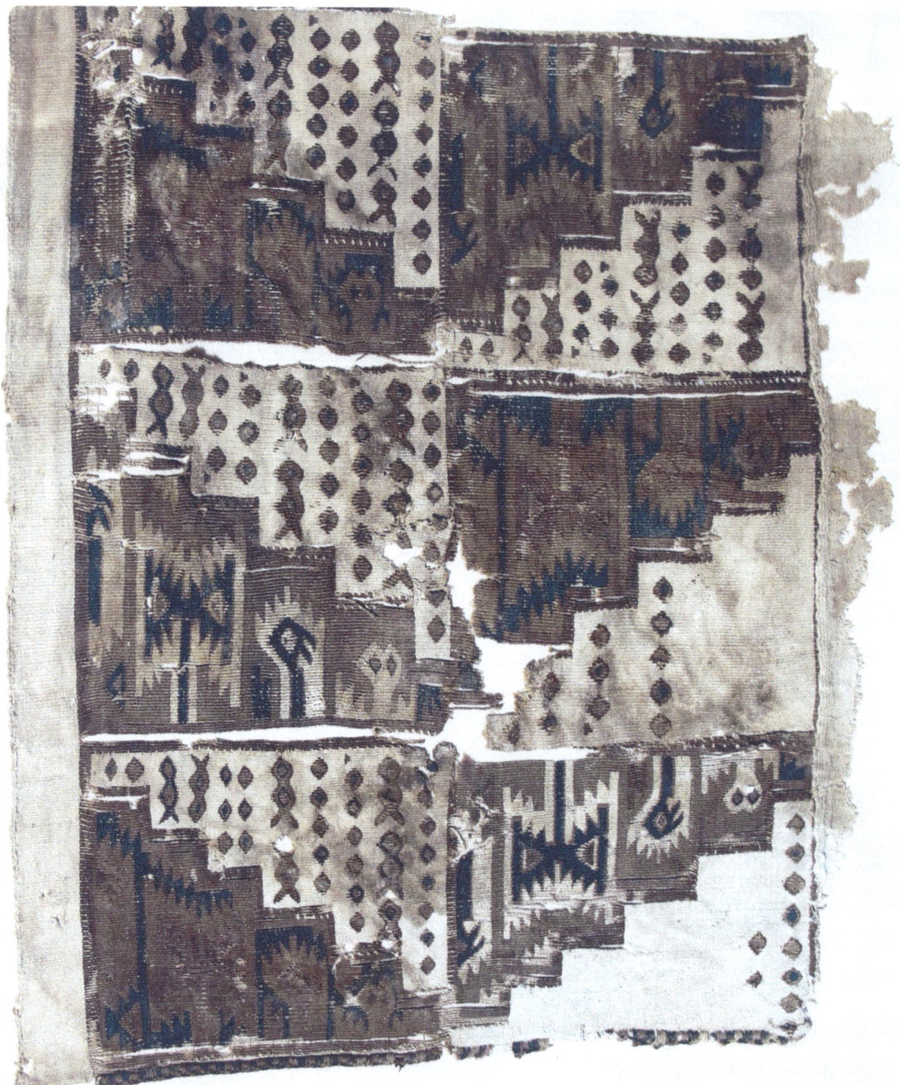

Museum number: V 8.990

Item: Fragment
Style: Inka
Size: 28 x 32 cm
Material/technique: A square, complete textile in tapestry. The warp is cotton 3Z (in one third of the textile two colors are twined together (brown + white) – in the rest of the textile the warps are monocolored. The wefts are mainly cotton Z and a few yarns of camelid fiber 2S. The threadcount is 12 x 50-60 per cm.
The tapestry fragment has 4 complete selvedges - over one weft-selvedge is a cross knit loop stitch embroidery.
Along one warp-end is a fragment of a plain weave cotton S textile. The threadcount of this textile is 28 x 20 per cm.

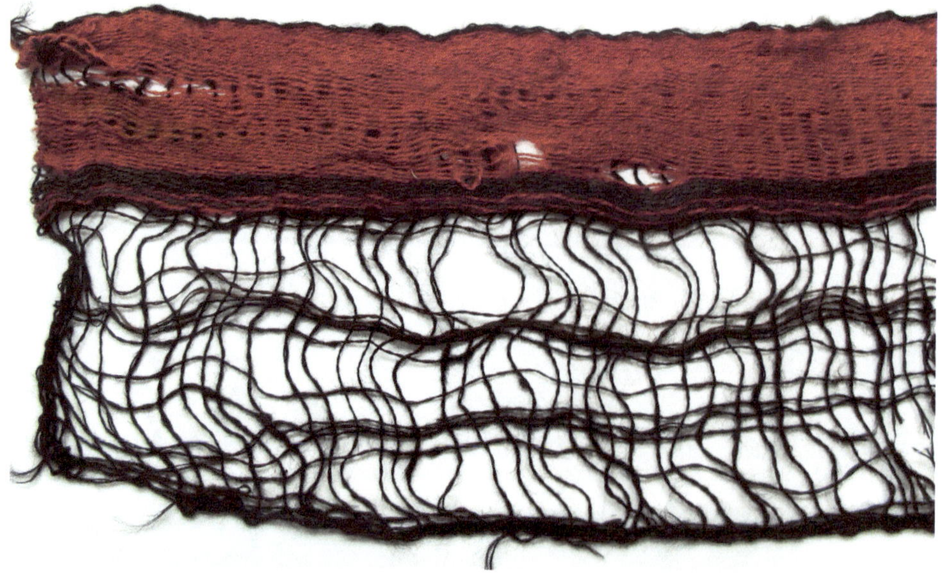

Museum number: V 9.151

Item: Headband
Style: Inka
Size: 115 x 17 cm
Material/technique: This headband is complete with warp- and weft-selvedges all around. It has 7 cm red camelid fiber warp rep and 10 cm coarse brown camelid fibers in plain weave (probably llama). All yarns are 2S.
See also V 9.136
Bibliography: similar headband Lena Bjerregaard, p.196, *PreColumbian Textiles in the Ethnological Museum in Berlin*, 2017, https://digitalcommons.unl.edu/zeabook/52/

Museum number: V 9.136

Item: Headband (complete)
Style: Inka
Size: 136 x 18

Material/ technique: This headband is complete with warp- and weft-selvedges all around. It has 7 cm red camelid fiber warp rep and 10 cm coarse brown camelid plain weave (probably llama). All yarns are 2S.
See also V 9.151.
Bibliography: similar headband Lena Bjerregaard, *PreColumbian Textiles in the Ethnological Museum in Berlin,* p. 196, 2017, https://digitalcommons.unl.edu/zeabook/52/

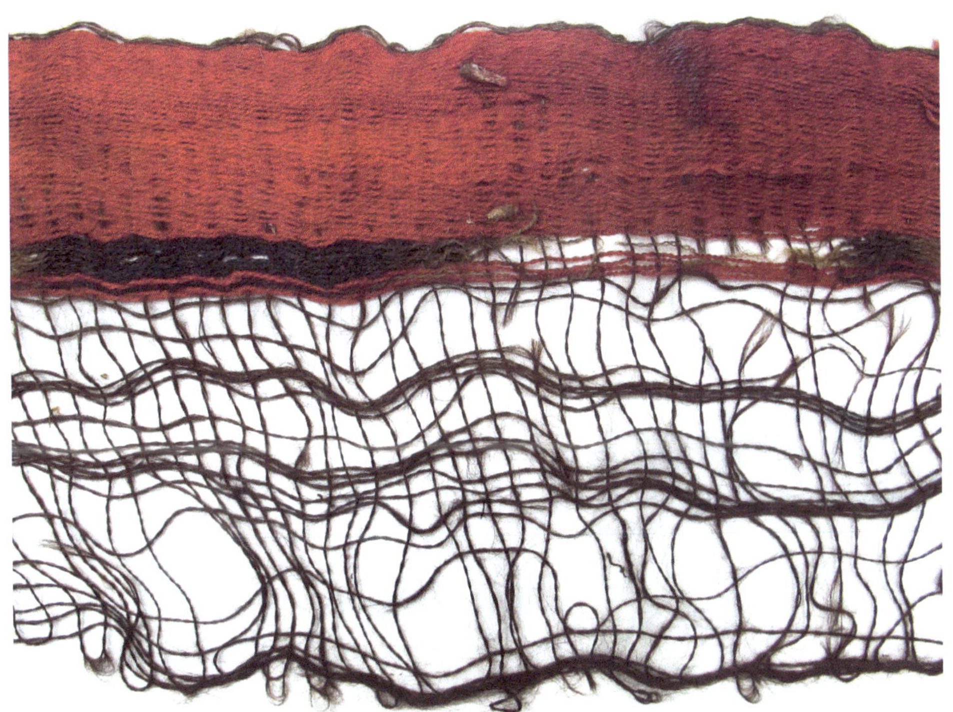

Museum number: V 11.262

Item: Kipu (complete)
Style: Inka
Size: 52 x 27 cm, (pendant strings on main string)
Material/technique: The kipu is all cotton – all strings are S plied.
Main string is complete and starts with a loop.
Knots: 8, single, long.
Groups of pendants: 5; 8; 6-6-6; 8,8,8
Strings: main, pendants, secondaries.

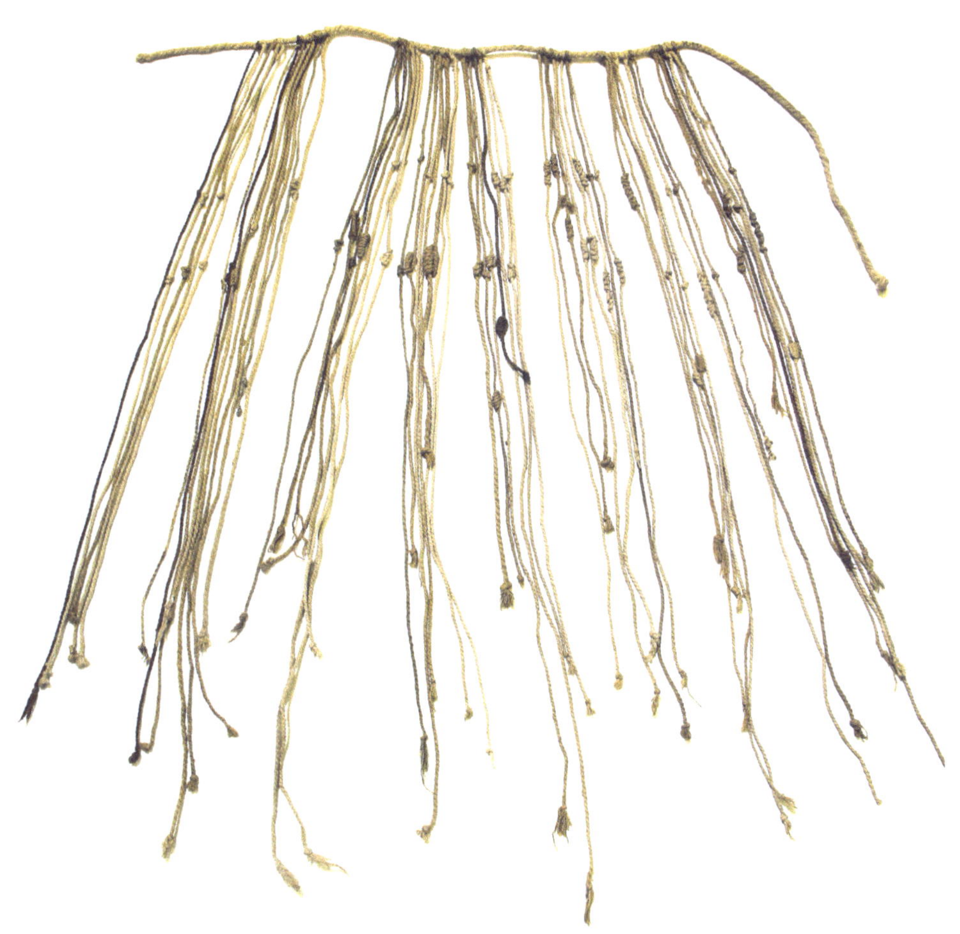

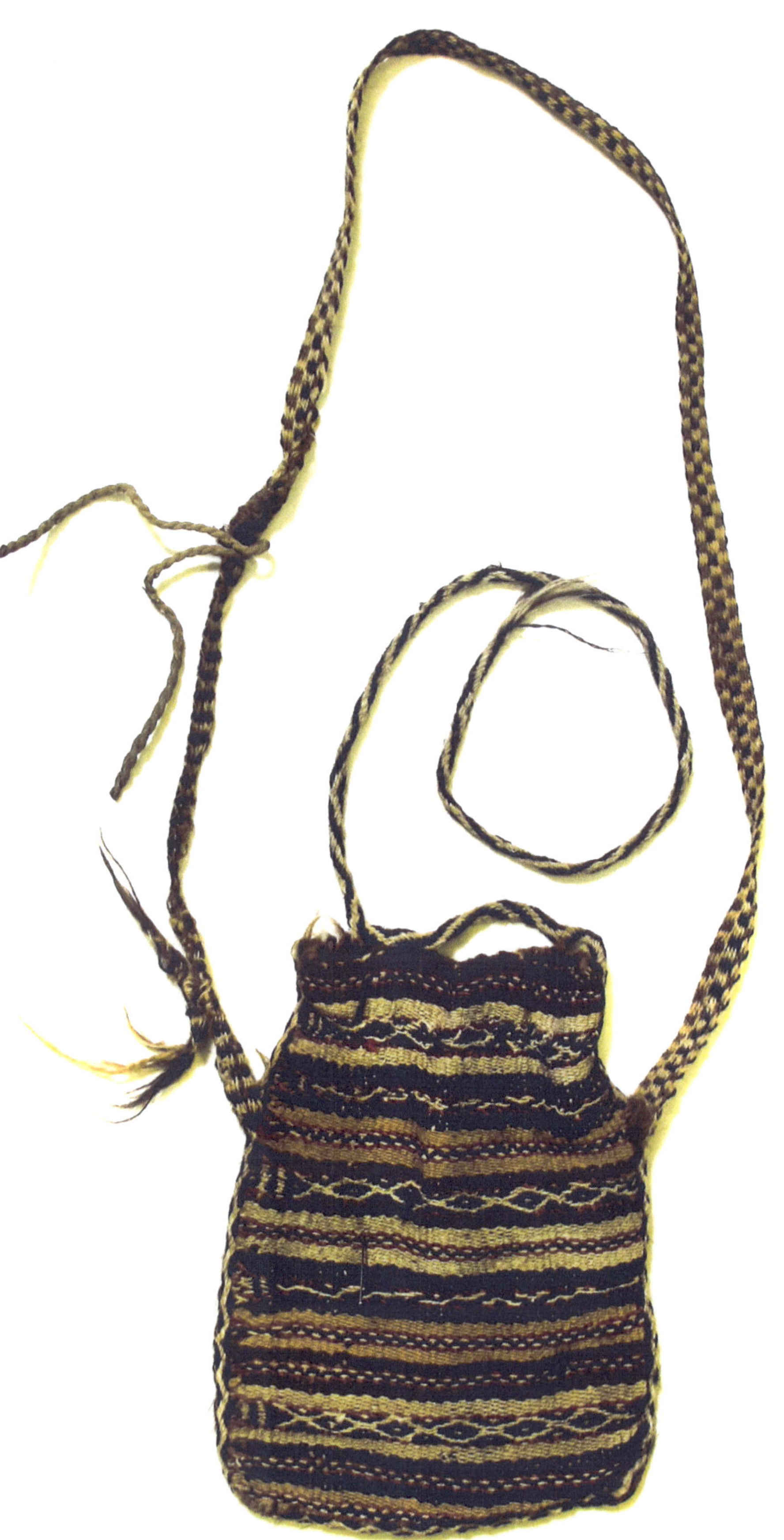

Museum number: V 9.331

Item: Bag
Style: Central coast, Inka
Size: 14 x 18 cm
Material/technique: All yarns are 2S camelid fiber.
The bag is in warp rep with stripes of complementary warp weave. The side and bottom are sewn together/ adorned with stem stitch embroidery. The warp is horizontal when worn.
The threadcount is 20 x 4 per cm.
The strap is 75 x 1 cm – woven in complementary warp patterning.
At top is a round fistbraided cord attached in 2 places of the top edge.

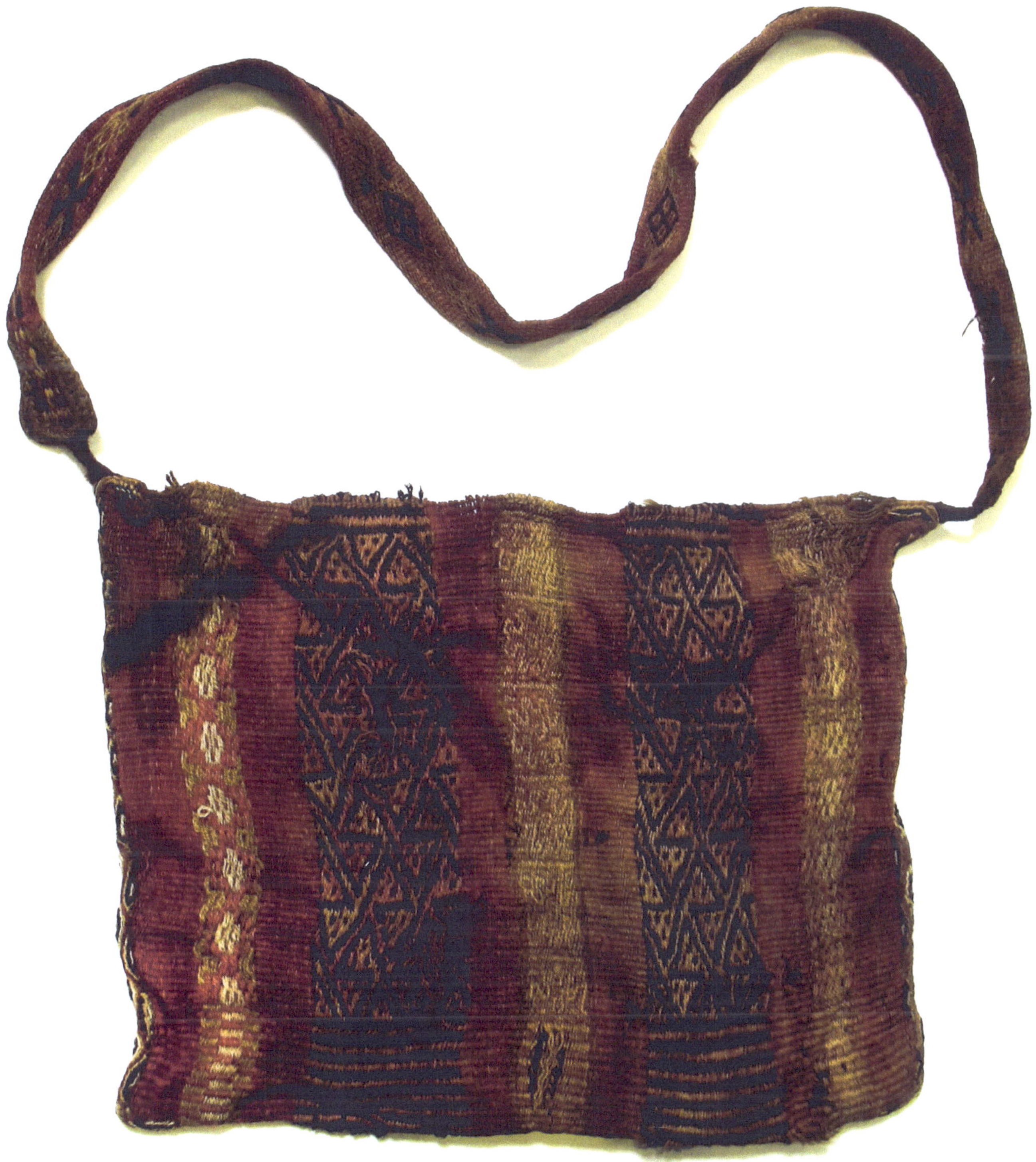

Museum number: V 9.333

Item: Bag
Style: Central coast, Inka
Size: bag, 20 x 27 cm; strap, 67 x 2 cm
Material/technique: Bag and strap are in camelid fiber 2S. Both have complementary warp patterns. The strap (double woven, complementary warp weave) is set up tubular, and the edges woven tubular. The bag has stem stitch embroidery along the sides.
The threadcount of the bag and strap (in plain weave) is 30 x 5 per cm
Bag has 4 selvedges and warp-selvedge at top.
The bag is complete.

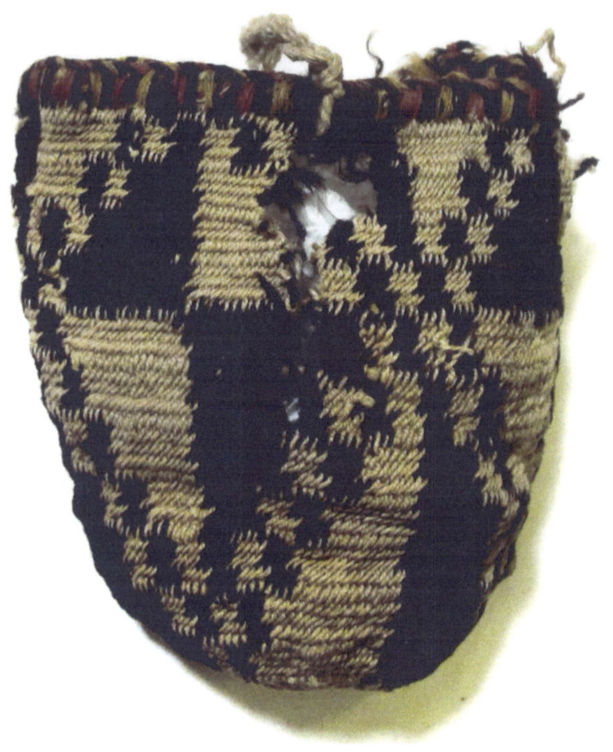

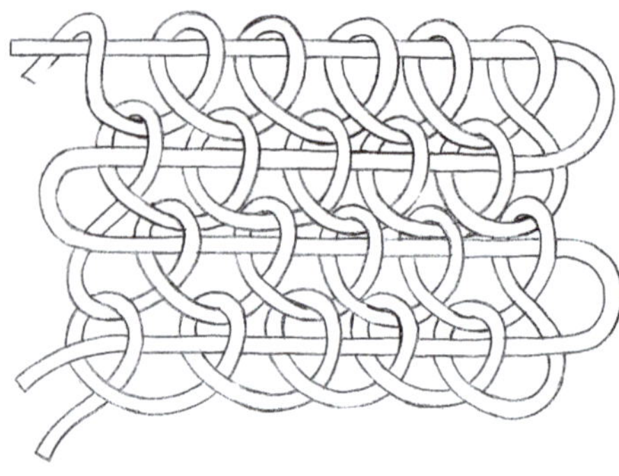

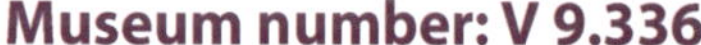

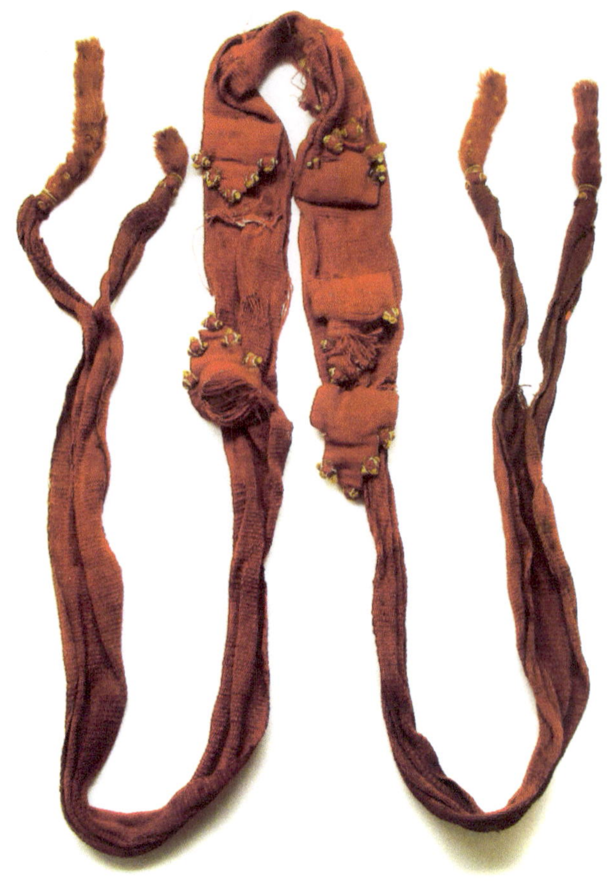

Museum number: V 9.336

Item: Bag
Style: Inka
Size: 11 x 12 cm
Material/technique: Spiral simple looping with extra acompanying yarn in camelid fiber 2S. The light and the dark yarns are alternatively hidden in the other. The upper edge is embroidered with cross knit looping stitches.

Museum number: V 9.340

Item: Hairband
Style: North/Central coast
Size: 200 x 8 cm
Material/technique: Band (warp camelid fiber 2S, weft cotton S). In the center part the band is decorated with little woven bags/pillows filled with unspun cotton fibers. The pillows are embroidered with 5 pointed tops.
At both ends are 11 cm tassel arranged on top of each other.

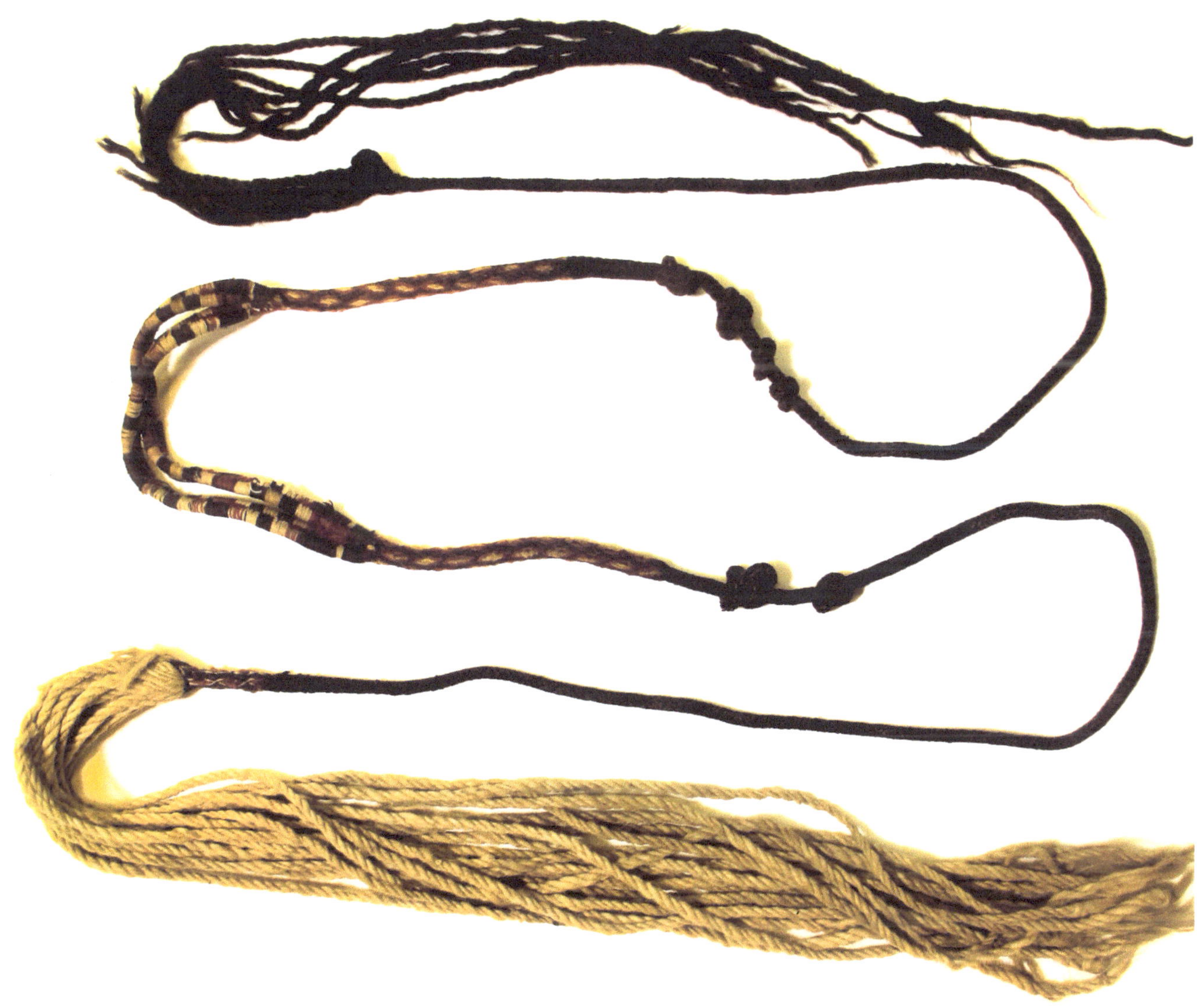

Museum number: V 9.343

Item: Sling (complete)
Style: Central/North coast, Late Horizon.
Size: 335 cm
Material/technique:

1. The sling has at boths ends a 60-67 cm tassel in camelid fiber 2S.
2. Following the white tassel is a round fistbraid of 4 cm.
3. Then follows a square braid of 8 strands (68 cm). At the end it has 2 knots – a single knot and a complicated (not kipu like).
4. Then follows a 14 cm round fistbraid.
5. The cradle is 4 bundles wrapped with a slit in the middle.
6. 14 cm round fistbraid.
7. 66 cm square braid of 8 strands – with at the beginning 4 knots (two single and two complicated).

The sling ends in a 66 cm long tassel.
All is camelid fiber 2S.

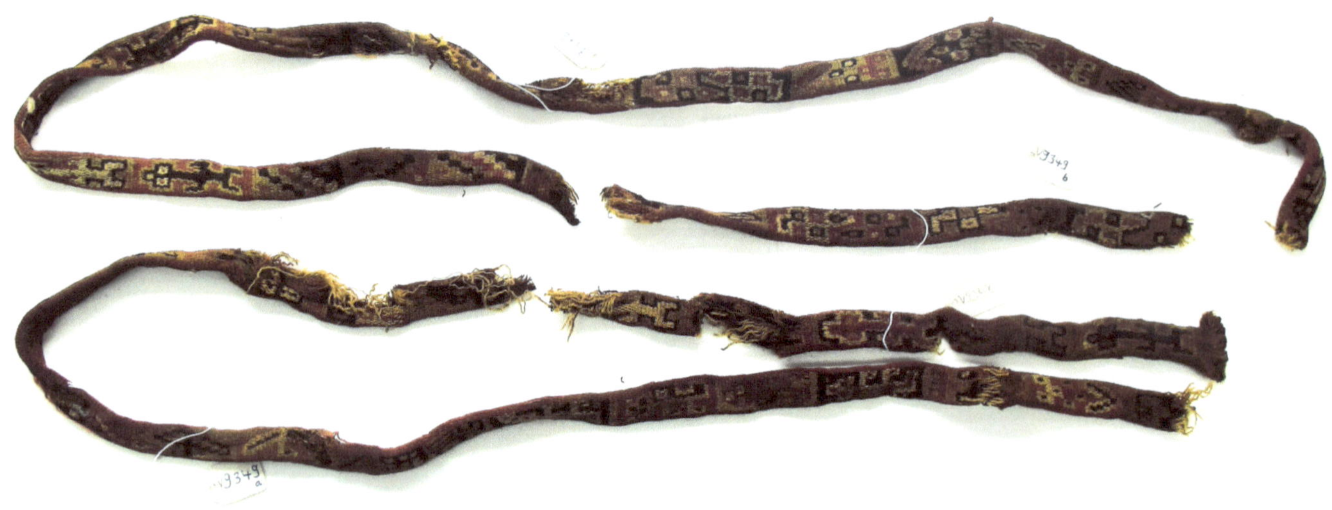

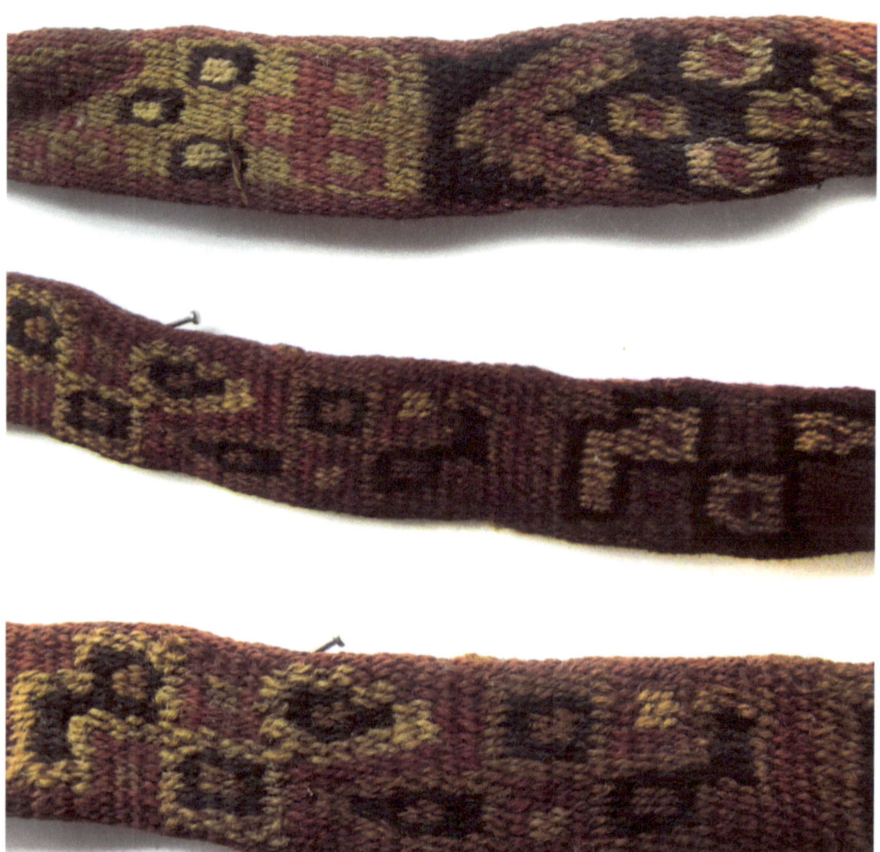

Museum number: V 9.346, V 9.348, V 9.349

Item: Tubular band
Style: Central Coast, Late Horizon
Size: V 9.346: 83 cm, V 9.348: 27 cm, V 9.349 a: 68 cm, V 9.349 b: 22 cm. All 1,5 wide.
Material/technique: Camelid fiber 2S yarns woven in tubular complimentary warp weave. The threadcount is 7 x 14 per cm.

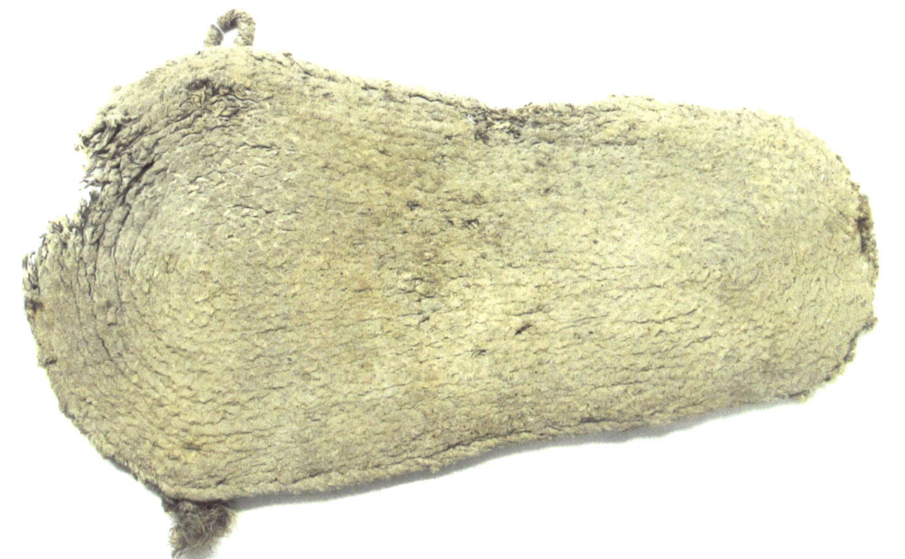

Museum number: V 9.330

Item: Shoesole
Style: Inka/ Central/North coast?
Size: 21 x23 cm
Material/technique: cotton 2Z, multiple paired yarns. The sole is stitched together from braids that are braided from 3 strands.

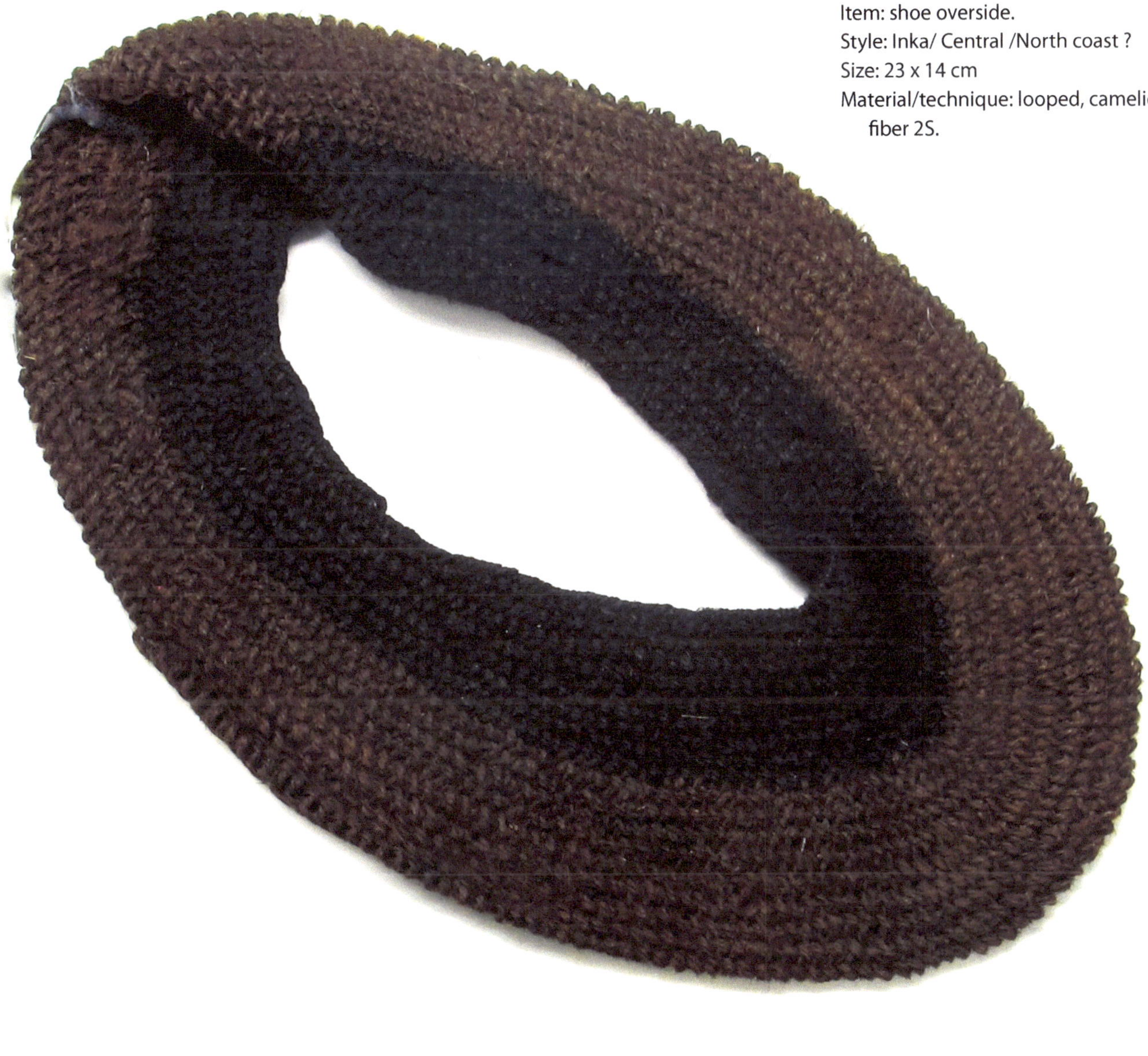

Museum number: V 9.337

Item: shoe overside.
Style: Inka/ Central /North coast ?
Size: 23 x 14 cm
Material/technique: looped, camelid fiber 2S.

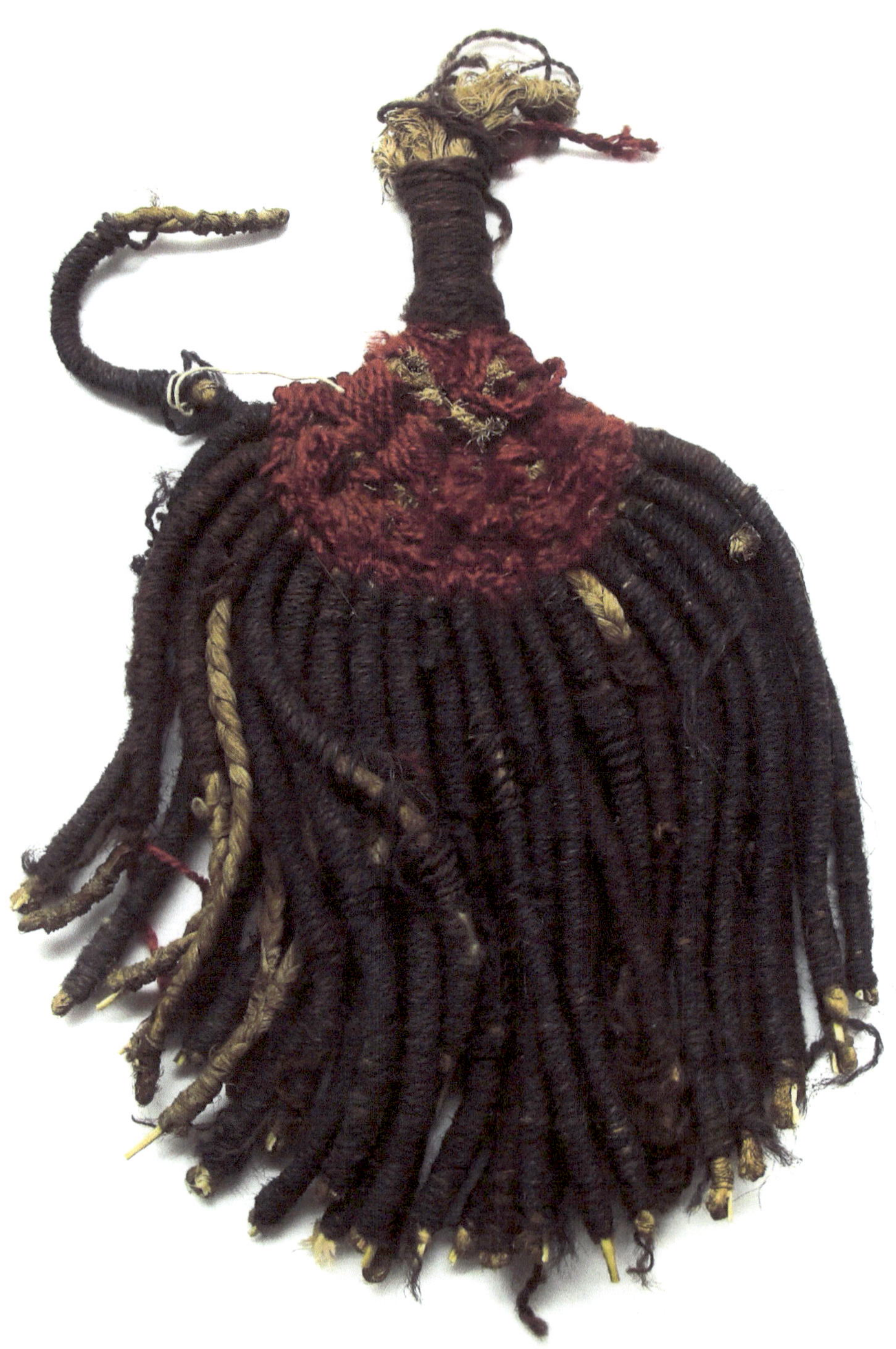

Museum number: VoNr 1829

Item: Tassel
Style: ?
Size: 18 x 13 cm
Material/technique: 3-braided plantfiber strings wrapped with 2S camelid fiber yarns.

COLONIAL 1600– 1700 AD

Museum number: V 9.000

Item: Complete textile.
Style: Colonial 16-1700 AD
Size: 76 x 61 cm
Material/technique: The textile is woven in interlocked tapestry with a warp in cotton 2S and a weft in camelid fiber 2S. The threadcount is 10 x 40-50 per cm.
Figures: pampas hare, birds, fish, puma, lizard, and symbolic animals: mermaid, fat scorpion.
The other half of the textile is in Textile Museum, Washington.
Published in: Helena Phipps, Johanna Hecht, Cristina Esteras Martín, *The Colonial Andes: Tapestries and Silverwork, 1530–1830*, Metropolitan Museum of Art Series, p. , 2004.

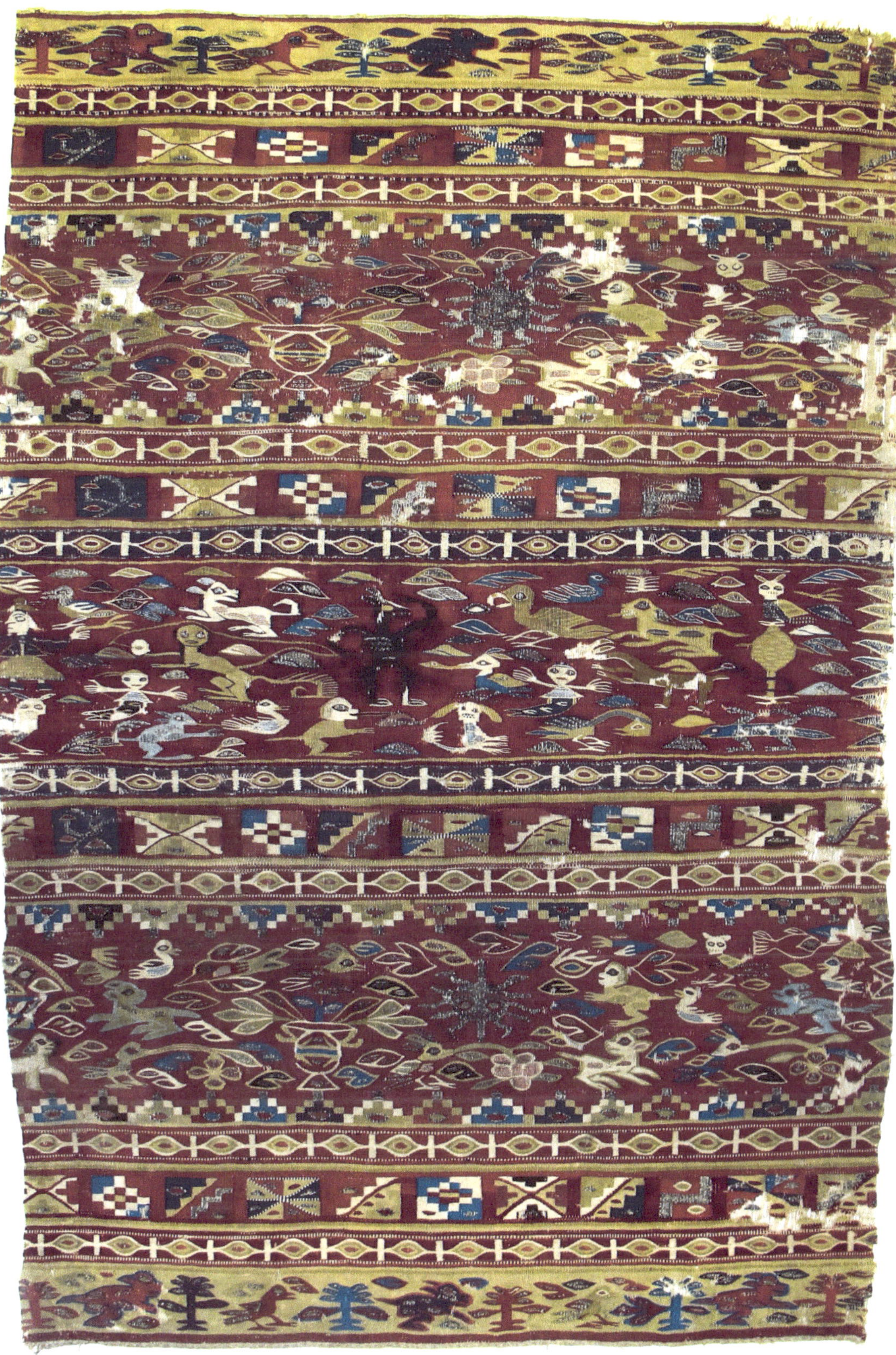

RECENT 1800-2000 AD

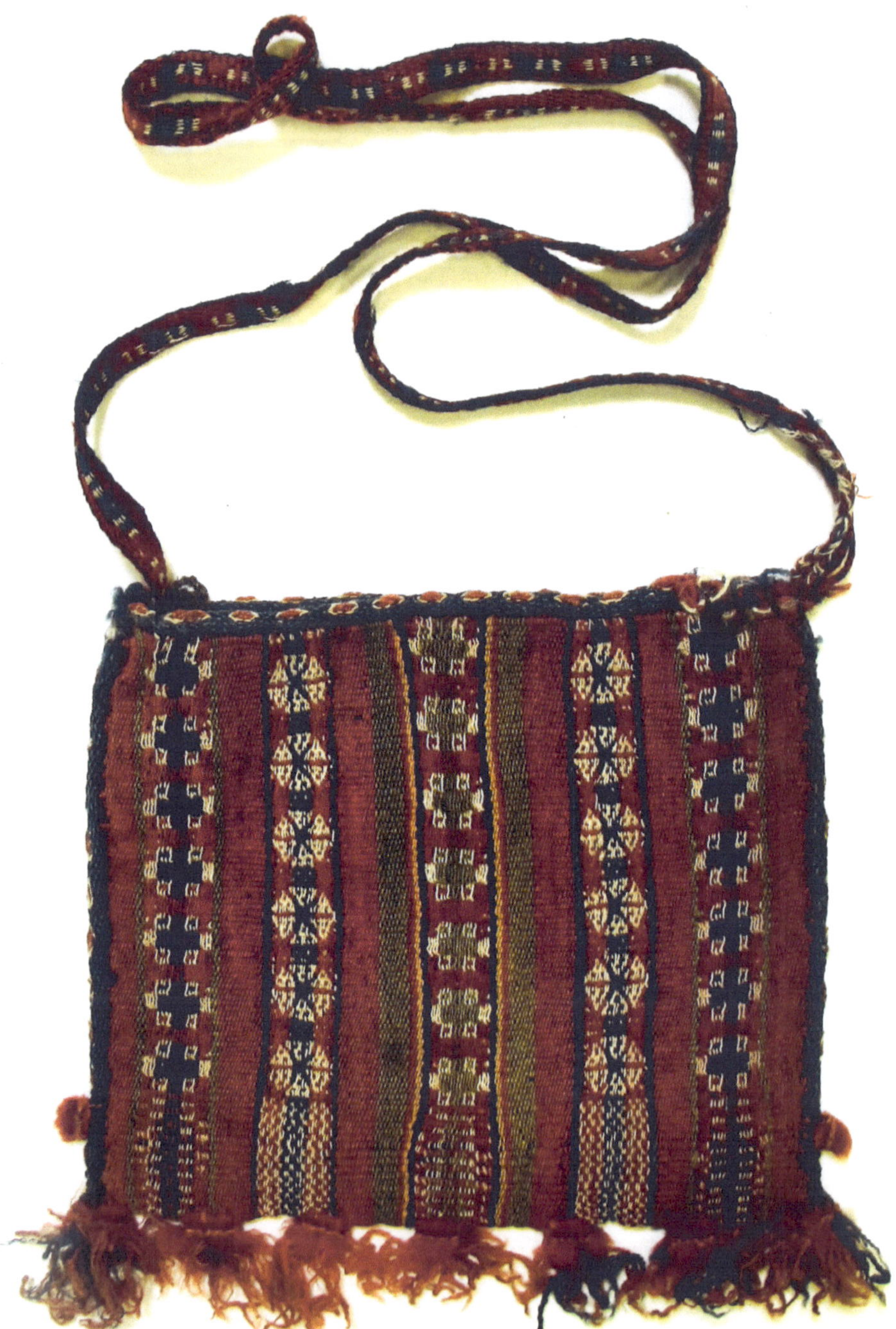

Museum number: V 3.168

Item: Bag for coca (coca inside)
Style: Colonial – mid 20. century.
Size: 19 x 20 cm – and strap 100 x 1 cm
Material/technique: Camelid fiber 2S.
Bag and strap are woven in complementary warp weave.
The edges of the bag has woven tube warp edgings at the sides and top opening.
An acrylic pink sewing thread is attaching the strap to the bag at one side.

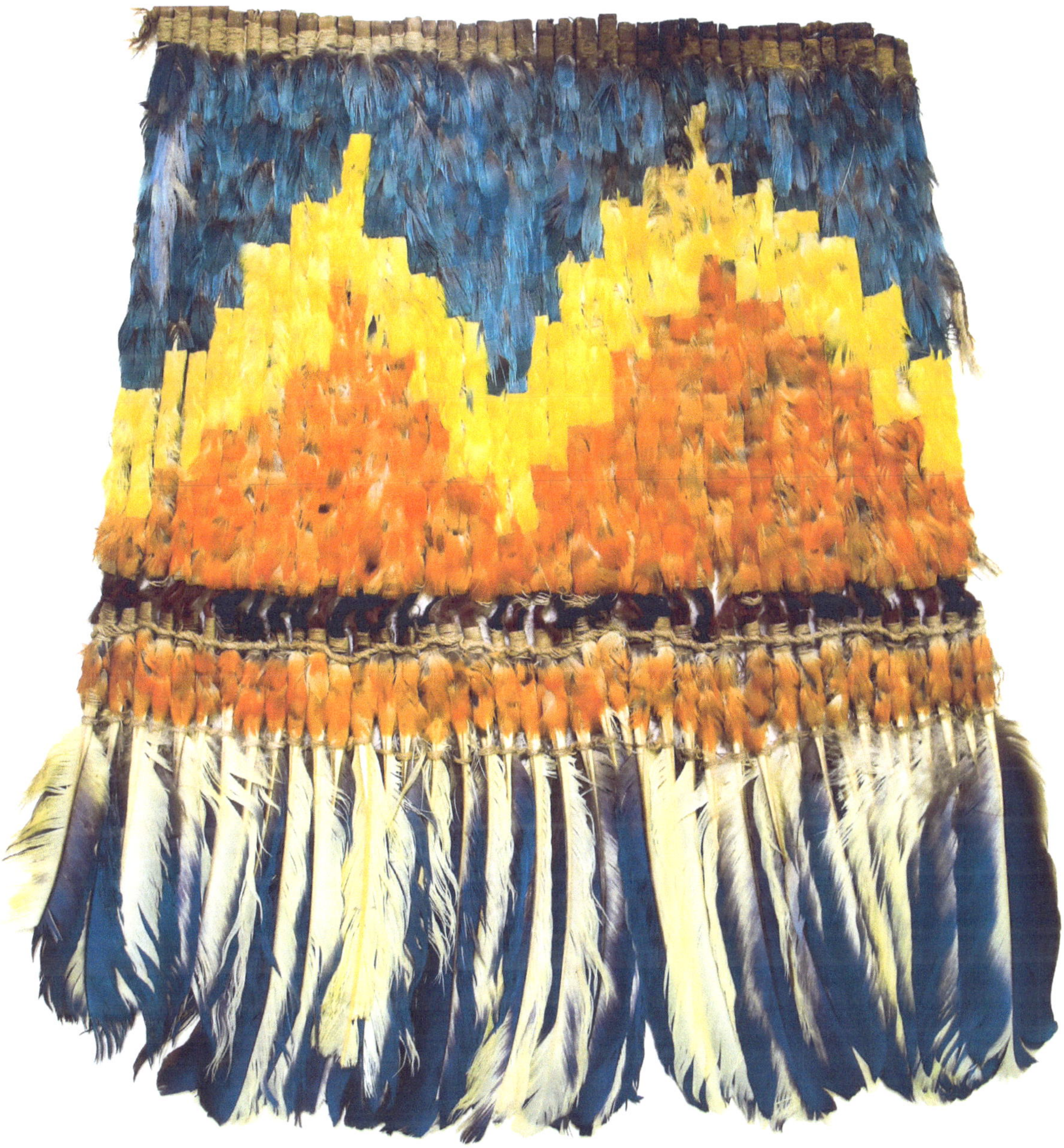

Museum number: V 10.399 b

Item: Feather apron ?
Culture: 19-20th Century, from Amazonia
Size: 41 x 40 cm
Material/technique: Split cane sticks (0,5 cm) are wrapped with 2S cotton yarns.
Feathers are secured in these wrappings.
At bottom a row of larger (17 cm) feathers.
Gift by the Museum Society on the occasion of the 150th anniversary of the Roemer-Museum, 1996

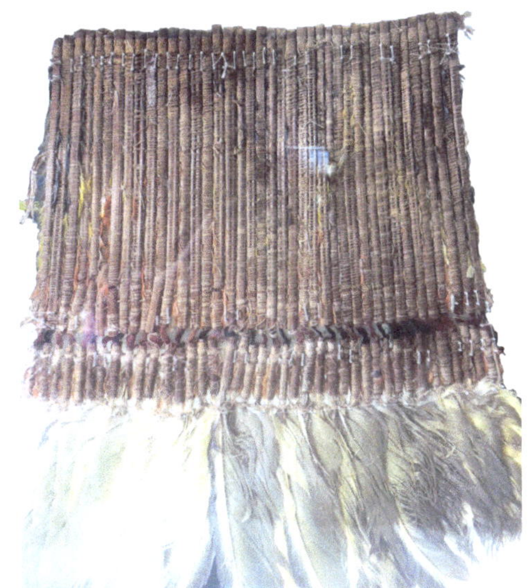

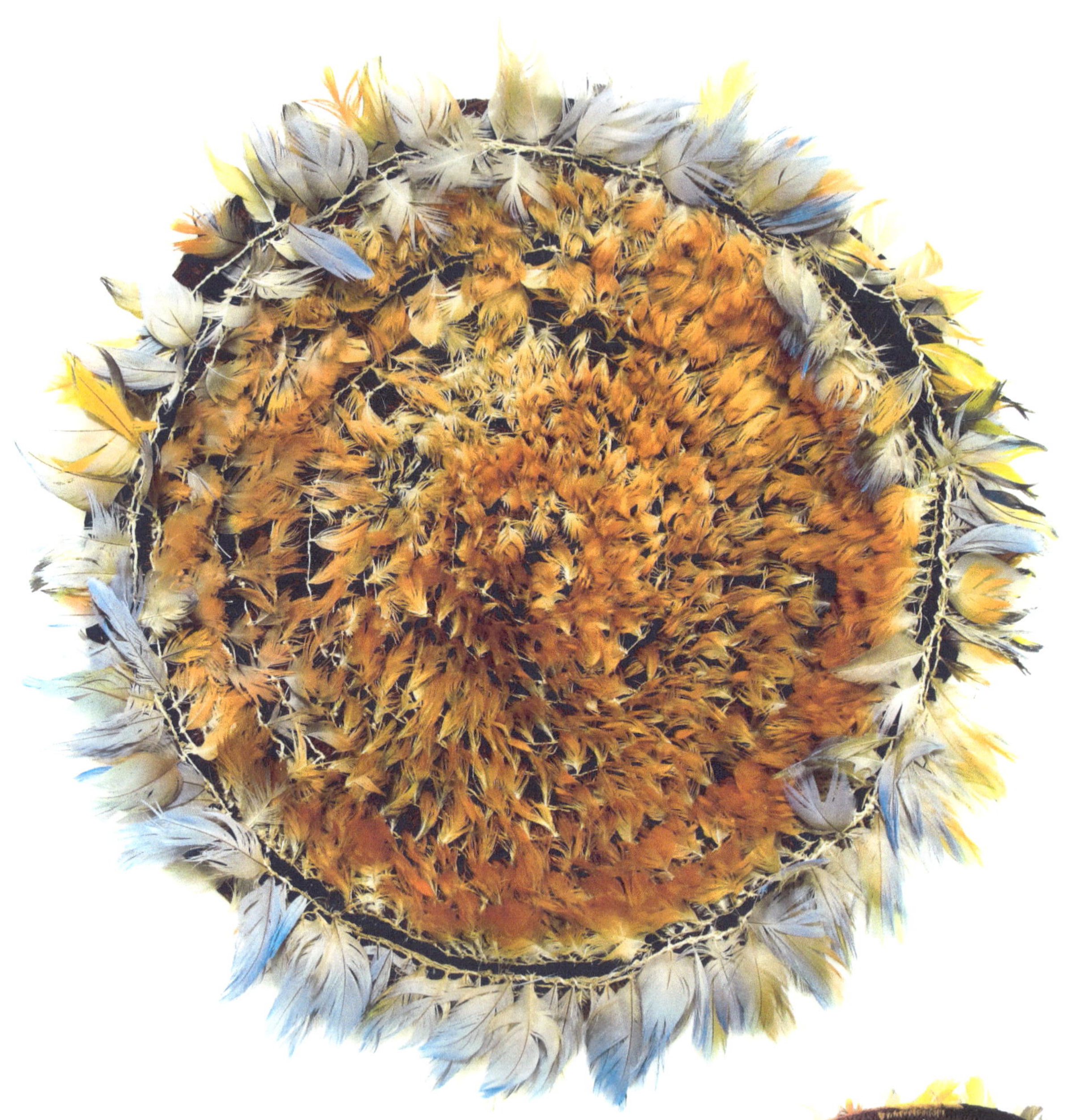

Museum number: V 10.399 c

Item: Feather-shield
Style: probably fake

Size: Ø 42 cm

Material/technique: A flat circular base made in looping. It consists of 1 cm wide spiral-looped stripes in different colors in 2S camelid fiber. On the front side of the "shield" strings of orange feathers are attached – the two outer rings are multicolored featherstrings.

Similar shields have not been found in the Andes region. The feather strings are probably preColumbian but very spacially sewn on – very unlike other preColumbian feather objects.

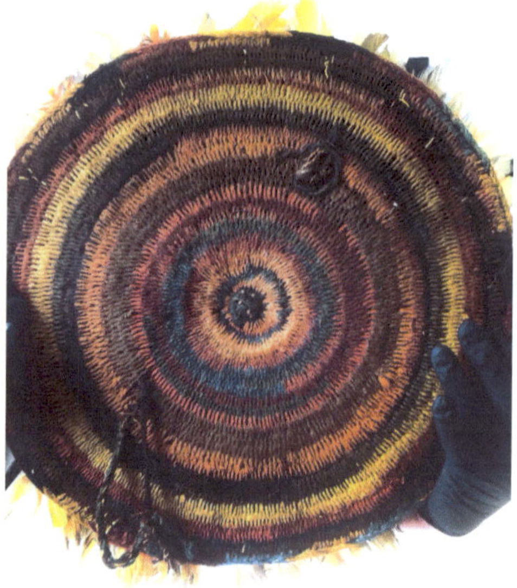

Museum number:
V 9.322

Item: False mummy head
Style:? Maybe a falsification???
Size: 83 x 30 cm
Material/technique: Maybe a "False mummy head" to attach on top of a mummy? It is made from plain weave cotton (S for warp, paired S for wefts). The threadcount is 12 x 5 per cm, stuffed with plant material. Plantfiber is attached as a wig. A long 180 x 8 cm, cotton 2S belt (with a threadcount of 20 x 3 cm) is tied on to the head with half of a fistbraided plantfiber sling and loose camelid fiber yarns. The belt has at either end a 10 cm long tapestry with 2S camelid fiber wefts.
At the back of the head is a 25 x 25 cm 4 selvedged cotton S textile made in plain weave. The threadcount of this textile is 12 x 12 per cm.
The materials are pre-Columbian, but usually the "false mummy heads" were closed pillows to set on top of a fardel. The long, loose textile seems odd…?

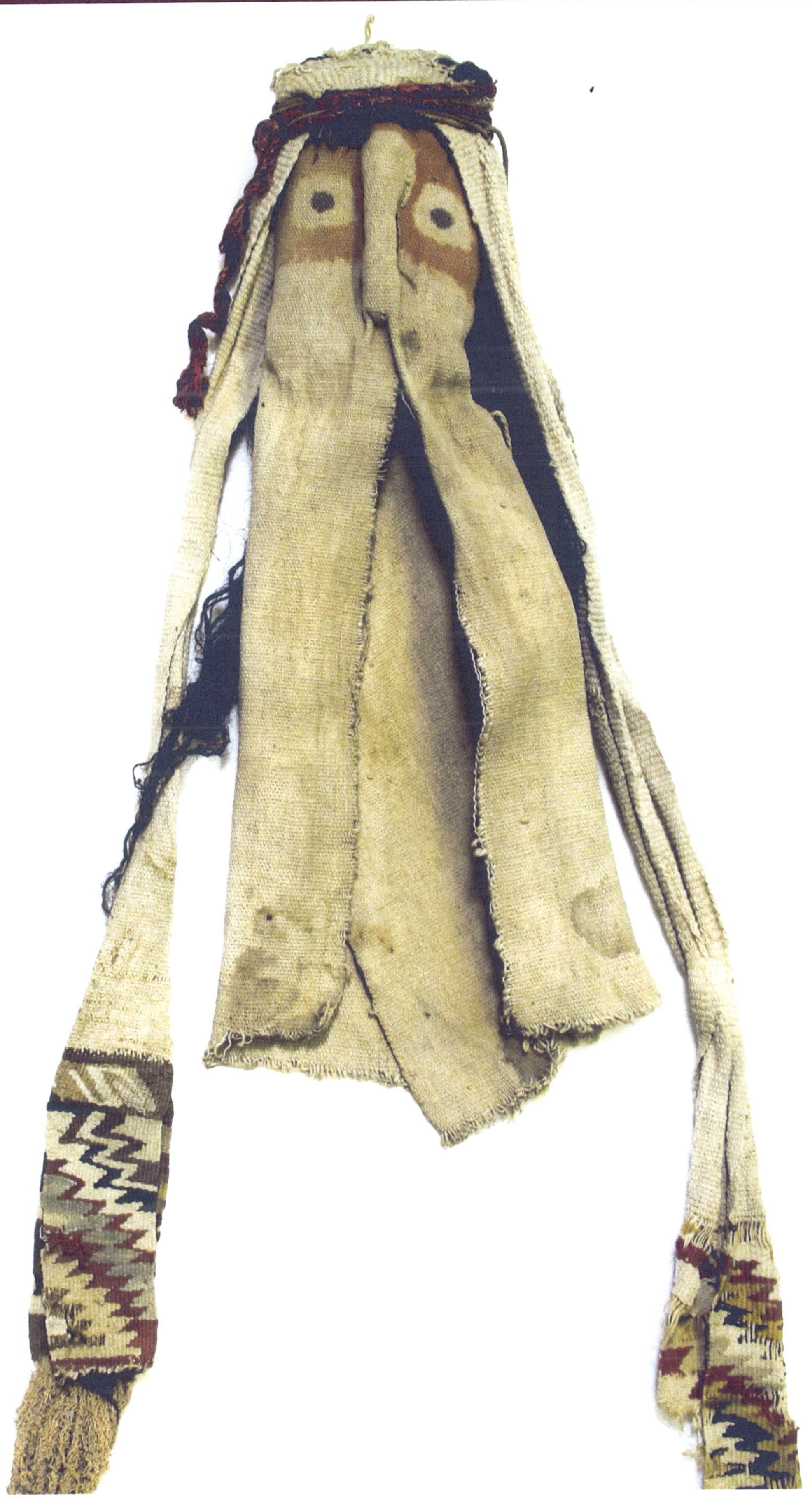

www.ingramcontent.com/pod-product-compliance
Lightning Source LLC
LaVergne TN
LVHW070130110826
845147LV00002B/228

* 9 7 8 1 6 0 9 6 2 1 6 6 7 *